COFFEE

A Guide to Buying, Brewing & Enjoying

Kenneth Davids

101

101 PRODUCTIONS

Publisher	Brete C. Harrison
Associate Publisher	James Connolly
Editors	Anna Morgan Pendergrass and Annette Gooch
Interior Designers	Linda Hauck and Charlene Mouille
Director of Production	Steve Lux
Illustrator	M.L. Duniec

Cover photography by Paul Schultz, Founder of Caffe Soma Coffee,
1601 Howard Street, San Francisco, CA 94103
Cover Design by Glenn Martinez & Associates

PLEASE NOTE: The advice for use of coffee apparatus given in this book is intended to complement the instructions provided by the manufacturers of those apparatus, not to substitute for those instructions. Please carefully read and observe the safeguards, cautions, and instructions that accompany your coffee apparatus before supplementing them with the advice given in this book.

Printed and bound in the USA
Published by 101 Productions/The Cole Group
4415 Sonoma Highway, PO Box 4089
Santa Rosa, CA 95402-4089

C D E F G H
3 4 5 6 7 8 9

Library of Congress Catalog Card Number in progress
ISBN 1-56426-500-5

Contents

Preface to the Fourth Edition

A couple of years ago American journalism discovered a new kind of modern problem: too much choice. Specialty coffees had the distinction of becoming a symbol for this latest crisis in contemporary consciousness: *The New York Times* cited the case of a 22-year-old man who entered a Boston market and was intimidated into paralysis when he was faced with choosing among 54 different kinds of coffee.

The editorial page of the *San Francisco Chronicle* later observed that this new kind of crisis was surely better than the one the newspaper observed 25 years earlier, when a survey determined that only one kind of coffee was served in San Francisco restaurants, and that was swill.

When the first edition of this book appeared 15 years ago, swill was still the dominant mode of coffee production, and specialty coffee roasters were pioneering idealists working mainly out of storefronts furnished in stained plywood and recycled coffee bags. In the years since then, specialty coffee has grown into a world of connoisseurship sufficiently complex to intimidate 22-year-olds and merit alarmed mention in the *New York Times*, and an industry sufficiently robust to have its own trade association, newsletter, and other accoutrements of an established player in the contemporary marketplace.

The various editions of this book have reflected the stages of those changes. In the first edition I was largely preoccupied with convincing readers that "coffee" was actually "coffees," and that making and drinking a cup was an act worthy of embellishing with choice and consciousness. Good, solid information was hard to come by for the first edition; if it had not been for the generous help of pioneers in San Francisco Bay Area specialty coffee business like Alfred Peet, Milt Mountanos, Tom Cara, and the late James Hardcastle, and the technical work of Michael Sivitz and others, the book hardly could have been written.

Now the problem is just the opposite: There are so many knowledgeable people in the specialty coffee business, and so much knowledge available, that the task has become one of selecting among too much information rather than ferreting out enough to make a useful book. And rather than proselytizing, I find myself increasingly assuming the role of philosophical (and sometimes skeptical) observer of a business and culture of connoisseurship testing its identity in several directions at once.

Despite the maturing of the specialty coffee business and the increasing sophistication of its clientele, this fourth edition retains the basic structure of the original book, which starts from scratch, assuming a reader with little knowledge of coffee but with a good palate, a literate turn of mind, and a consuming, indeed almost insatiable, interest in the subject.

Those already familiar with aspects of fancy coffee will want to tread swiftly and lightly through the opening couple of chapters before wading in. For these more experienced aficionados in particular I've tried to deliver useful information on newer developments in specialty coffees: flavored coffees, new decaffeination methods, more sophisticated home espresso paraphernalia, estate and organic coffees, and the like.

Specialty coffee roasters, importers, and retailers are the true authorities in this book. If in my observation they present a consensus on an issue, I have tried to reflect that consensus, making it clear whenever my own view deviates from it. If there is no consensus on an issue, as there is not, for example, on the value of flavored coffees, I have tried to reflect the various points of view as fully and sympathetically as I can.

What I have not deviated from is my conviction that specialty coffee is a superb way of enriching a small but real pleasure in life, and my equally strong admiration for the mavericks and idealists who created the culture of specialty coffee and continue to shape and nurture it. Despite the astonishing growth in the business over the past few years, that feisty passion appears to be intact. May it always be so.

This is my first opportunity to thank some of the coffee idealists who have shared their knowledge and passion with me over the past 15 years. If I were to name everyone who, from the first edition of this book through this one, helped me with a crucial piece of information or allowed me to try a piece of equipment or a coffee, the list would be as long as many of the chapters in the book. I can only touch on a few names. I have already mentioned Alfred Peet, Milt Mountanos, Tom Cara, and James Hardcastle, who were of such help in preparing the first edition of this book. Later editions are particularly indebted to younger members of the Mountanos coffee clan, Mike Mountanos of Mountanos Brothers Coffees and broker Mark Mountanos of South San Francisco; James Reynolds of Peets Coffee & Tea in Berkeley; Michael Sivitz; Jay Endres and Bob Barker of the Roastery Development Group in San Mateo, California; Christopher Cara of Thomas Cara in San Francisco; Richard Grame of Western Flavors & Fragrances in Livermore, California; and George Howell of The Coffee Connection in Boston. I have also gotten valuable advice from many equipment buyers over the years; for this most recent edition I am particularly indebted to Lucy Tetraut, Deborah McGraw, and Terry Watson of Peet's, and Alice Harrison of Fante's in Philadelphia. Finally, I have always found the columnists and writers in the *Tea & Coffee Trade Journal* invaluable sources of information and opinion.

Ultimately, everything of value in this book derives from these individuals and the many others who generously took a moment to assist me; only the mistakes and prejudices are completely mine.

Finally, I want to thank Jackie Killeen of 101 Productions, who nursed three editions of this book into print, and the various bright and patient people at Cole Publishing, particularly my editor, Annette Gooch, who put up with me and all of my last-minute revelations and coffee-fueled brainstorms during the production of this latest edition.

Introducing It

*More than a wake-up pill;
the perfect cups; specialty
versus commercial coffees*

When the first edition of this book appeared in the mid-1970s, finding a bag of freshly roasted specialty coffee was an act of esoteric consumerism often requiring miles of freeway travel and journeys into select corners of certain large American cities. If you wanted a decent cappuccino, you were in even bigger trouble; you might have to trek halfway across town, or in some cases halfway across the country.

The recent culinary revolution in the U.S. has changed all that. Today there seems to be a specialty coffee store on every gentrified street corner and a cappuccino machine in every restaurant. Furthermore, the transformation seems to have reached deeper than fad or fashion; it appears to have touched a part of our sensual being.

To give you a statistic: When I sold my café in Berkeley, California, in 1975, it was one of about five or six such establishments in the entire town, and one of three putting out a decent cappuccino. In 1987, there were thirty cafés on one side of the University of California campus alone, brewing close to 40,000 cups of Italian coffee a day, or 1.2 cups per student, per day, a figure that includes tea drinkers and puritans.

Whereas the current Europeanizing of American habits may be based on a genuine sensual perception of quality, such was not the case even a few years ago. At that time, I kept running across the Jamaican Blue Mountain syndrome: well-meaning middle-class families, with no idea what fine coffee really tasted like, buying fancy coffee at $18 a pound to impress their guests, and then storing it in their refrigerators for two months, where it went terminally rancid. I also witnessed small specialty roasters changing hands and going big time, in the process replacing attention to quality with attention to marketing.

Today there appears to be a counter-reaction. Better-educated consumers have led to more responsible retailing practices in the specialty coffee industry. If there is a fall-off in quality today, it is probably happening at the level of the coffee producer and distributor. If you are a grower with a famous coffee on your hands—with Japanese, North Americans, and Germans all bidding for it—you may want to produce more of that coffee, more than is commensurate with maintaining the quality that made it famous in the first place. Or if you are a wholesaler facing the same demand, you may begin to make discreet substitutions: Costa Rican in place of more expensive Hawaiian Kona, for instance, or lower-priced Ethiopian coffees mixed in with somewhat similar, but higher-priced, Yemen Mocha coffees.

Still, the implicit theme of this book is on its way to prevailing: Coffee is a sensual experience as well as a wake-up pill, and if it is drunk at all, it should be drunk well and deliberately, rather than swilled half cold out of Styrofoam cups while we work. Enjoying good coffee may not save the world, but it certainly won't hurt.

Nevertheless, there remains something of a discrepancy between aspiration and fulfillment. Recently, I was in a department store in Berkeley researching prices on the latest espresso machines. A few years before, there would have been two or three machines on display and passersby would have asked me what to do with them. Now there were at least twenty machines on display, and I was asked a series of detailed technical questions by a group of rather well-informed consumers. Their questions revealed that this cross-section of Northern California department-store browsers knew what a good cappuccino tasted like, but still were uncertain about the exact steps needed to produce one at home. They wanted advice on details: about which machine to choose, about frothing milk, and about choosing and grinding espresso coffees. They knew what they wanted, but needed a little advice about how to achieve it. The same might be said for visitors to specialty-coffee stores: Customers are convinced, for instance, that freshly roasted, whole-bean coffees taste better than canned, but still seem tentative on details.

This book is addressed to those coffee drinkers who are interested in the details, as well as to casual, unconverted readers who may doubt that coffee offers a world of pleasure and connoisseurship as rich and interesting as wine, although considerably more accessible. It is not another gift cookbook filled with recipes that you try once, during the week between Christmas and New Year's. It is a practical book about a small but real pleasure, with advice about how to buy better coffee, make better coffee, enjoy coffee in more ways, avoid harming yourself with too much caffeine, and, if you care to, talk about coffee with authority. Throughout, I've tried to blend the practical and experimental with the historical and descriptive, and to produce a book simultaneously useful in the kitchen and entertaining in the armchair.

A note on price: In the years since this book first appeared, coffee prices have fluctuated, often dramatically. But even at its most expensive, fine coffee has remained a bargain, perhaps too much a bargain from the point of view of the growing countries. A cup of one of the world's premier coffees today costs less than the same amount of Pepsi-Cola, and is *fifteen or twenty times* cheaper than a wine of the same distinction.

I sometimes think that coffee has remained inexpensive because Americans want to keep it that way. They are willing to pay for quality in coffee, but not snobbery in coffee. Whereas wine carries with it an aristocratic culture of nostalgia, Americans have insisted on keeping coffee the people's drink, with the search for the "perfect cup" a quest for a Holy Grail that is accessible to everyone; no knighthood necessary. It has often been noted how consistently coffee has been associated with democracy in America's cultural history. From the defiant American embrace of coffee after the Boston Tea Party to the "good cup of Java" refrain on the cult television series "Twin Peaks," coffee has represented an arena where plain folks can pursue and recognize quality without needing to put on airs or drop a lot of cash. Coffee offers connoisseurship at a good price, without pretension.

The Perfect Cup

I used to stay at a little run-down hotel in Ensenada, Mexico, overlooking the harbor. The guests gathered every morning in a big room filled with threadbare carpets and travel posters of the Swiss Alps, to sit on broken-down couches, sip the hotel coffee, and look out at the harbor through sagging French doors.

Nachita, the old woman who ran the hotel, made the coffee from very cheap, black-roasted, sugar-glazed beans. I assume the beans were the carelessly picked and primitively processed type called *naturals* in the coffee trade, because the coffee had the rank bitterness associated with such beans, a taste that, once experienced, is never forgotten. Nachita's tendency to lightly boil the coffee didn't help much either. By the time the coffee got to us, it was dark, muddy, and sourly bitter, with a persistence no amount of sugar could overcome nor canned milk obscure.

By anyone's standards it was bad coffee. But—you can guess the rest—the morning, the sun on the sea, the chickens in the backyard, the mildewed smell of Nachita's carpets and the damp smell of old stone walls, the clumsy bilingual conversations, the poems about mornings and Mexico I never put on paper, got mixed up with that sour bitterness and turned it into something perfect. I loved it; I even loved the tinny sweetness of the condensed milk. After all, there wasn't any other cup of coffee, and I was happy.

A cup of coffee is as much a moment caught in the matrix of time and space as it is a beverage: the "perfect" cup of coffee to whom and when?

Of course, there are certain universals in good coffee making, which run through this book like comforting refrains: good water, good beans properly roasted and freshly ground, careful brewing, and so on. All of these fortunately do not depend on sleazily exotic mornings in Ensenada and work even at five o'clock on rainy Sundays in Cleveland.

There is plentiful indication, for instance, that the steady decline in coffee drinking in the United States (the near three cups a day the average American drank 20 years ago has shrunk to fewer than two cups today) results from the widespread use of instant coffees that lack both flavor and aroma. Why else would the consumption of quality coffees be increasing spectacularly, while the consumption of commercial coffees continues to decrease?

Nevertheless, consumers of the average tasteless, thin-bodied instant may be in for a bit of a surprise when they taste their first cup of one of the world's great, rich, full-bodied coffees. If one gets used to living in a studio apartment, a mansion may feel

ARABIAN COFFEE ROASTING

a little uncomfortable—for the first week.

Furthermore, the best cup of, say, Middle Eastern-style coffee, will taste like a cross between cough syrup and ice cream topping to a coffee drinker in the United States, whereas a Middle Easterner faced with the contents of the American's Chemex would probably wonder why they served the wash water along with the coffee. Even with good coffee, tastes differ.

The Three Great Coffee Traditions

Coffee drinkers worldwide can be divided by habit and preference into three great traditions: first, the Middle East; second, southern Europe and Latin America; and third, northern Europe, America north of the Rio Grande, and the rest of the English-speaking world.

Middle Easterners adhere closest to the basics. They roast their coffee dark, generally; grind it to a powder, generally; bring it to a boil several times, always; and produce a small, bittersweet cup heavy with sugar and sediment. The little cups are sipped with a ceremonious air, at all times of the day, and nobody rushes.

Southern Europeans or city-dwelling Latin Americans have two perfect cups, one for morning and one for afternoon or evening. They prefer their coffee dark-roasted, bittersweet, often nearly burned. It is best dribbled out of espresso machines in small servings, dark, heavy-bodied, and foamy on top, with a little, not a lot, of sediment in the cup. In the morning, a small, stiff serving of this stuff is mixed with hot milk in a bowl or large glass, something coffee drinkers can really get their hands around. They want to warm their palms and fill their nostrils with it; if it were physically possible, they would probably take a bath in it. In the afternoon or at night, however, the southern Europeans' perfect cup is as small as the Middle Easterners', perhaps one-fourth the size of the morning bowl, black, but just as strong and sweet.

The perfect cup of coffee in the English-speaking world is at the furthest remove from the Middle Easterners'. First, the beans are roasted brown, not black, without a trace of the burned, bitter tang of coffee in southern Europe or the Middle East. The beverage must be clear (without sediment), light, smooth, and so delicate that milk or even sugar tends to overwhelm any pretense to body or flavor.

Typical North American coffee drinkers neither immerse themselves in big bowls every morning nor save their coffee for after dinner, nor do they take quick little sips out of tiny cups with ceremonial deliberation. They drink the stuff all day out of office urns or carry a half-filled cup around while doing housework. As has often been pointed out, North Americans' coffee is beverage as well as dessert; they not only finish meals with it, but are liable to start and middle with it, too.

Finally, there is another, separate tradition that is dangerously close to swamping all the other three: dumping a spoonful of brown powder into a Styrofoam cup of hot water and drinking it while walking out the door into the smog. This tradition has become well established in all parts of the world. A friend reports that she was unable to find anything except Nescafé instant coffee in the cafés of Guatemala Antigua, the home of one of the world's finest coffees. The final blow, however, came in Guadalajara, where she ordered a cappuccino and then watched in stunned silence as the counterman turned away from the gleaming espresso machine to dump a spoonful of brown powder into a cup of frothed milk.

One reason for such a paradox, of course, is that the best Mexican and Central American coffee is bought by the United States, whereas the locals can afford only the cheapest grades of local coffee and may prefer a decent instant instead. But I can't help but feel the reasons are more than economic; I feel sure that instant coffee is part of the anti-sensual, compulsive work ethic of industrialism, creeping over the world like the shadow of a giant billboard. After all, instant makes for considerably shorter coffee breaks.

At any rate, readers of this book need not feel limited by any tradition. The preparing of a cup of coffee, like any other gesture, can be enriched by choice and consciousness. The following pages offer you not the perfect cup, but the perfect cups.

Specialty Versus Commercial Coffees

All the coffees I advise you to buy are known in the trade as *specialty coffees*. The opposite of specialty is *commercial coffee*. From the consumer's viewpoint, the most immediately noticeable difference between commercial and specialty coffees is packaging: Commercial coffee comes in little bottles of instant or is already ground and packed in a tin or a collapsed, plastic-encased brick. Specialty coffee comes as whole beans, either in one-pound bags or in bulk, and needs to be ground before it's brewed.

Commercial coffee is usually roasted and packed in large plants, under nationally advertised brand names. Specialty coffee is usually roasted in small stores or factories, using traditional methods and technology, and is often sold where it's roasted.

Specialty coffees offer considerably more choice than commercial coffees. You can buy coffee by the place where the bean originated (Kenya, Colombia), by roast (French roast, Italian roast), or by blend designed for the time of day, price, or flavor. Commercial coffees offer only a very limited selection of blend and roast, and little possibility of buying straight, unblended coffees.

Specialty coffees offer more opportunity for consumers to participate in the creation of their pleasure; commercial coffees are *fait accompli* in tins or bags.

Admittedly, these once-clear distinctions have become a bit fuzzy of late. Since more and more consumers are buying specialty coffees and fewer and fewer are buying commercial coffees, commercial coffee companies have been attempting to co-opt the specialty market with a sort of compromise product: whole-bean coffees in tins or bags. Although these are usually high-quality, well-prepared beans, they fail to qualify as specialty coffees in other respects. They are not as fresh (bagged coffee, which is

usually handled like a canned product with a long shelf life, is particularly likely to be sold stale). They do not offer the same variety of choice (large commercial coffee concerns could never market the more exotic coffees of the world because supply is inconsistent and demand is small). And the purported European dark roasts tend to be under-roasted to cater to mainstream taste (a "French" roast by Maxwell House, for example, is about as French as the contents of a carafe in an all-night diner).

On the other side of the coin, some large wholesale specialty roasters (those specialty roasters who sell their coffees through other retailers and supermarkets) have invaded the commercial market with cans and two-ounce, single-serving bags of pre-ground coffee. These products are usually superior to the corresponding commercial products because of the specialty roasters' tradition of quality and smaller scale of operation, but they still are a compromise product, and do not represent the absolute best in specialty coffee roasting.

The final, most important difference between commercial and specialty coffees is the way they taste and smell. The best commercial blended coffees are good. The worst are atrocious. The best specialty coffees, bought fresh and brewed correctly, are more than good; they are superb, and superb in a variety of ways. In the next few pages I explain why.

Main Coffee Categories

Coffee buyers divide the world's coffee production into three main categories: *high-grown mild, Brazilian*, and *robusta*.

High-grown mild coffees demand the highest prices on the world market. The coffee tree will not tolerate frost, nor will it flourish in extremely high temperatures. This means coffee grows best in certain well-watered, mountainous regions of the tropics. High-grown mild coffees, no matter where they come from, are cultivated at altitudes over 2,000 feet above sea level, usually between 4,000 and 6,000 feet. They are produced from berries that are picked only when ripe and are prepared with care. The responsible specialty-coffee roaster uses only the finest high-grown mild coffees.

Use of the term *Brazilian* to describe the next most preferred group of coffees is misleading, since Brazil also produces excellent mild coffees. The trade term, however, refers to lower-grade coffees that are grown at low altitudes on vast plantations and are mass harvested. These coffees at best have a middle-of-the-road, neutral flavor, with a flat aroma. Most decent commercial blends contain large proportions of Brazilian, with smaller additions of high-grown milds.

Both high-grown mild and Brazilian coffees are produced from plants that belong to the botanical species *Coffea arabica*. The arabica is the original coffee plant; it still grows wild in Ethiopia and was first cultivated in Yemen at the southern tip of the Arabian peninsula. *Coffea arabica* was then carried around the world by coffee-hooked devotees, much as European wine grapes spread to form the basis of the world's wine industry. All specialty coffees come from *Coffea arabica* stock, which still makes up the majority of the world's production.

Many other species of coffee tree grow wild in Africa, however, and one, the *Coffea robusta*, has grown to major importance in world markets. The main advantages of the robusta are that it resists disease and that it grows successfully at lower altitudes than *Coffea arabica*. The bean, however, does not have the fragrance or flavor of the best arabica, or even a decent Brazilian, and in general demands the lowest prices in the world market. It also packs 30 to 40 percent more caffeine than *Coffea arabica*. Robusta is used as a component in the cheapest American commercial coffees, especially instant coffees.

The coffee bean, like all beans, is a seed; it grows at the heart of a small berry, about the size of the end of your little finger. Before the coffee can be shipped and roasted, the bean must be separated from the berry. Nature has been particularly lavish in its protection of the coffee bean, and removing the three sets of skin and one layer of pulp from around the bean is a complex process. If done properly, the coffee looks better, tastes better, and demands a higher price.

The worst preparation would be as follows: The coffee berries are stripped—leaves, unripe berries, and all—onto the ground. This mixture is then scooped up,

sifted, and dried in big piles, and some time later the hardened berry is stripped off the bean. Some beans are small and deformed, shriveled, or discolored. In poorly prepared coffee all the beans, good and bad, plus a few twigs, a little dirt, and some stones, are shipped together. The various flavor taints associated with cheap coffee—sourness, mustiness, harshness—all derive from careless picking and drying.

The best preparation would run like this: The beans are selectively picked as they ripen. The outer skin is immediately scraped loose, exposing the pulp. The beans are then soaked, and the sweet pulp fermented off the bean. More soaking, or more properly, washing, follows before the bean is dried and the last layers of skin, now dry and crumbly, are stripped off the bean. In some cases, the beans are further tumbled and "polished" to improve their appearance.

Between these two extremes are coffees that are dried in the old-fashioned way, with the bean still inside the fruit, but are picked selectively, and dried and cleaned with care. These also can be excellent coffees.

Coffee is graded according to three basic criteria: quality of bean (altitude and species), size of bean, and quality of preparation. An additional criterion is simply how good the coffee tastes and smells, what coffee people call "cup quality."

Again, the responsible specialty-coffee seller buys only the best grades of coffee, which means high-grown mild beans, excellent preparation, with high cup quality. When you buy from a responsible specialty-coffee seller, you should be buying top quality, no matter what country of origin or roast you choose.

KALDI & the DANCING GOATS

CHAPTER 1

How It Started
The odyssey of the bean

The most famous version of the origin of coffee goes like this: Once upon a time in the land of Arabia Felix, there lived a goatherd named Kaldi. Kaldi was a sober, responsible goatherd whose goats were also sober, if not responsible. One night, Kaldi's goats didn't come home, and in the morning he found them dancing with abandoned glee near a shiny, dark-leafed shrub with red berries. Kaldi soon determined that it was the red berries on the shiny, dark-leafed shrub that caused the goats' eccentric behavior, and it wasn't long before he was dancing too.

Finally, a learned imam from a local monastery came by, sleepily, no doubt, on his way to prayer. He saw the goats dancing, Kaldi dancing, and the shiny, dark-leafed shrub with the red berries. Being of a more systematic turn of mind than the goats or Kaldi, the learned imam subjected the red berries to various experimental examinations, one of which involved parching and boiling. Soon neither the imam nor his fellows fell asleep at prayers, and the use of coffee spread from monastery to monastery, throughout Arabia Felix, and from there to the rest of the world. We never find out whether Kaldi and his goats dropped dead from exhaustion and caffeine poisoning, or learned to control their habit.

Owing to stories like this one, coffee was first thought to have originated near the southern tip of the Arabian peninusla, in what is now Yemen, on the Arabian peninsula, where Europeans first found it growing. But botanical evidence indicates that *Coffea arabica* originated on the plateaus of central Ethiopia, several thousand feet above sea level, where it still grows wild, shaded by the enormous umbrella-like trees of the rainforest. How it got from Ethiopia across the Red Sea to Yemen is uncertain. Given the proximity of the two regions and a sporadic trading relationship that goes back to at least 800 B.C., no specific historic event needs to have been involved. But if one were to be cited, the leading candidate would appear to be the successful Ethiopian invasion of Southern Arabia in 525 A.D. The Ethiopians ruled Yemen for some fifty years, plenty of time for a minor bit of cultural information like the stimulant properties of a small red berry to become part of Yemeni experience, and eventually, its agricultural practices. At any rate, *Coffea arabica* seems to have been cultivated in Yemen from about the sixth century on. Black African cultures also used coffee beans, but as a solid food, combined with animal fat, for instance, or chewed like nuts.

In Arabia, coffee was first mentioned as a medicine, then as a beverage taken in connection with meditation and religious exercises by dervishes. From there it moved into the streets and virtually created a new institution, the coffeehouse. Once visitors from the rest of the world tasted it in the coffeehouses of Cairo and Mecca, the spread of *Coffea arabica*, by sixteenth-century standards, was electrifyingly rapid. The extraordinary story of the dissemination of *Coffea arabica* from the seed of possibly one tree to the entire world is full of the sort of passion and sacrifice that must come from deeper springs than greed alone. Everywhere people tasted coffee, they wanted it and went through extraordinary pains to bring some home with them.

The Spread of Coffee

The amazing odyssey of the arabica plant was possible only because of its stubborn botanical self-reliance; it pollinates itself, which means mutations are much less likely to occur than in plants that have a light pollen and require cross-fertilization.

Most differences in flavor between arabica beans are caused not so much by differences in the plants themselves, but by the subtle variations wrought by soil, moisture, and climate. The plant itself has remained extraordinarily true to itself through five centuries of plantings around the world.

Legend has it that the Arabs, protective of their discovery, refused to allow fertile seed to leave their country, insisting that all beans first be parched or boiled. All this jealous care was doomed to failure, however, and it was inevitable that someone, in this case a Moslem pilgrim from India named Baba Budan, should sneak some seeds out of Arabia. Tradition says that sometime around A.D. 1650 he bound seven seeds to his belly, and as soon as he reached his home hermitage, a cave in the hills near Chikmagalgur in south India, he planted them and they flourished. In 1928, William Ukers reported in his encyclopedic work *All About Coffee* that the descendants of these first seeds "still grow beneath gigantic jungle trees near Chikmagalgur," doubtless keeping other hermits alert during their religious exercises. Today, offspring of the original trees are officially known as *var. Old Chick*, and still produce around a third of India's coffee.

The French became interested in the Indian coffee, but their attempt to propagate coffee in southern France, near Dijon, failed because the tree does not tolerate frost. The more enterprising Dutch, however, carried the descendants of the first seven seeds of Baba Budan to Java, where, after some effort, coffee growing was established on a regular basis.

At this point in history, coffee made its debut as the everyday pleasure of nobles and other Europeans rich enough to afford exotic luxuries. Coffee was available either from Mocha, the main port of Yemen, or from Java. Hence the famous blend of Mocha-Java, which in those days meant putting together in one drink the entire world of coffee experience.

Now comes one of the most extraordinary stories in the spread of coffee: the saga of the noble tree. Louis XIV of France, with his insatiable curiosity and love of luxury, was of course by this time an ardent coffee drinker. The Dutch owed him a favor and managed, with great difficulty, to procure him a coffee tree. The tree had originally been obtained at the Arabian port of Mocha, then carried to Java, and finally back across the seas to Holland, from where it was brought overland to Paris. Louis is said to have spent an entire day alone communing with the tree before turning it over to his botanists. The first greenhouse in Europe was constructed to house the noble tree. It flowered, bore fruit, and became one of the most prolific parents in the history of plantdom.

This was 1715. From that single tree sprung billions of arabica trees, including most of those presently growing in Central and South America. But the final odyssey of the offspring of the noble tree was neither easy nor straightforward.

The first sprouts from the noble tree reached Martinique in the Caribbean in about 1720, due to the truly heroic efforts of Chevalier Gabriel Mathiew de Clieu, who assuredly follows Baba Budan into the coffee hall of fame. De Clieu first had difficulties talking the authorities in Paris into giving him some trees (he finally stole them), but this was nothing compared with what he went through once at sea. First, a fellow traveler tried to rip up his trees, a man who, de Clieu writes, was "basely jealous of the joy I was about to taste through being of service to my country, and being unable to get this coffee plant away from me, tore off a branch." Other, more cynical commentators suggest the potential coffee thief was a Dutch spy bent on sabotaging the French coffee industry.

Later, the ship barely eluded pirates, nearly sunk in a storm, and was finally becalmed. Water grew scarce, and all but one of the precious little seedlings died. Now comes the most poignant episode of all: De Clieu, though suffering from thirst himself, was so desperately looking forward to coffee in the New World that he shared half of his daily water ration with his struggling charge, "upon which," he writes, "my happiest hopes were founded. It needed such succor the more in that it was extremely backward, being no larger than the slip of a pink."

Once this spindly shoot of the noble tree reached Martinique, however, it flourished. Fifty years later there were 18,680 coffee trees in Martinique, and coffee

cultivation was established in Haiti, Mexico, and most of the islands of the Caribbean.

De Clieu became one of coffee's greatest heroes, honored in song and story (songs and stories of white Europeans, that is; what the Africans and Indians working the new coffee plantations thought about coffee is not recorded). Pardon, in *La Martinique*, says de Clieu deserves a place in history next to Parmentier, who brought the potato to France. Esmenard, a writer of navigational epics, exclaims:

> With that refreshing draught his life he will not cheer;
> But drop by drop revives the plant he holds more dear.
> Already as in dreams, he sees great branches grow,
> One look at his dear plant assuages all his woe.

The noble tree also sent shoots to the island of Réunion, in the Indian Ocean, then called the Isle of Bourbon. This plant was found to be a somewhat different variety of arabica, with smaller beans, and was named *var. bourbon.* The famed Santos coffees of Brazil and the Oaxaca coffees of Mexico are said to be offspring of the Bourbon tree, which had traveled from Ethiopia to Mocha, from Mocha to Java, from Java to a hothouse in Holland, from Holland to Paris, from Paris to Réunion, and eventually back, halfway around the world, to Brazil and Mexico. For the final irony, we have to wait until 1893, when coffee seed from Brazil was introduced into Kenya and what is now Tanzania, only a few hundred miles south of its original home in Ethiopia, thus completing a six-century circumnavigation of the globe.

Finally, to round out our set of coffee notables, we add the Don Juan of coffee propagation, Francisco de Mello Palheta of Brazil. The emperor of Brazil was interested in cutting his country into the coffee market, and in about 1727 sent de Mello Palheta to French Guiana to obtain seeds.

Like the Arabs and the Dutch before them, the French jealously guarded their treasure, and Don Francisco, whom legend pictures as suave and deadly charming, had a hard time getting at those seeds. Fortunately for coffee drinkers, Don Francisco so successfully charmed the French governor's wife that she sent him, buried in a bouquet of flowers, all the seeds and shoots he needed to initiate the billion-dollar coffee industry of Brazil.

CHAPTER 2

Buying It
What the names mean;
choosing coffee by roast

The first decision in drinking coffee is where to buy it. There are roughly four strategies for purchasing specialty coffees: First, you can order by mail, which is at best an expedient and should be indulged in only if there are no specialty-coffee suppliers in your area. Second, you can buy from a supermarket with a selection of whole-bean coffees and a do-it-yourself grinder. Third, you can buy from a gourmet food market or the fancy foods section of a large department store. Fourth, you can buy from a specialty-coffee store.

The price may be lowest at the supermarket for all the well-advertised reasons (lower markup, brisker competition, higher volume). The same coffee at a specialty-coffee store may cost up to 10 percent more, but you have several advantages: You can request special blends, impress the clerk with your knowledge of coffee, sample new coffees, and wander around staring at the little machines and gadgets. And if the store is a good one, you can be sure that the management cares too much about what is sold to carry stale or badly roasted beans. As for the third alternative, whole-bean coffees found in the gourmet food market or department store are often excellent, but if sales volume is low and the manager disinterested, you may be buying a stale coffee held too long on the shelf. Most stores specializing in coffee, or in coffee and tea, care too much about their products to sell them less than fresh.

Your next concern may be finding a specialty-coffee store or choosing among them. With kitchen fundamentalists, new-wave gourmets, and jet-age cosmopolitans transforming our food-shopping habits, most good-sized North American cities now have dozens of specialty-coffee and tea sellers. You can find them listed in the yellow pages under "Coffee Dealers, Retail." If there are none, you could call supermarkets to see whether they handle whole-bean coffees or check the back of this book for mail-order sources. If you really enjoy coffee and are isolated from convenient sources, you should consider roasting your own, an enjoyable and surprisingly simple procedure (see pages 93–97).

Kinds of Specialty Store

Specialty-coffee stores usually fall into one of the following categories: (1) stores that roast their own coffee on the premises or nearby; (2) outlets of a chain that roasts coffee at a central location; (3) stores that buy their coffee from other specialty roasters; (4) stores that buy their coffee green and have it roasted for them.

To me, stores in the first category are the most exciting, and I suggest that in general you buy your coffee as close as possible to the person who does the roasting. The coffee usually will be fresher, the salesperson a bit better informed, and the shop more interesting.

Then, of course, you can visit shops and taste their coffees. Some specialty-coffee stores, peculiar though it may sound, brew their coffees so badly, it's hard to tell anything about their beans from their samples. On the other hand, many specialty stores brew fresh samples of their coffees to order for potential customers. The most common practice is to keep two coffees brewing at a time and to rotate the choices.

If roasting machinery is not in evidence, you can ask where the shop obtains its coffee. Half—perhaps all—the stores in your area may get their coffee from the same roaster.

Even two shops that buy from the same supplier may differ in their handling of coffees. Staling begins the moment a coffee leaves the roasting machine, and a coffee sold by one shop a week after roasting will be significantly better than the same coffee sold elsewhere after three weeks. Look for well-established shops, large volume, and a proprietor who cares.

In cities with large European neighborhoods, one occasionally finds stores or cafés where a few (sometimes only one) fine coffees are roasted and sold as they were before the proliferation of convenience foods and canned coffees. These places often produce excellent coffee, though you must go elsewhere for a wide range of coffees and equipment.

The Coffee Lexicon

Many stores carry as many as 30 varieties of coffee. Each one has a name, plus a few aliases. Take heart, however. No matter how many names there are, they all refer to

28

the degree to which the bean is roasted, the place the bean came from before it was roasted, the dealer's name for a blend of beans, or a flavoring that was added to the beans after they were roasted.

European Names

Suppose you are in a specialty-coffee store examining the beans in the glass-fronted bins. Some, you notice, are darker in color than others. You may also note that most names given these darker coffees are European: *French, Italian, Viennese, Continental.* These names do not refer to the origin of the beans. Rather, these coffees are distinguished by the length of time the bean is roasted. Italian roast, for instance, is usually darker and has been roasted longer than Viennese. Increasingly, specialty-coffee sellers specify the coffee that they have chosen to dark-roast; in this case the coffee is given a double label such as *Dark-Roast Colombian* or *Italian-Roast Mexican.* In other cases, however, the coffee a roaster chooses for dark roasts is a blend of coffees from a variety of countries, and the name refers only to the roast, not to the origin of the bean.

Non-European Names

Next to the coffees with European names, you will note coffees that have a light-to-medium brown color and carry non-European names, such as *Sumatran, Kenya,* or *Mexican.* Unlike the coffees with European names, these coffees are usually roasted about the same length of time, or to what the roaster feels is the optimum roast to bring out the distinctive qualities of the coffee. The difference is not the roast, but the origin of the bean. A coffee labeled *Sumatran,* for instance, should consist entirely of beans from a single crop in a single country, Sumatra. Since coffee can be grown successfully only in or very near the tropics, such straight varietal coffees tend to carry names of an exotic and sultry timbre.

Straight coffees, in addition to the name of the country in which they originated, often carry qualifying names: *Guatemala Antigua, Kenya AA, Java Arabica, Colombia Plantation, Costa Rica La Minita.* Most of these qualifying terms are either grade designations (*AA*), or market names referring, however indirectly, to coffee-growing regions (*Antigua*). A few, such as *Arabica,* describe a botanical species or variety, and epithets like *Plantation* or *Estate* indicate coffee grown on a large farm rather than peasant plots. Very occasionally, the specific name of a particularly famous or well-publicized estate (*La Minita*) will appear.

Market Names

I discuss market names at length in Chapter 3, under the countries to which they refer. There are literally thousands in the coffee trade, but only the most famous find their way into the vocabulary of the specialty-coffee retailer. Some derive from the name of a district, province, or state; others from a mountain range or similar landmark; others from a nearby important city; and still others from the name of a port or shipping point. *Oaxaca* coffees from Mexico are named for the State of Oaxaca; the *Kilimanjaro* coffees of Tanzania for the slopes of the mountain on which these coffees are grown. The *Harrar* coffees of Ethiopia take their name from the old city of Harrar; the *Santos* coffees of Brazil from the name of the port through which they are shipped.

Grade Names

Retailers may also qualify coffee labels by grade name. Grading is a device for controlling the quality of an agricultural commodity so that buyer and seller can do business without personally examining every lot sold. Coffee grading terminology is, unfortunately, varied and obscure. Every coffee-growing country has its own set of terms, and few are distinguished by logical clarity. *Kenya AA* is an exception: Clearly *AA* is better than *A* or *B*. But though the Colombian terms *excelso* and *supremo* are both laudatory, one could hardly determine by reason alone that *supremo* is the single highest grade of Colombian coffee, and *excelso* a more comprehensive grade consisting of a mixture of supremo and the less desirable extra grade. Although one may be aware that altitude is a prime grading factor in Central American coffees, one could hardly guess without coaching that *strictly hard bean* refers to Guatemalan coffees grown on plantations situated at altitudes of 4,500 to 5,000 feet, and *hard bean* to those at 4,000 to 4,500 feet. The higher the altitude, the slower-maturing the bean, and the harder and denser its substance—hence *hard bean.*

Estate Names

The latest development in the specialty coffee world is the marketing of coffee by estate, rather than by regional name, market name, or grade. A coffee estate is simply a coffee farm, something larger than a "peasant plot," but perhaps smaller than a "plantation." The term *estate* has a long history in the coffee business, but the latest use in the specialty coffee trade clearly is based on analogy with the wine industry's "estate-bottled" idea.

Apparently, what is meant by an "estate coffee" is a coffee that has been grown, and in most cases processed, on a single farm or estate, and is offered to the importer or roaster unmixed with coffees from other locations. The most celebrated traditional estate coffee is the famous Wallensford Blue Mountain of Jamaica. A good example of an estate with a more recently acquired reputation is La Minita farm of the Tarrazu district of Costa Rica. The owner, William McAlpin, has been successful over the past several years in establishing his farm, or "estate," in the consciousness of the specialty coffee trade. In addition to obsessive preparation of his coffee, his efforts include a color brochure supplied with his coffees and a well-made documentary video tape. The success of La Minita in publicizing itself may be encouraging other estate owners to similar efforts.

The marketing of a coffee by estate is clearly of advantage to the grower, because an estate coffee commands higher and more consistent prices than coffees not similarly recognized, and puts the grower less at the mercy of fluctuations in supply and other exigencies. Estate coffees also offer an advantage to roasters and importers, because presumably these coffees will be more consistent in their character and quality than similar coffees of more vaguely identified origin.

Nevertheless, the opportunity for abuse remains, perhaps intensifies, with estate coffees. If a grower does succeed in creating a separate identity for a coffee, and if demand for that coffee eventually exceeds the possibility of supply, why not simply buy some cheaper coffee from somewhere over the hill, and ship it as your own?

Furthermore, the estate concept lends itself to substituting hype for substance, and names for quality. For every farmer who, like William McAlpin, works just as hard on making his coffee taste good as he does on publicizing it, there may be others who decide to skip the taste part and just go for the publicity.

Still, the buyers who handle specialty coffee always have their noses in the air sniffing for rats, and estates that do abuse their reputations risk losing them just as rapidly as they managed to establish them in the first place. Or let's hope so.

Estate coffees share the cup characteristics of the growths in the region where the estate is located. The estate coffee, if it is a good one, will simply be a better, more consistent exemplar of those characteristics.

There is little way of determining through deduction alone whether a given name is a general market name or a more specific estate name, unless retailers help you out by sticking "estate" into the description somewhere, which, fortunately, they usually do. I have noted a few of the better-known estates in the discussion of coffees by country in Chapter 3.

Flavoring Names

Flavored coffees are good but inexpensive coffees, roasted a medium brown, and mixed with liquid flavoring agents that soak into the beans. The flavorings are a modified version of those used throughout the food industry. You may see actual bits of nuts, fruit, or spice mixed in with the beans, but these components merely dress up the mix and give it a natural look. The real flavoring is done by the added liquids. Some specialty-coffee sellers refuse to carry flavored coffees for various practical and philosophical reasons, but let's assume that our hypothetical coffee store does carry them. You will immediately notice that they bear names easily identified as part of the American pop gourmet lexicon. If it sounds like a name of a candy (*hazelnut creme*) or a bar drink (*piña colada*), for example, it's a flavored coffee. Or if its name includes the words *creme, vanilla, chocolate*, or the name of any nut, fruit, or spice, you can be certain it's a flavored coffee. To my knowledge, the only country to appear in the flavored-coffee lexicon is Ireland, and it should not require much experience or reflection to deduce that *Irish Creme* does not describe a coffee grown in Ireland. I discuss flavored coffees in detail in Chapter 3.

Surmounting the Confusion

To return to the traditional coffee lexicon, the average specialty-coffee retailer's use of terminology in labeling coffees is seldom logical or consistent, even when dealing with straight or varietal coffees. Ideally, one ought to be made aware of the country and region where a coffee originated, its grade, its botanical variety, its market name, when it was harvested, and the name of the farm or co-operative where it was grown and processed. Unfortunately, some of this information is not known to the retailer, and what is known tends to be communicated in sincere but somewhat arbitrary fashion. The labels attached to coffees in signs and lists are particularly vague. We usually are given the name of the country and one or two qualifying adjectives. Some retailers may choose the most significant qualifying adjectives, others the most romantic, but the end result is still confusion. Readers of the next chapter should be able to manage the terminology fairly well and at least be in a position to make intelligent deductions.

To find out how capable you are of surmounting such confusion at this point, try this: *Kenya.* A tropical name, therefore a straight coffee from Kenya, roasted medium brown to American tastes. *Kenya AA.* The qualifying adjective, *AA*, doesn't sound like a place and has a superlative ring to it, so you figure it must be a grade. Of course, you're correct. *Sumatran Mandheling.* A tropical name, therefore a straight coffee from Sumatra roasted medium brown. Since *Mandheling* doesn't sound like a grade, nor have you heard it mentioned as a botanical variety, you may assume it is a market name referring to a specific coffee-growing region in Sumatra. You have deduced correctly. *Mexican Altura Coatepec.* Another straight coffee roasted medium brown, from Mexico. *Coatepec* sounds like a regional name. *Altura* has that superlative ring associated with grades, and if you're at all familiar with Spanish you'll know it refers to height, so you assume it's the name of a grade based on the altitude at which the coffee is grown. Correct. *Murasaki Estate-Grown Kona.* Everybody knows *Kona* is a place in Hawaii, and Hawaii is tropical; therefore, you conclude that this is a straight coffee roasted medium brown from the Kona district of Hawaii, specifically from an estate or farm called *Murasaki.* Outstanding deduction. *Passion fruit.* Well, *passion fruit* is definitely a tropical name, but it's a name of a fruit and not a place, so you assume that this is a coffee of unspecified origin, roasted medium brown, and flavored with something that tastes like passion fruit. Absolutely correct. *French.* Coffee is not grown in France, so this must be a roast, darker than usual. Pick any prize on the lower shelf. *French-Roast Mexican Oaxaca Pluma.* First of all, a straight coffee from Mexico roasted darker than usual. Since Oaxaca is a city in Mexico, you figure (correctly) that *Oaxaca* refers to the region in Mexico where the coffee was grown. That leaves *Pluma,* which must be either a botanical variety or a grade; you guess grade and you're right. Any prize on the top shelf, including the pandas.

Names of Blends

Deduction is even more in order when dealing with blended coffees. Blends, of course, are mixtures of two or more straight coffees. There are two reasons to blend beans: One is to create a coffee with a flavor that is either better and more complete than, or at least different from, the flavor produced by a straight coffee. The other is to cut costs while producing a palatable drink.

Nearly all commercial coffees sold in cans or bags are blended. Commercial roasters might want to market a pure Sumatran coffee, for instance, but they can't count on obtaining an adequate supply of the same coffee month after month to warrant the expense of getting a name that is accepted by the public.

With many blends found in specialty-coffee stores, the name gives some clue to the origin of the coffees involved. The simplest to interpret is the famous mixture of one-third Yemen Mocha and two-thirds Java Arabica, the *Mocha Java* of tradition. Such a blend is not designed to save money, but rather to combine two coffees that complement one another: Yemen Mocha is a sharp, distinctive, medium-bodied coffee, whereas Java is smoother, deeper toned, and richer. Together the two coffees make a more complete beverage than either one on its own.

Other blends are named after the dominant straight coffee and combine an inexpensive neutrally flavored coffee with a more costly name coffee. Thus we have *Jamaican Blue Mountain* blends or *Mocha* blends. The characteristics of the name coffee still come through, less intensely than in a straight coffee, but distinctively enough if the blending is done right. There is also a savings for the consumer (and a profit for the seller). In other cases, the blender may use lesser-known coffees to mimic the characteristics of a more famous and hard-to-find or expensive coffee; thus we have *Jamaica Style* coffee or *Kona Style* blends.

Another tendency in blend nomenclature might be called the generally geographical. We find a *Central American* blend, or a *Caribbean* blend. Or, we meet blends named for the time of day we presumably might drink them: *Breakfast* blend usually means a blend of brisk, light-bodied coffees roasted more lightly than *after-dinner* blends, which generally consist of heavier-bodied coffees carried to a darker roast.

House Blends

At this point we reach the ultimate test: the mysteriously named house blends, the beloved children of the proprietor or roaster, baptized with names of his or her personal fantasy. A specialty roaster may have one such child or a dozen. Some of these offspring may have been a tradition in a coffee-roasting family for a couple of generations; others may have been born yesterday; a few may be unique, but most are standard blends well known in the coffee business, with slightly different proportions and fanciful names. Occasionally the name gives us a clue to content, but most often we're faced with the arbitrary romance of the proprietor, whose preferences may run from mountaineering (*Tip of the Andes Blend*) to the elegantly British (*Mayfair*), to the darkly Latin (*Orsi*). Lately there seems to be a trend to naming blends after colleagues and loved ones; an excellent Northern California roaster carries a blend named after one of his children, and another offers blends chosen by and named for employees.

I confess to mixed feelings about vaguely named blends. Romance and imagination are marvelous qualities and should be encouraged, but I also think the consumer deserves to be informed in a direct and unpatronizing way. Fortunately, responsible specialty-coffee roasters increasingly do offer descriptions of their blends; and although these one-liners are sometimes colored by wine label romance, they do at least name the constituent coffees, if not their proportions and precise provenance.

Organic Coffees

Narrowly defined, organic coffees are those coffees certified by various international monitoring agencies as having been grown without the use of harmful chemicals. Some retailers may call a coffee *organic* because laboratory tests have shown it to be free of residues of harmful agricultural chemicals, but such coffees should be called *chemical-free* rather than *organic*. *Organic* connotes an entire agricultural and environmental program, not simply a product that tests have shown to be free of chemical residues. Organic coffees should be identified by origin and roast, just like any other straight coffee. I discuss organic coffees generally in Chapter 3, and take up related consumer health concerns in Chapter 9.

Brand Names

A few commercial-style brand names are beginning to slip into the specialty-coffee lexicon. These names are catchy, evocative, always accompanied by a logo, and usually appear on well-designed bags in more sophisticated supermarkets and gourmet and natural food stores. Some have been developed in an effort to create an identity for various certified organically grown coffees. *Cafe Altura* and *Cafe Tierra* are two of the oldest and best established of these specially named organic coffees.

More recently, they have been joined by others, including *Cafe Tierra Madre* and *Aztec Harvest*. By the time this book is published there may be a dozen more. One could say, only partly facetiously, that if a name is vague, poetic, Latin American, and comes with a good but sincere-looking logo, it is probably a brand name for an organic coffee.

Caffeine-Free Coffees

Decaffeinated, or caffeine-free, coffees have had the caffeine soaked out of them; they are sold to the roaster green, like any other coffee. Roasters in most metropolitan centers offer a variety of decaffeinated straight coffees, roasts, and blends. The provenance of the bean should still be designated: *Decaffeinated French-Roast Colombian*, for instance.

The names used for the various methods of decaffeination may cause some confusion. *Water-only* or *Swiss -Water Process* decaffeinated coffees have had the caffeine removed from them by first soaking the green beans in hot water, then removing the caffeine from the water by means of activated charcoal filters, then finally restoring the remaining chemical constituents to the green beans by re-immersing them in the same hot water. *Conventional process, traditional process,* or *European process* all refer to methods in which the caffeine has been removed from the hot water (not from the beans themselves) by means of a solvent, rather than by charcoal filters. The solvent is either methylene chloride or ethyl acetate. Ethyl acetate is derived from fruit, so you may see beans decaffeinated by processes using it described as naturally decaffeinated coffees. Finally, coffees are beginning to appear that have been decaffeinated by direct treatment of the bean with a compressed, semi-liquid form of carbon dioxide (CO_2). I'm told that this is technically the best process of all, but I'm not sure what these coffees will be called if they become established in the specialty coffee lists. *CO_2-processed* has too chemical a ring to it; *gas-processed* sounds murderous. How about *air-processed*, or better yet, *naturally air-processed*? I'm sure that we'll hear from the advertising industry soon enough on this important issue of nomenclature. For a detailed discussion of decaffeination processes and the health and quality issues involved, see Chapter 9.

Some Last Slippery Terms

A last few terms that are particularly ambiguous: *Turkish coffee* refers to neither coffee from Turkey nor roast. The name designates grind of coffee and style of brewing. *Turkish* is a common name for a medium- to dark-roast coffee, ground to a powder, sweetened, boiled, and served with the sediment still in the cup. *Viennese* is a slippery designation. It can mean a somewhat darker-than-normal roast, or a blend of roasts (about half dark and half medium), or, in Great Britain, a blend of coffee and roast fig. *New Orleans coffee* is usually a dark-roast coffee mixed with chicory root, or a dark-roast, Brazilian-based blend without chicory.

Coffee Roasts and Flavor

Given a good-quality bean, roasting is probably the single most important factor influencing the taste of coffee. The significant variable is the length of time the coffee is roasted. The longer the roasting, the darker the bean. The darker the bean, the more tangy and bittersweet the flavor. When this flavor settles onto the uninitiated coffee drinker's palate, the usual response is to call it *strong*.

Now for a first plunge into the taste jungle and the wilds of nomenclature. *Strength* in coffee properly refers to the proportion of coffee to water, not the flavor of the bean. The more coffee and the less water, the stronger the brew. So you could make a light-roasted, mild-flavored coffee very strong, and brew a dark-roasted, sharp-flavored coffee very weak.

I would rather call this dark-roasted flavor *dark, bittersweet, tangy, sharp*, or maybe *European*. Anything but *strong*, since we need that word for later. This flavor occurs in degrees, depending on how dark the bean is roasted, and eventually becomes a virtually new flavor when the bean is roasted entirely black. To understand the chemistry behind the change, one needs to know what happens when a coffee bean is roasted.

Roasting Chemistry

The green coffee bean, like all the other nuts, kernels, and beans we consume, is a combination of fats, proteins, fiber, and miscellaneous chemicals. The aroma and flavor that make coffee so distinctive are present only potentially, until the heat of roasting simultaneously forces much of the moisture out of the bean and draws out of the base matter of the bean fragrant little beads of a volatile, oily substance variously called *coffee essence, coffee oil,* and *coffeol.* This substance is not properly an oil, since it (fortunately) dissolves in water. It also evaporates easily, readily absorbs other less desirable flavors, and generally proves to be as fragile a substance as it is tasty. Without it, there's no coffee, only sour brown water and caffeine; yet it constitutes only one two-hundredth of the weight of the bean.

The roasted bean is, in a sense, simply a dry package for this oil. In medium- or American-roasted coffee, the oil gathers in little pockets throughout the heart of the bean. As the bean is held in the roaster for longer periods and more moisture is lost, the oil develops further and begins to rise to the surface of the bean, giving dark roasts their characteristic oily appearance.

Beneath the oil, the hard matter of the bean develops a slightly burned flavor, which adds the bittersweet undertone so attractive to dark-roast aficionados. Eventually, the bean turns to charcoal and tastes definitely burned; this ultimately roasted coffee is variously called *dark French*, *Italian*, or *heavy roast*, and has an unmistakable charcoal tang.

Dark roasts also contain considerably less acid and somewhat less caffeine than lighter roasts; these substances go up the chimney with the roasting smoke. Consequently, dark roasts lack that slightly sour snap or bite coffee people call *acidy*. Some dark-roast coffees taste bitter or sour, but this results from the cheaper coffees used in the blend rather than the roast, and such sourness should not be confused with either the dry snappy bite of a good acidy coffee or the bittersweetness of a good dark roast.

Roast Terminology

Back to terminology for a moment. Coffee drinkers are so habitual that whole nations march from coffee initiation to grave knowing only one roast. This uniformity accounts for the popular terminology for describing roasts: *French roast* and *Italian roast*, which vie for the darkest; *Viennese* or *light French*, a slightly darker roast than *American*; and so on down to what we might call *American roast*, which by country is the lightest of all.

This assigning of national names to coffee roasts is a bit arbitrary, but is based on the sound fact that southern Europeans roast their coffee darker than northern Europeans or North Americans. I'll leave the question of whether the darkness of roast has some correlation to the relative intensity of nocturnal habits among the various

nations of coffee drinkers to those who may want to consider the issue over their second cup of dark-roast coffee.

The common terms for roasts among most coffee sellers are the standard, usually unnamed, *American roast* (medium brown); *Viennese* or *light French* (slightly darker than American with the merest undertone of dark tang); *Italian, espresso*, or *continental* (dark brown, definitely dark-flavored and bittersweet); and *Italian* or *dark French* (nearly black).

Of course, the "standard" medium roast varies greatly by region and by roaster. The West Coast generally prefers a darker standard than the East Coast, with the Midwest appropriately somewhere between. As a rule, Atlanta roasts lighter than New Orleans and northern California darker than southern California. As for roasters, all vary the roast slightly to bring out what they regard as the unique characteristics of each coffee, but this perfect moment varies according to the philosophy of the roaster. Roasters who lean to the darker end of the spectrum often use the traditional term "full-city" to describe their roast, which usually means that a few slight patches of oiliness appear on the bean, whereas beans roasted by those favoring the lighter end of the spectrum will exhibit a completely dry surface. To roasters who adhere to the dark end of the spectrum, lighter-roasted coffees taste too acidy and almost sour; to those who adhere to the light end, darker-roasted coffees taste too muted or charred. Neither is incorrect; these variations are part of the delight and challenge of specialty coffees.

Your best bet is to learn to associate flavor with the color and appearance of the bean rather than with the name alone, but for reference I've condensed everything you'll need to know about the names of roasts in a table page 41.

Blends of Roasts

You can either buy a coffee roast as dark as you care to drink it or make a blend of roasts. If you wish to blend roasts, buy a good, straightforward acidy coffee such as a Colombian, medium roasted. Then begin adding French- or Italian-roast beans, a few at a time, every time you grind yourself some coffee. Eventually, by adding and subtracting, you'll arrive at proportions that please you, and you can mix your own blend, a half-pound at a time. Of course, you may be the mercurial type who likes drinking a different blend every time, in which case, carry on.

If you don't have a grinder, have the coffee-store clerk make a blend for you before grinding. I'd suggest you start with half dark-roast (the darkest) and half American-roast Colombian, and work the proportions up or down from there. The next step in determining your personal blend is to experiment with the light-roast coffee; substitute some winy Kenya or heavy-bodied Sumatran for the Colombian, for instance. But for that, read on.

At this point, a reader with a logical turn of mind might ask: Why don't specialty stores offer a whole line of dark-roasted straight coffees? Dark-roasted Mexican, for instance, dark-roasted Sumatran, and so on. Some stores do. Those that do not argue that since dark roasting burns out many acids and other chemicals, with them go the subtle differences in flavor that distinguish one straight coffee from another. Thus, it wouldn't be worth a specialty-coffee roaster's effort to dark-roast a variety of beans.

It is true that virtually all distinctions in flavor are burned out with a very dark, black-roasted preparation. But with the medium-dark roasts from categories 3 and 4 (see page 41), certain distinctions remain. Dark-roast Kenya may not taste like Kenya, but it will taste different from dark-roast Colombian. Heavy-bodied coffees make heavy-bodied dark roasts, for instance. Some coffees dark-roast sweeter than others. Many Mexican and Peruvian coffees, for example, make a particularly sweet dark roast.

Also, roasters have different tastes in assembling their dark-roasted blends. Many Latin Americans, for instance, like a hint of sourness in their blends; it reminds them of the coffee from their childhood. So most dark-roast coffees blended for the Latin American taste have a touch of the medicinal flavor called *Rioy*. The same holds true for "authentic" New Orleans coffee. Most Italian roasters do not consider an espresso blend authentic unless it contains 10 to 50 percent high-caffeine, heavy-bodied Robusta, as well as some earthy Brazilian coffees, whereas most North American specialty roasters won't let either of these coffees inside their warehouses.

Consequently, once you learn to distinguish between roasts, you may want to pick out a dark-roast blend that suits you best. Ask the clerk whether the dark-roast coffee for sale is a straight coffee or a blend. If it's a blend, it may range from bitter to almost sweet, depending on the tastes of the blender. The bitterness I'm describing here, of course, is different from the distinctive tang that comes from roasting coffee darkly in the first place. It is a quality of the coffee itself, rather than a flavor acquired through roasting.

If you love dark-roast coffee—in fact, if you love any kind of coffee—you may want to learn to roast your own. You can buy the best beans, roast them precisely to your taste, drink exquisitely fresh coffee, and save considerable money.

Coffee Roasts: Names, Colors, Taste

1	Light brown; dry surface.	Cinnamon New England Light	Tastes more like toasted grain than coffee, with distinct sour or acidic tones.
2	Medium brown; dry surface.	Regular American Medium-high Medium Brown	For an American, the characteristic coffee flavor, the grain flavor is gone; a definite acidy snap, but richer toned and sweeter than category 1.
3	Slightly darker brown; patches of oil on the surface.	Light French High Viennese* City Full-city Light espresso	A slight, dark-roasted, bittersweet tang almost indistinguishable. Less acidy snap than 2.
4	Dark brown; oily surface.	Italian Espresso European** French After-dinner Continental Dark Spanish	A definite bittersweet tang; all acidy tones gone.
5	Very dark brown, almost black; very shiny, oily surface.	Dark French French Italian Neapolitan Heavy Spanish	Burned or charcoal tones plus the bittersweet tang; all acidy tones gone.

Viennese also sometimes refers to a blend of about one-third dark-roasted beans (4 or 5) and about two-thirds medium-roasted beans (2).

European sometimes refers to a blend of about two-thirds dark-roasted (4 or 5) and one-third medium-roasted beans (2).

CHAPTER 3

Tasting It
What to taste for; choosing coffee by country and market name; flavored coffees

Learning to distinguish roast is a first, relatively simple step in learning to taste and buy coffee intelligently. Once we move from distinguishing roast to discriminating among coffees by country of origin, we enter a more ambiguous realm. Signs and brochures bombard us with light and full bodies; mellow, acidy, bright, and distinctive flavors; rich and pungent aromas; and on into the mellow, full-bodied tropical sunset.

Most stores carry 15 to 30 varieties of straight coffee, all of which have to be described somehow or other on a sign or brochure. By the middle of the list, you sense a certain strain; by the end, the writer sounds desperate: "stimulating and vibrant," writes one; "an exotic coffee with a lingering aftertaste, full-bodied and provocative," writes another; "stands apart in its own special way," adds still another. Perhaps. Is the emperor wearing his new clothes? Do these coffees really taste different?

They do. Differences stand out on a coffee-educated palate as clearly as do sugar and salt. Experienced coffee tasters can distinguish the general origin of most coffees in a blend simply by smelling and tasting. The problem is twofold and has to do with communication. First, the public doesn't understand coffee language—that is, doesn't associate terms in the brochures with sensations in the mouth. Second, in their effort to make every coffee sound absolutely different from every other coffee, brochure writers often resort to mealymouthed romanticisms and wine label clichés in place of genuine description.

The comedian George Carlin once pointed out that there is no name for the two little ridges under the nose. The world is full of unnamed phenomena, and the closer we get to the heart of what it means to be alive, the more unnameable things become. The subtle differences in flavor and aroma among coffees are as real as the chair you're sitting in, but the words don't exist to describe them. One slings a word at a flavor and feels like a Sunday painter trying to copy a sunset with a tar brush. So we're back to the same old refrain: The only thing to do is taste.

Coffee tasting is in many ways more crucial to buying quality coffee than wine tasting is to buying quality wine. The reason: Wine is labeled fairly specifically, whereas coffee is labeled vaguely. For instance, we can learn from its label that a given wine is from France, a country; from Beaujolais, a region; and from Moulin-à-Vent, a small area in Beaujolais whose vineyards produce a particularly sturdy and rich red wine. Finally, the bottle tells us what year the grapes were grown and the wine bottled. Suppose, however, that one buys a coffee from Ethiopia. More than likely it will simply be labeled *Ethiopia* or *Ethiopian*. This tells us nothing and would be analogous to simply labeling all wines from France, from the cheapest *vin ordinaire* to aged Lafite-Rothschild, as *French*.

Some specialty roasters might go further and label a coffee *Ethiopian Harrar*. *Harrar*, like *Beaujolais*, is a region or market name, so we're getting closer. But few specialty roasters will tell us more. We are seldom told what plantation, estate, cooperative, or village a coffee comes from, for example, even though this may be the most important piece of information of all. Nor are we told when the coffee was harvested, or how long the coffee was held in warehouses before roasting, or by what method it was processed.

So a wine book can be much more specific in its recommendations than can a coffee book, not only because wine labels are themselves more specific, but also because coffee demands a closer collaboration from retailer and consumer, from delivery in this country to the point of actually being drunk. A bottle of wine can be affected by how it is stored, transported, and handled, but the fact remains that it is bottled and ready to be enjoyed (at however remote a date) when it leaves the winery. Coffee is subject to three crucial operations—roasting, grinding, and brewing—by parties who are thousands of miles away from the tree on which the bean originated. Thus, coffee even from the same crop and estate may taste different after having been subjected to the tastes of different roasters and a variety of grinding and brewing methods.

Furthermore, conditions in growing countries change in ways beyond the control of any roaster or importer. A coffee from a certain heretofore reliable estate, cooperative, region, or even country may become unavailable or suddenly deteriorate in quality, sending your buyer scurrying for a substitute.

In the mid-1980s, for example, Ethiopian Harrar was almost universally substituted for the then unavailable Yemen Mocha. However, by the end of the decade war and drought had cut off our supply of Ethiopian coffees, whereas the coffee politics that had kept Yemen Mocha out of the warehouses were resolved. Consequently, if you bought a good Mocha-Java blend in 1985, chances are the Mocha was an Ethiopian coffee; if you bought the same blend at the same dealer in 1991, the Mocha was probably a true Yemen coffee. Similar smaller-scale substitutions and trade-offs are repeated daily in the tasting rooms of the best brokers and roasters, as they attempt to maintain the consistency their customers expect, while conditions of supply constantly change.

Finally, there is always the question of whether a coffee actually is a Sumatran Mandheling, or a Yemen Mocha, or a Jamaican Blue Mountain. Particularly with high-priced coffees, a temptation exists at every step, from the exporter to the importer to the roaster, to substitute lower-priced or more readily available coffees for those represented in signs and brochures. Thus, coffee thrusts the consumer into a more active, and possibly more satisfying, role than does wine, but frustrates those who might prefer memorizing to tasting.

Learning to Taste

Consequently, anyone interested in coffee must learn to taste. There is no traditional tasting ritual for the lay coffee drinker as there is for the wine drinker. Professional tasters slurp coffee off a spoon, roll it around in their mouths, and spit it into a bucket, which isn't common after-dinner behavior. I suggest when you're tasting that you make coffee in your ordinary way, sample the aroma, taste some black, and then enjoy it. If you normally add cream and/or sugar, do so after the first sampling.

You may well want to compare samples of various coffees at the same sitting, however, so you have an idea of what coffee terminology actually describes. Remember that dark roasting mutes or eliminates distinctions in flavor, so make certain you taste coffees that have been roasted to standard North American taste: light to medium brown. It's best to buy all of your samples from the same supplier, so that your palate won't be confused by differences in style of roast. You can either make individual samples with a small pot or a one-cup filter cone, or brew the way professional tasters do. In either case, use the same amount of each coffee, ground the same and brewed identically.

If you want to proceed as professional tasters would, assemble a clean cup or shallow glass for each coffee to be sampled; a soup spoon, preferably silver plated; a glass of water in which to rinse the spoon between samplings; and something to spit into. Put one standard measure (2 level tablespoons) of each coffee to be sampled, freshly and finely ground, in each cup; pour 5 to 6 ounces of near-boiling water over each sample. Some of the grounds will sink to the bottom of the cup, and some will form a crust on the surface of the coffee. Wait a couple of minutes for the coffee to steep, then test each coffee for aroma. Take the spoon and, leaning over the cup, break the crust. Virtually stick your nose in the coffee, forget your manners, and sniff. The aroma will never be more distinct than at this moment. If you want to sample the aroma a second time, lift some of the grounds from the bottom of the cup to the surface, and sniff again.

After you've broken the crust, most of the grounds should settle to the bottom of the cup. Use the spoon to scoop up whatever remains floating on the surface and dump it into the improvised spittoon. Top off the cup with fresh hot water. Now take a spoonful of each coffee, lift it to a point just below your lips, and suck it violently into your mouth. The purpose is to spray coffee all over your tongue in order to experience a single, comprehensive jolt of flavor.

This inhaling of coffee spray should give you a notion of flavor. Now roll the mouthful of coffee around your tongue, bounce it, chew it even. This exercise should give you a sense of both the body and the acidity of the sample, concepts that I attempt to define in a page or two. Also note how the sensation of the coffee develops after the first impression; note whether it changes and deepens, or whether it becomes weaker or flatter. After all this, spit out the coffee, noting the aftertaste. Continue this procedure until you can distinguish the qualities I discuss in the following pages. It's a good idea to concentrate successively on each of the broad tasting categories; i.e. taste all three samples for acidity; then taste all three for body; then for flavor; and finally for finish, or aftertaste. Continue to taste as the coffee cools. Some characteristics reveal themselves most clearly in a cooler coffee. If your palate becomes jaded or confused, sip some cold water or eat a bit of bread.

Coffee Families

The following page contains a list of most of the straight, or varietal, coffees you will encounter in specialty-coffee stores in the United States. There are five sections. Each of the first three represents a family of coffees. First are the Latin American coffees, characterized by a bright, brisk acidity and clean, straightforward flavor.

Second is the Arabian and African family of coffees, characterized by a distinctive winy acidity. Third are the coffees of the Malay Archipelago, which have both heavy body and a lower-toned, richer acidity. In each case I've put the countries producing the most distinctive and famous coffees first. The fourth heading includes a pair of coffees that have nothing in common except a subtle difference from all the other coffees of the world. The fifth gives some categories of coffees distinguished by factors other than geography.

Latin American
    Guatemala: *Antigua, Cobán, Huehuetenango*
    Costa Rica: *Tarrazu, Tres Rios, Herediá, Alajuela*
    Jamaica: *Blue Mountain, High Mountain*
    Colombia
    Mexico: *Coatepec, Oaxaca Pluma, Chiapas*
    Venezuela: *Maracaibo*
    Peru: *Chanchamayo*
    Brazil: *Bourbon Santos*
    Haiti
    El Salvador
    Dominican Republic; Santo Domingo
    Nicaragua
    Ecuador

Arabian Peninsula and African
    Yemen; Mocha
    Kenya
    Ethiopia: *Harrar, Ghimbi, Sidamo, Yirgacheffe*
    Zimbabwe
    Tanzania
    Uganda: *Bugishu*

Indonesian and New Guinea
    Sumatra: *Mandheling, Ankola*
    Sulawesi or Celebes: *Toraja*
    New Guinea
    Java

Individualists
>Hawaii: *Kona*
>India: *Mysore, Monsooned Malabar*

Special Categories
>Maragogipe
>Peaberry
>Aged coffees
>Organic and progressive coffees

When you begin tasting, I suggest you choose one coffee from each of the first three lists, if possible a good Mexican coffee, a Yemen Mocha, and a good Sumatran coffee. After you've made three cups, begin smelling and tasting. You should eventually attempt to distinguish the following qualities:

Acidity

Taste those high, thin notes, the dryness the coffee leaves at the back of your palate and under the edges of your tongue? This pleasant tartness, snap, or twist is what coffee people call *acidity*. It should be distinguished from *sour*, which in coffee terminology means an unpleasant sharpness. The acidy notes should be very clear and bright in the Mexican, a little softer and richer in the Sumatran, and overwhelming in the Yemen Mocha. Aged coffees, and some old crop, low-grown coffees, have little acidity and taste almost sweet.

You may not run into the terms *acidity* or *acidy* in your local coffee seller's signs and brochures. Many retailers avoid describing a coffee as *acidy* for fear consumers will confuse a positive acidy brightness with an unpleasant sourness. Instead you will find a variety of creative euphemisms: *bright, dry, sharp, vibrant,* etc.

An acidy coffee is somewhat analogous to a dry wine. In some coffees the acidy taste actually becomes distinctively winy; the winy aftertaste should be very clear in the Yemen Mocha. In brochures you may find the aftertaste that I call *winy* described with other terms; *fruity* and *grapy* are favorites. Fruit connotes sweetness, however; I find the better analogy is to the sharpness of a dry wine, hence my preference for the term *winy*. The main challenge is to recognize the sensation, however; once you do that, you can call it anything you like.

Body

Body or mouth feel is the sense of heaviness, richness, and thickness at the back of the tongue when you swish the coffee around your mouth. The coffee is not actually heavy; it just tastes that way. To follow a wine analogy again, burgundies and certain other red wines are heavier in body than clarets and most white wines. In this case wine and coffee tasters use the same term for a similar phenomenon. The Mexican coffee should have the lightest body and the Sumatran the heaviest, with the Yemen Mocha somewhere in the middle. If you can't distinguish body, try pouring milk into each coffee. Note how the flavor of the heavy-bodied Sumatran carries through the milk, whereas the flavor of the Mexican dies away. If you drink coffee with milk, you should buy a heavy-bodied coffee. If you drink black coffee, you may prefer a lighter-bodied variety.

Aroma

Strictly speaking, *aroma* can't be separated from acidity and flavor. Acidy coffees smell acidy, and richly flavored coffees smell richly flavored. Nevertheless, certain high, fleeting notes are reflected most clearly in the nose of a coffee, as some tasters say. There is frequently a subtle floral note to some coffee that is experienced most clearly in the aroma, particularly at the moment the crust is broken in the traditional tasting ritual. Of the three coffees I recommend for your tasting, you are most likely to detect this fresh floral note in the Yemen Mocha, but depending on the roast and freshness of the coffee you could experience it in any of the three samples. The best Colombian and Kona coffees are particularly noted for their floral aroma.

Finish

If aroma is the overture of the coffee, then *finish* is the resonant silence at the end of the piece. *Finish* is a term relatively recently brought over into coffee tasting from wine connoisseurship; it describes the aftertaste that lingers on the palate after the coffee is spit out or swallowed. It is in part a reflection of body; heavier-bodied coffees like the Sumatran will have a much longer finish than lighter-bodied coffees like the Mexican.

Flavor

Flavor is the most ambiguous term of all. Acidity has something to do with flavor, and so do body and aroma. Some coffees simply have a fuller, richer flavor than others, whereas other coffees have an acidy tang, for instance, that tends to dominate everything else. One can also speak of a distinctively flavored coffee, a coffee whose flavor characteristics stand out. Of the three coffees I suggest that you sample, the Yemen Mocha is probably the most distinctive, the Mexican the least distinctive, and the Sumatran the richest.

The following are some terms and categories often used to evaluate flavor. Some are obvious, many overlap, but all are useful.

Richness.   *Richness* partly refers to body, partly to flavor; at times even to acidity. The term describes an interesting, satisfying fullness. Of the coffees I suggest you try, the Sumatran should be the richest in body and the Yemen Mocha should have the richest acidity. The term *rich* would probably not be used in any context with the Mexican coffee.

Complexity.   I take *complexity* to describe flavor that shifts among pleasurable possibilities, tantalizes, and doesn't completely reveal itself at any one moment; a harmonious multiplicity of sensation. The Yemen Mocha definitely should be complex; if the Sumatran is a good one it should also be complex; the Mexican is undoubtedly the least complex coffee of the three.

Balance.   This is a difficult term. When tasting coffees for defects, professional tasters use the term to describe a coffee that does not localize at any one point on the palate; in other words, it is not imbalanced in the direction of some one (often undesirable) taste characteristic. As a term of general evaluation, *balance* appears to mean that no one quality overwhelms all others, but there is enough complexity in the coffee to arouse interest. It is a term that on occasion damns with faint praise. The Mexican sample should be most balanced, but it has less to balance than the other two coffees. If you tasted the Yemen Mocha against a standard Ethiopian Harrar you would probably sense how the Yemen coffee is similar to the Harrar, but much more balanced.

Varietal Distinction or Character

This one is easy. If the coffee has characteristics that both set it off from other coffees, yet identify it as what it is, it has *varietal distinction*. In one sense, all of your three samples are distinctive, because they probably embody the best and most characteristic traits of the growing region from which they came. In another sense the Yemen Mocha and Sumatran could be seen as much more distinctive than the Mexican, simply because the Mexican embodies what for North Americans is a version of the normative coffee taste, whereas the other two coffees have characteristics that set them off from that norm. The rich, winy acidity of the Yemen Mocha immediately suggests that it is either a Yemen coffee or a good Ethiopian, for example; the heavy body and rich finish of the Sumatran identifies it as a good Indonesian coffee. It would be difficult to distinguish the Mexican coffee from a Peruvian, for example, or from any one of several other Latin American coffees.

Earthiness, Wildness. *Earthiness* and *wildness* are flavor defects deriving from careless, primitive processing that in some contexts may be seen as virtues. Some Harrar coffees sold in specialty stores may have a hint of wildness or earthiness to them. Roasters from Italy often like to include some earthy-tasting Brazilian coffees in their espresso blends. If a New Orleans blend is at all authentic it also should have some Brazilian wildness in it. If the earthy taste dominates to the point that the coffee tastes distinctly sour or harsh, this quality becomes a flavor defect; you won't find such coffees in specialty stores. Your Sumatran sample could have a hint of earthiness or mustiness to it, but it shouldn't.

Flavor Defects. *Harshness* and *sourness* are two of the most widely used negative epithets. Harshly flavored coffees are unpleasantly bitter, sharp, or irritating. Terms like *grassy, hidey, barnyard fermented, musty,* and *Rioy* (medicinal) describe even more dramatically undesirable flavor characteristics. All of these characteristics derive from careless processing. Presumably the coffees you taste will be superior, hence free from such defects.

Coffee by Country

Anyone who reads a newspaper is aware of how arbitrary the concept of nation state can be. National boundaries often divide people who are similar, and cram together those who are different. A Canadian from Vancouver has considerably more in common culturally with an American from across the border in Seattle than with a fellow Canadian from across the continent in Quebec, for example.

The concept of country often plays a similarly arbitrary and misleading role in coffee connoisseurship. Countries tend to be large, and coffee growing areas small; Ethiopian coffee that is gathered by hand from wild trees and processed by the dry method hardly resembles coffees from the same country that have been grown on estates and processed by the wet method. On the other hand, some families of taste-alikes transcend national boundaries. In the big picture, for example, high quality coffees from Latin American countries generally resemble one another, as do coffees from East Africa and the Arabian Peninsula. And both tend to differ from coffees from Indonesia and New Guinea.

But the notion of generally labeling coffee by country of origin is inevitable and well established. Hence the organization of the next section of this chapter by continent and country. It is well to keep in mind, however, that in tasting coffee, as in thinking about history, the notion of country is no more than a convenient starting point.

Mexico: Coatepec, Oaxaca Pluma, Chiapas

Most Mexican coffee comes from the southern part of the country, where the continent narrows and takes a turn to the east. Vera Cruz State, on the gulf side of the central mountain range, produces mostly lowland coffees, but coffees called *Altura* (High) *Coatepec*, from a mountainous region near the city of that name, have an excellent reputation. Other Veracruz coffees of note are *Altura Orizaba* and *Altura Huatusco*. Coffees from the opposite, southern slopes of the central mountain range, in Oaxaca State, are also highly regarded, and marketed under the names *Oaxaca* or *Oaxaca Pluma*. Coffees from Chiapas State are grown in the mountains of the southeastern-most corner of Mexico, near the border with Guatemala. The market name traditionally associated with these coffees is *Tapachula*, from the city of that name. Most Mexican coffees currently in specialty stores appear to come from either Oaxaca or Chiapas.

Don't expect any of these coffees to taste like the coffee you may have tasted while visiting rural Mexico. The brew most village-dwelling Mexicans drink is made from primitively processed coffees that have been passed over by the exporters; these cheaper beans are usually dark-roasted and glazed with sugar. They make a sweet, heavy brew with a peculiar sour twist, which appeals to some visitors and turns others into temporary tea drinkers. If you have acquired a taste for such coffee, you must pursue it outside the confines of the specialty-coffee store. Look for canned coffees from the southern United States, or coffees sold in Puerto Rican, Mexican, or Cuban markets under Latin-sounding names.

But the fine coffees of Mexico are a different matter. They are not among the world's greatest coffees, because they often lack richness and body, but at their best they are analogous to a good light white wine—delicate in body, with a pleasantly dry, acidy snap. If you drink your coffee black and like a light, acidy cup, you will like the best Mexican coffees.

Mexico's Chiapas State is also the origin of many of the organically grown coffees now appearing in the specialty stores. These are coffees certified by various independent monitoring agencies to be grown without the use of pesticides, fungicides, herbicides, or other harmful chemicals. For more on organic coffees, see pages 75-77 in this chapter and Chapter 9.

Guatemala: Antigua, Cobán, Huehuetenango

The central highlands of Guatemala produce some of the world's best and most distinctively flavored coffees. The most famous regional market names are *Antigua*, from the countryside west of the old capital of Guatemala; *Cobán*, from Alta Verapaz, a district a hundred or so miles northeast of Antigua; and the less celebrated *Huehuetenango*, from a district about a hundred miles northwest of the old capital. The Antigua coffees are most famous, but some specialty roasters feel that they have become inconsistent owing to the complacency of many of their producers, and prefer the similar but lesser-known coffees of Huehuetenango. Some shops may advertise their Guatemalan coffees by grade; the highest grades are *strictly hard bean*, indicating coffees grown at altitudes of 4,500 feet or higher, and *hard bean*, indicating those grown between 4,000 and 4,500 feet. Well-known Guatemalan estates include San Miguel, Capitillo, San Sebastián, and Los Volcanos.

The best Guatemalan coffees have a very distinct, spicy or, better yet, smoky flavor that sets them apart from all other coffees. They are very acidy, and the spiciness or smokiness comes across as a twist to the acidy tones. The finest Guatemalan coffees are medium to full in body and rich in flavor. You will like Guatemalan coffees if you like their smoky, distinctive flavor and fairly rich cup.

The Guatemalan government recently embarked on an apparently well-organized effort to increase Guatemalan coffee production and coffee exports. Like the extraordinarily successful effort the Colombian government started 30 years ago, the Guatemalan plan is designed to simultaneously increase awareness and a market for Guatemalan coffee in the United States and other consuming countries, while improving agricultural methods and the living conditions of the Guatemalan peasant farmers who raise coffee. The difference between the Colombian and the Guatemalan efforts is that the Guatemalan is aimed at the specialty-coffee market in the United States, whereas the Colombian effort was aimed at the high end of the commercial market. Both are pursuing similar tactics on the growing end, however: introducing new, higher-bearing, disease-resistant varieties of coffee, improving access to quality coffee processing, tightening grading criteria, and establishing improved living and

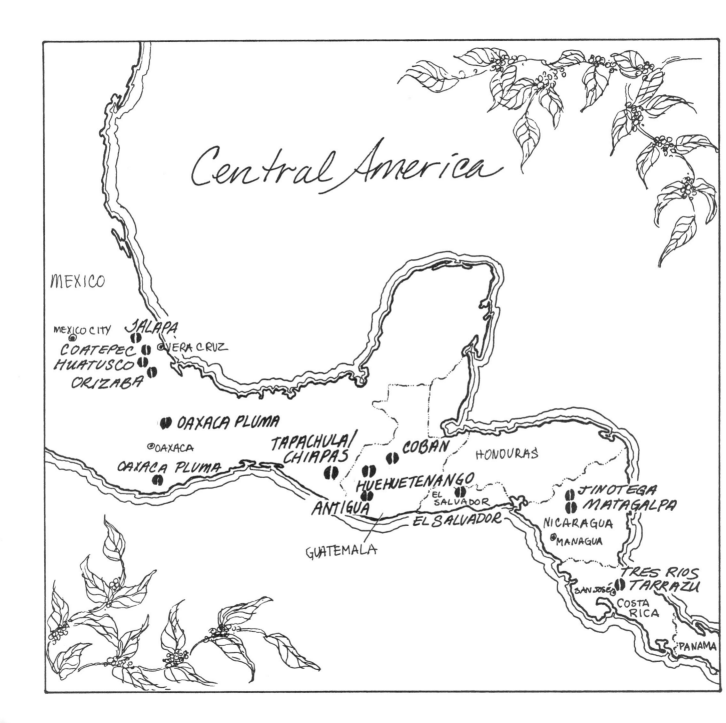

medical conditions for small growers.

Whether the effort to introduce new, higher-bearing and durable varieties of coffee will result in higher yields but poorer cup quality, as has happened in Colombia, remains to be seen.

El Salvador

Although the recent misfortunes in El Salvador have presented many opportunities for stirring journalism, coffee from this country poses a contrasting problem for writers of coffee brochures: They don't know what to say about it. The general consensus is that El Salvadoran coffee has a flavor somewhere between neutral and mild. One brochure calls it slightly sweet, which is about the most positive comment I've heard about it. I'd say El Salvadoran coffee has decent body but lackluster flavor. The best grade is labeled *strictly high grown.*

Nicaragua

For several years in the 1980s, Nicaraguan coffee was not imported into the United States because of the political differences between the U.S. and Nicaraguan governments. It is now widely available again.

Nicaraguan coffee presents still another challenge for coffee describers. One brochure tells us it's like the coffees of Mexico, but different. In general, I find it as middle-of-the-road as El Salvadoran: decent, straightforward flavor, fairly acidy, with medium to light body. Jinotega and Matagalpa produce the best-known Nicaraguan coffees.

Costa Rica: Tarrazu, Tres Rios, Herediá, Alajuela

Costa Rican is a classically complete coffee; it has everything and lacks nothing. The best displays an exceptionally full body and robust richness. Good Mexican coffees are brisk; good Costa Rican coffees are hearty.

Costa Rican coffee is grown primarily in the countryside surrounding the capital, San José. Four of the most famous coffees by district are *San Marcos de Tarrazu, Tres Rios, Herediá,* and *Alajuela.* Altitude may be a more important factor in determining flavor than district; *strictly hard bean* indicates a Costa Rican coffee grown above 3,900 feet; *good hard bean* from 3,300 to 3,900. Unlike many coffees of the world, Costa Rican growths generally are identified either by the estate or farm (*finca*) on which they were grown, or by cooperative or processing facility (*beneficio*) where they were processed. This piece of information, which is usually available to the roaster or importer, is seldom passed on to the consumer except in the case of well-known estates like Bella Vista or La Minita.

La Minita Farm has become particularly prominent owing to the quality of its almost fanatically prepared coffee and the skillful publicity efforts of its owner, William McAlpin. The La Minita coffee appearing in specialty stores is likely to be so labeled: *Costa Rica La Minita, La Minita Tarrazu,* etc.

But again, it's better not to become too absorbed in names and labels. If the coffee you taste is rich and hearty, analogous to a good burgundy, and you like it, it is a good Costa Rican coffee.

Jamaica: Blue Mountain, High Mountain

Jamaican coffee is a story of extremes: The lowland coffees of Jamaica are so ordinary that they are seldom sold in the United States except as fillers for cheap blends. On the other hand, the highland coffees traditionally rank among the world's most distinguished, and *Jamaican Blue Mountain,* however one defines that name, is the world's most celebrated, most expensive, and most controversial coffee.

Some years ago it was not entirely clear whether any high-quality coffee from the Blue Mountain district of Jamaica was entitled to be marketed as *Jamaican Blue Mountain,* or whether the name properly applies only to coffees grown on a single plantation, the Wallensford Estate. Today, responsible roasters designate estate-produced coffees grown at over 3,000 feet in the *Blue Mountain* district of Jamaica as authentic Blue Mountain. Most will be either Wallensford (best) or Silver Hill Estate Mountain. If you want to know where a store's Blue Mountain comes from, you can always ask. *Jamaican High Mountain* usually describes a somewhat lesser coffee than *Blue Mountain,* grown at lower altitudes in other parts of the island.

The Jamaican situation has been complicated by the many people who, in one way or another, are attempting to profit from the extraordinary prices demanded for Blue Mountain. In particular, other plantation owners in the high mountains of Jamaica are trying to produce a coffee that will ride on the coattails of the original into the pocketbooks and onto the palates of the Americans and Japanese. These entrepreneurs appear honest and well meaning; less admirable, however, are the American roasters who market a "Blue Mountain Style" coffee that has the taste characteristics of Blue Mountain, but may not contain a single bean of actual Blue Mountain.

Today it appears that either Wallensford Blue Mountain has greatly fallen off in quality, or we are drinking something else in a Wallensford Blue Mountain barrel.

The original Wallensford coffee from fifteen years ago was an understated masterpiece, a quintessentially classic coffee with enough of everything: rich flavor and aroma, full body and moderate acidity in perfect, subtle balance. The Blue Mountain coffees shipped today retain the body and richness, but lack the acidity; they are smooth, well-bodied, moderately rich coffees deserving to be drunk, but not to be carried on about.

And even if the real thing appeared in the stores tomorrow, would it be worth the prices currently being asked? I would say probably not. Blue Mountain was a great coffee, and some of it may still be great, but at this point it appears to represent still another minor chapter in the long history of vanity, snobbery, and the sacrifice of substance to pretense.

Dominican Republic; Santo Domingo

Coffee from the Dominican Republic is often called *Santo Domingan*, after the country's former name, perhaps because *Santo Domingo* looks romantic on a coffee bag and *Dominican Republic*, pedestrian. Coffee is grown on both slopes of the mountain range that runs on an east-west axis down the center of the island. The four main market names are *Cibao, Bani, Ocoa,* and *Barahona*. All are well prepared, washed coffees. The last three names have the best reputation. Bani makes a soft, mellow cup much like Haiti; Barahona a more acidy and heavier-bodied cup, closer to Jamaican High Mountain in quality and characteristics.

Haiti

Haiti, which shares the island of Hispaniola with the Dominican Republic, has a coffee industry built on contradiction. On the one hand, most of its coffee is raised on tiny peasant plots and processed by the most primitive of methods. On the other, the Haitian government has tended to promulgate extraordinarily detailed sets of laws and prohibitions apparently intended to upgrade coffee quality by sheer force of edict. Owing to continuing internal political problems, Haitian coffees are difficult to find.

The best of many grades is *strictly high-grown washed;* second best is *high-grown washed.* The heavy rainfall and deep volcanic soil combined with the low altitudes may account for the mellow sweetness that distinguishes the best Haitian coffee. It has fair body and acidity to go with the pleasantly soft, rich flavor.

Colombia

The Colombian coffee industry is the giant of the fine, mild, coffee-producing countries of the world. Although it ranks second to Brazil—with about 12 percent of the world's total coffee production compared with Brazil's 30 to 35 percent—most of Colombia's 12 percent is excellent coffee, grown at high altitudes on small peasant holdings, carefully picked, and wet-processed.

Central Colombia is trisected from north to south by three *cordilleras,* or mountain ranges. The central and eastern *cordilleras* produce the best coffees. The principal coffees of the central *cordillera* are *Medellín, Armenia,* and *Manizales,* all named for the towns or cities through which they are marketed. Medellín, the most famous coffee of the three, is known for heavy body, rich flavor, and fine, balanced acidity; Manizales and Armenia are, in general, thinner in body and less acidy. For the purposes of large-scale marketing in the United States, these three coffees are often grouped together as *MAM,* an acronym for Medellín-Armenia-Manizales. If your coffee seller is not clear about the precise provenance of a Colombian coffee, it was probably sold as MAM, which means it could be any of the three.

The two most famous coffees of the eastern *cordillera* are *Bogotá,* from the region surrounding Colombia's capital city, and *Bucaramanga,* marketed through the town of the same name. Bogotá, considered one of the finest coffees grown in Columbia, is less acidy than Medellín, but equally rich and flavorful. Bucaramanga is a soft-bean coffee, with some of the character of fine Sumatran coffees: heavy body, low acidity, and rich flavor tones.

The highest grade of Colombian coffee is *supremo.* Again, to simplify matters for commercial coffee buyers, the Colombians combine two grades of coffee—*supremo* and the second best, or *extra*— into one more comprehensive grade, *excelso.*

In recent years, Colombia has been replacing the older strains of arabica with newer, faster-growing and heavier-bearing strains. These new trees generally produce a rounder, flatter bean, which many roasters and importers feel is inferior to the classic Colombian coffees from the older trees. Although tasting against memory is tricky, I would tend to agree.

Nevertheless, Colombian coffee at its finest is, like Costa Rican or the best Kona, a classic. No quality is extreme. This coffee is generally full-bodied, but not so full-bodied as a Sumatran; acidy, but not nearly so acidy as an Ethiopian or Kenyan; richly flavored, but not quite so rich as a Sumatran or the best high-mountain Jamai-

CUBA

JAMAICA

DOMINICAN REPUBLIC

HAITI

BLUE MOUNTAIN

HAITIAN

SANTO DOMINGO

PUERTO RICO

Caribbean

&

Upper South America

MARACAIBO

CARACAS

CARACAS

TRUJILLO

MÉRIDA

CÚCUTA

PANAMA

TÁCHIRA

YENEZUELA

COLOMBIA

BUCARAMANGA

MEDELLÍN

ARMENIA

MANIZALES

BOGOTÁ

BOGOTÁ

can. The best Colombians even have a slight winy tone reminiscent of African coffees, but these winy tones are elusive and never dominate.

Venezuela: Maracaibo

At one time, Venezuela ranked close to Colombia in coffee production, but in the 1960s and 70s, as petroleum turned Venezuela into the richest country in South America, coffee was relegated to the economic back burner. Today Venezuela produces less than one percent of the world's coffee, and most of it is drunk by the Venezuelans themselves. Now that petroleum has failed to bring lasting prosperity, the Venezuelan government is attempting to promote coffee growing and exporting again as a means of diversifying and stabilizing its economy.

The best Venezuelan coffee comes from the far western corner of the country, the part that borders Colombia. Coffees from this area are called *Maracaibos*, after the port through which they are shipped, and include one coffee, *Cúcuta*, that is actually grown in Colombia, but is shipped through Maracaibo. Coffees from the coastal mountains farther east are generally marked *Caracas*, after the capital city, and are shipped through La Guaira, the port of Caracas.

The best-known Maracaibo coffees, in addition to Cúcuta, are *Mérida, Trujillo,* and *Táchira.* Mérida is the most distinctively Venezuelan and most likely to be found in specialty stores in the United States. Trujillo is rather lifeless, only a step above the cheap Brazilian coffees. Táchira and Cúcuta are a group in themselves, since their rich acidity makes them resemble Colombian coffees. Regardless of market name, the best grade is *Lavado Fino.*

The most characteristic Venezuelan coffees, in surprising contrast to the neighbor coffees from Colombia, are strikingly low in acidity. At worst they are spiritless, at best sweet and delicate. The finest, such as the Méridas, have fair to good body and an unemphatic but pleasant flavor with hints of richness. Venezuelan, if you can find it, is a good coffee to balance sharply acid coffees in blends and a comfortable coffee drunk straight.

Ecuador

Ecuador produces substantial amounts of coffee, but little seems to appear in specialty stores in the United States. This is another unremarkable coffee, with thin to medium body and occasional sharp acidity.

ECUADOR

ECUADOR

NORTHERNS

PERU

LIMA

CHANCHAMAYO

URUBAMBA

South America

BRAZIL

SANTOS

RIO

SÃO PAULO

RIO DE JANEIRO

SANTOS

PARANA

Peru: Chanchamayo

Generally a mildly acid coffee, light-bodied but flavorful and aromatic, *Peruvian* generally resembles the coffees of Mexico. Like Mexican, it is considered a "good blender" owing to its pleasant but understated character. Peruvian also is often used in dark roasts and as a base for flavored coffees. Wet-processed coffee from the Chanchamayo Valley, about 200 miles east of Lima in the high Andes, has the best reputation of the Peruvian coffees.. The Cuzco region, particularly the Urubamba Valley, also produces a respected washed coffee, and some good certified organic coffees from Northern Peru are now appearing in specialty-coffee stores. These coffees, certified by independent monitoring agencies to be organically grown, are promoted not only as a way of protecting the American consumer's health, but more important, as a way of supporting sustainable agriculture and a better and healthier life for those Peruvians involved in the cooperatives producing the coffees. For more on organic coffees, see, pages 75-77 in this chapter and Chapter 9.

Brazil: Bourbon Santos

When not suffering catastrophic frosts, Brazil produces 30 to 35 percent of the world's coffee. Vast plantations of millions of trees cover the hills of south-central Brazil. For the commercial coffee industry, Brazil is of supreme importance, a giant in every respect, but for the specialty-coffee trade, it shrinks to something smaller than El Salvador. Despite all the coffee produced in Brazil, none ranks close to the world's best. The Brazilian coffee industry has concentrated from the beginning on producing "price" coffees: cheap, fairly palatable, but hardly distinguished.

Of the many market names for Brazilian coffee, only one, *Santos*, is of importance for the specialty-coffee trade. Another, *Rio*, is significant mainly because it lends its name to a peculiar medicinal flavor that coffee people call *Rioy*.

Santos coffees are grown mainly in the state of São Paulo. In the nineteenth century, the harsh flavor of Rio coffee competed for popularity with the mild Santos. Much of the famous New Orleans coffee was Rio coffee, with chicory added, and some coffees dark-roasted in the United States today for the Latin taste may still include Rio coffee. This is because Latins, who drank the cheap, Rioy-tasting natural coffees at home while the more expensive, washed milds were being sold to the United States, may still crave a bit of the old home-country harshness in their dark-roast blends.

Santos coffee, named for one of the principal ports through which it is shipped, comes mainly from the original Bourbon strain of *Coffea arabica* brought to

RED SEA

YEMEN

MOCHA

MOCHA

ADEN

GULF OF ADEN

ETHIOPIA

GHIMBI

HARRAR

DJIMAH

SIDAMO

YIRGACHEFFE

SUDAN

UGANDA

KENYA

SOMALIA

ZAÏRE

BUGISHU

MT ELGON

LAKE VICTORIA

MT KENYA

KENYA NAIROBI

NAIROBI

KIVU

RWANDA BURUNDI

MT KILIMANJARO

MT MERU

MOSHI

MOMBASA

ARUSHA

LAKE TANGANYIKA

KILIMANJARO

TANZANIA

INDIAN OCEAN

Africa

MBEYA

LAKE MALAWI

Brazil in the eighteenth century from the island of Bourbon, now Réunion. For the first three or four years these trees produce a small, curly bean that coffee people call *Bourbon Santos*. This is the highest-grade coffee Brazil produces, and it will more than likely be the coffee a store sells as *Brazilian*. After three or four years, the beans begin to grow larger and flat; this coffee is called *Flat Bean Santos* and is cheaper and less desirable than Bourbon Santos. Bandeirante is a particularly good and consistent Brazailian estate-grown coffee that appears frequently on specialty coffee lists.

Bourbon Santos is smooth in flavor, medium in body, with moderate acidity—in short, another decent but hardly extraordinary coffee. Since it generally sells for about the same as more distinguished, unusual coffees, I see little reason to buy it except gourmet curiosity. The cheaper Brazilian coffees are occasionally for sale in specialty stores, presumably to be used by consumers to save money in their private blends.

Arabian Pennisula and African Yemen; Mocha

Mocha is one of the more confusing terms in the coffee lexicon. The coffee we call *Mocha* today is grown as it has been for hundreds of years in the mountains of Yemen, at the southwestern tip of the Arabian Peninsula. It was originally shipped through the ancient port of Mocha, which has since seen its harbor blocked by a sandbar. The name *Mocha* has become so permanently a part of the world's coffee vocabulary that it stubbornly sticks to a coffee that today would be described more accurately as Yemen or even Arabian.

The other ambiguity derives from the famed chocolate aftertaste of Arabian Mocha, which caused an enthusiast to use the same name for the traditional mixture of hot chocolate and coffee. So the term *Mocha* is an old-fashioned nickname for coffee, a common name for coffee from Yemen, and the name of a drink made up of coffee and hot chocolate in equal parts.

Aside from the wild coffees of Ethiopia, Arabian Mocha is the most ancient and traditional of coffees and still one of the best. It is the bean that literally sold the world on coffee. The true Arabian Mocha, from North Yemen, is still grown as it probably was over a thousand years ago, on irrigated terraces clinging to the sides of semiarid mountains; water is directed through little rock-lined channels to the roots of the plants, which are shaded from the desert sun by rows of poplars. The beans are also processed as they have been for centuries; even the best grades (*Mocha Extra*) are natural coffees, dried with the fruit still attached to the beans. The dried husk is later removed by millstone or other primitive methods, which accounts for the rough, irregular look of the beans. The names in Yemen coffee are also irregular; no two authorities agree as to whether they properly indicate grade, district, or variety of bean. Of the market names that most often appear on the lists of American specialty stores, *Mattari* usually represents a more acidy, winy version of the Mocha style than the lower-toned, more balanced *Sanani*.

The best coffees of Arabia and Ethiopia, and some from Kenya and Tanzania, are the most distinctively flavored coffees in the world. The acidity leaves an unmistakable dry, winelike aftertaste on the palate. If the coffees of Mexico can be compared with dry white wines, Mochas and Ethiopians are the Bordeaux of the coffee world. In addition to its rich winy quality, Mocha has its own particular flavor note, which some people, with more imagination than accuracy, I believe, associate with chocolate. Don't be disappointed if it doesn't taste like Hershey's. Rather, it is a peculiar rich edge to the aftertaste that lurks very clearly but subtly behind the winy acidity. The stronger you make the coffee, the more clearly you will taste the "chocolate" flavor.

During most of the 1980s, Yemen Mocha was not available in the United States, owing to the politics and quotas of the International Coffee Agreement (ICA). Stores either openly or clandestinely sold Ethiopian Harrar as a substitute. The Ethiopian coffee, like the Yemen a well-prepared but dry-processed coffee, is often excellent, but not as rich or as balanced as the Yemen. With the breakdown of the ICA quota system in 1989, Yemen Mocha is again available, offsetting the loss of many Ethiopian coffees owing to drought and civil war.

Since Mocha is such a distinctive coffee, everyone has something interesting to say about it: unique, sharp flavor; mellow body; creamy, rich, distinctive winy flavor. Despite its distinctiveness, I find Mocha a very balanced coffee, with a medium to full body, good but not overwhelming acidity, and a rich flavor with those tantalizing chocolate undertones. The aroma is overwhelming and delicious, heady with winy and acidy notes. Mocha is a fine coffee: If you can find the real thing, try some. It is also an excellent alternative for those who wish a coffee grown without chemicals. Yemen Mocha is as organic as it was over a thousand years ago when the first trees from Ethiopia were established.

Ethiopia: Harrar, Ghimbi, Sidamo, Yirgacheffe

Coffee was first cultivated in Yemen, but the arabica tree originated across the Red Sea in Ethiopia, on the mountain plateaus where tribespeople still harvest the wild berries. Ethiopian coffees are now among the world's most varied and distinctive, and at least one, Yirgacheffe, ranks among the best. All display the winy or fruity acidity characteristic of African and Arabian coffees, but they play a rich range of variations on this theme.

The Harrar coffees are the most widely available of fancy Ethiopian coffees. They are grown on small peasant plots and farms in the Eastern part of the country near the old capital of Harrar, at about 5,000 to 6,000 feet. You may see these coffees called *longberry Harrar* (large bean), *shortberry Harrar* (smaller bean), or *Mocha Harrar* (peaberry, or single bean). The *Harrar* may become *Harari, Harer,* or *Harar.* In Great Britain, Harrar is sold as *Mocha,* adding to the confusion surrounding that abused term. Some retailers cover both bases by calling this coffee *Moka Harrar.* Like Yemen Mocha, Harrar is a "handmade" coffee, processed carefully by the traditional dry method. It is grown on such a small scale and by such simple methods that it is almost certainly free of chemicals, and like Mocha a good choice for those who wish a traditional organically grown coffee.

Ethiopian Harrar can range from an extremely rough, winy coffee, gamey and light-bodied, to a coffee in which the wine quality becomes rich, fragrant, and fruit-like, and the body heavier, much like the best Yemen Mochas. Differences in quality of preparation probably have much to do with these variations.

Washed coffees from the western part of Ethiopia, usually sold as *Ghimbi* or *Gimbi,* share the pronounced winy tones of the Harrar coffees, but at best envelop them in a richer, more balanced profile and somewhat heavier, longer- finishing body.

The washed coffees of southern Ethiopia exhibit related but different flavor tendencies. These coffees may show little sign of the characteristic gamey and winy qualities of their compatriot coffees. Instead they tend to be gentle, and the wine tones turn distinctly fruit-like and flowery. They may appear in specialty stores described either by the district in which they're produced (*Sidamo, Washed Sidamo*), or by terms like *Ethiopian Fancies* or *Ethiopian Estate Grown.* The most celebrated of these coffees is called *Yirgacheffe* or *Yrgacheffe.* This coffee virtually has a cult following in the United States, and for good reason. Like the best Sumatran and Yemen coffees it is rich, teasing, and mysterious on the palate, with a very long, resonant finish. Like Sumatran, its acidity vibrates inside the richness of the body, but Yirgacheffe adds a soft, fragrant, flowery note so distinctive that it may make this the most unique among the world's coffees.

The recent terrifying misfortunes of the Ethiopian people, including drought, famine, and civil war, have reduced the availability of all Ethiopian coffees, particularly the washed varieties. Those Ethiopian coffees that do make it to the store bins will probably be expensive, but still worth every penny.

Kenya

Although Kenya is only a few hundred miles south of Ethiopia and Yemen, coffee growing came late here. The native Kenyans have taken up what the British started, and made their coffee industry even more modern and efficient than the Colombian. The coffee is raised both on small peasant plots and on larger plantations.

The main growing area stretches south from the slopes of 17,000-foot Mt. Kenya almost to the capital, Nairobi. There is a smaller coffee-growing region on the slopes of Mt. Elgon, on the border between Uganda and Kenya. Most Kenyan coffee sold in specialty stores appears to come from the central region around Mt. Kenya and is sometimes qualified with the name of the capital city, Nairobi. Grade designates the size of the bean; *AA* is largest, followed by *A* and *B*.

Kenyan coffee is usually sold purely on the basis of grade. Recently a West Coast importer with strong African connections has been bringing into the United States Kenya AA coffees explicitly selected by district or cooperative. These coffees are qualified by very specific and wonderfully exotic market names: *Kahuhia, Thunguri, Mungala*, etc. At this writing none of these names have established distinctive enough reputations in the specialty coffee trade to appear regularly on signs or brochures, but they may well do so in the future.

Kenyan, like the Arabian Mocha and the Ethiopian Harrar to the north, has a distinctive dry, winy aftertaste. At its best, however, it has a full-bodied richness that Ethiopian and even Mocha lack. Furthermore, it is improving, as growers respond to government incentives encouraging quality. This is a fine coffee for those who like the striking and unusual, not so winy as Ethiopian Harrar, fuller-bodied but more intense than Yemen Mocha.

Tanzania

The coffee industry of Tanzania initially was closely tied to that of Kenya, since early in their national histories they shared exploiters: first the Germans, then the British. Over the last decade the Tanzanian coffee industry has languished, however, while the Kenyan continues to improve and prosper.

Most Tanzanian arabicas are grown on the slopes of Mt. Kilimanjaro and Mt. Meru, near the Kenyan border. These coffees are called *Kilimanjaro* or sometimes *Moshi* or *Arusha* after the main towns and shipping points. Smaller amounts of arabica are grown much farther south, between Lake Tanganyika and Lake Nyasa, and are usually called *Mbeya*, after one of the principal towns, or *Pare*, a market name. In all cases, the highest grade is *AA*, followed by *A* and *B*.

Most Tanzanian coffees share the characteristically sharp, winy acidity typical of African and Arabian coffees. They tend to be medium- to full-bodied and fairly rich in flavor. In Great Britain I've encountered Tanzanian coffees from the Kilimanjaro region that exhibit the soft, floral richness of Yirgacheffe and similar washed Ethiopian coffees, but they seem not to be imported into the United States.

Uganda: Bugishu

The main part of the Uganda coffee production is robusta, used in instant coffees and as cheap fillers in blends. Uganda does produce one excellent arabica, however: Bugishu or Bugisu, from the western slopes of Mt. Elgon, on the Kenya border. It is another typically winy African coffee, close to Kenyan coffees in flavor but lighter in body.

Zimbabwe

Zimbabwe, formerly Rhodesia, has been exporting an excellent coffee to the United States in recent years. It is a washed coffee grown on medium-sized farms, and still another variant on the acidy, winy-toned coffees of East Africa. Some importers rank Zimbabwe with the best Kenyan coffees. Samples I have tasted were not so full-bodied or rich, but it is a fine and improving African-style coffee.

India: Mysore, Monsooned Malabar

About 80 percent of India's coffee is grown in the southern state of Karnataka, and is often sold as *Mysore*, after the former name of that state. At its best, Indian Mysore

is a lesser version of the Indonesian coffees: rich, sweet, and full-bodied. At its worst, it is heavy and lifeless.

Monsooned Mysore coffees have been exposed for several weeks to the moist winds of the monsoon, which yellows the bean and reduces the acidity, imparting a heavy, syrupy flatness reminiscent of aged coffees (see page 74). Monsooned coffees are considered a delicacy by many, perhaps because of the romance of the name and the process. They strike me as mainly useful in blends to mellow and give richness to rougher, more acidy coffees. They do not appear very often in American specialty stores. If you are curious, try an aged Indonesian coffee, which tastes fairly similar. If aged coffees are not available at your local stores, they can be ordered by mail from Peet's Coffee & Tea in Berkeley, California (see Sending for It). The best monsooned coffee is called *Monsooned Malabar*.

Sumatra: Mandheling

Some of the most famous coffees of the world are grown on the gigantic islands of the Malay Archipelago: Sumatra, Sulawesi or Celebes, and Java in Indonesia, and Papua New Guinea. Whereas Central American coffees are distinguished by their dry, winy aftertaste, the coffees of Indonesia and New Guinea are noted for their richness, full body, long finish, and an acidity that, though pronounced, is deep-toned, gentle, and enveloped in the complexity of the coffee. These are ideal coffees for those who want a beverage heavy enough to carry its flavor through milk. There is something warm and reflective about the best Indonesian coffees; they suggest gigantic meals and wicker chairs.

Many consider the Mandheling and Ankola coffees of Sumatra the world's finest. They are often hard to find, but still moderate in price. Of the two, Mandheling is the more admired, and the Lintong mark of Mandheling probably the most admired of all. Both Ankola and Mandheling are grown near the port of Padang in west-central Sumatra, at altitudes of 2,500 to 5,000 feet. Mandheling is probably the most full-bodied coffee in the world; you can feel the richness settling in the corners behind your tongue. It has a relatively low acidity, but enough to keep the cup vibrant and interesting. The flavor, like the body, is rich, smooth, and full.

These are dry-processed coffees, but the dried husk of the fruit is removed by washing in hot water, giving the coffee a more uniform appearance than is the case with many other dry-processed coffees. It may be that the unusual preparation of Sumatran and Sulawesi coffees, which combines prolonged contact of coffee bean with dried fruit characteristic of the dry method, and the meticulous cleaning and sorting

Indonesia & New Guinea

BORNEO
(KALIMANTAN)

CELEBES
(SULAWESI)

TORAJA

ANKOLA/MANDHELING

PADANG

SUMATRA

NEW GUINEA

JAVA

JAVA ARABICA

NEW GUINEA

usually associated with the wet method, contributes to the unique flavor characteristics of these fine coffees.

Sulawesi or Celebes: Toraja

The island of Sulawesi, formerly Celebes, spreads like a four-fingered hand in the middle of the Malay Archipelago. The Celebes coffee most likely to be found in specialty stores today is Toraja, from the mountainous area near the center of the island, in the palm of that hand. Celebes Toraja is a splendid coffee very similar to the best Sumatran coffees, though perhaps a little less rich and full-bodied, and a bit more acidy and vibrant in the upper tones. Like Sumatran, it is arguably one of the world's finest coffees.

Java

The Dutch planted the first arabica trees in Java early in coffee history, and before the rust disease virtually wiped out the industry, Java led the world in coffee production. Most of this early acreage has been replaced by disease-resistant robusta, but, under the sponsorship of the Indonesian government, arabica has made a modest comeback on several of the old estates originally established by the Dutch.

Java, like New Guinea, shares the low-toned richness of the other Indonesian and New Guinea coffees, but tends to be more obviously acidy, a bit lighter in body, and quicker to finish. Lurking in the acidity is a slight smoky or spicy twist.

Of the revived "old" estates that provide most of the good Java arabica, Djampit is the most likely source of the Java coffee in your specialty store.

Old Government, Old Brown, or simply *Old Java* describe Java arabica that has been held in warehouses for two to three years. Such matured coffee turns from green to light brown, gains body and sweetness, and loses acidity. Old Java was one of the world's great gourmet coffees until it disappeared from the market after World War II. It has recently been revived, although it remains difficult to obtain in the United States. Similar coffees are readily available in Great Britain, however, and visitors there should take the opportunity to sample them. Old Java is a fine variation on the Indonesian theme: heavy-bodied, rich, and darkly sweet.

New Guinea

Coffee labeled *New Guinea* usually comes from Papua New Guinea, which occupies the eastern half of the island of New Guinea. These coffees are grown in peasant patches and small plantations throughout the rugged mountain highlands. The best New Guinea coffee is estate- or plantation-grown. In general, New Guinea is a low-key version of the great Indonesian coffees: not as full-bodied as the best Sumatra, less acidy and aromatic than the best Celebes, but a comfortably rich cup. Coffee marketed as *Arona* seems to be the currently preferred New Guinea coffee among specialty roasters.

Hawaii: Kona

Kona, on the southwest coast of Hawaii, the largest island of the Hawaiian chain, produces the most famous and the most traditional of Hawaiian coffees. Coffee has been grown in smaller quantities elsewhere on the islands since the early days of European settlement, but encouraged by the impending closure of sugar and pineapple plantations and the tourism-induced popularity of Hawaiian coffee, large commercial concerns now have established plantations on the islands of Kauai and Molokai. Similar efforts soon may follow on other islands.

The original Kona coffee was, and still is, grown on small farms above the Pacific on the lower slopes of Mauna Loa. The coffee trees are shaded by a cloud cover that appears regularly most afternoons (the famous "automatic shade"), just in time to protect them from the full devastation of the tropical sun.

In years past, the original Kona coffee appeared to be on the way to becoming a luxurious memory. A tourist-inflated economy, low coffee prices, and an aging population of grower-landowners appeared to be conspiring to doom the Kona coffee industry. In addition, local schools no longer timed their vacations to coincide with coffee-picking season. But that was before the coffee price hikes of 1977, before a flood of tourists began carrying the romance of Kona coffee back to their kitchens, and before a new generation of small, quality-oriented coffee producers appeared to consolidate and capitalize on the revival. That revival is now in full swing. Whether it has produced a better Kona coffee or simply more of it is still subject to debate, but the tourists are happy and the little coffee towns are humming again.

In the process Kona has become a bit pricey, perhaps too pricey when compared with some of the world's great and undervalued coffees, such as the best Sumatran, Guatemalan, and Kenyan. Furthermore, its cost has created an equivalent to the Jamaican Blue Mountain syndrome: We now have commercial roasters producing Kona style coffee, Kona blend coffee, and coffee vaguely labeled *Kona* that probably consists in large part of Central American beans. At present most "Kona

Blend" coffees sold in Hawaii contain at most 5 percent actual Kona. Proposed regulations up the minimum percentage required by law to 51 percent.

Regardless of the hucksterism surrounding it, Kona is a unique and valuable American phenomenon, and at its most authentic is medium-bodied, fairly acidy, with some subtle winy tones, very richly flavored, and overwhelmingly aromatic when fresh. If you like to tantalize yourself with coffee fragrance before you drink, or find Indonesian coffees too rich, African coffees too winy, and Central and South American coffees too sharp, Kona may be the coffee for you.

The best grade is *extra fancy*, followed by *fancy* and *number one* grades. There are many excellent small estates in the Kona district. I am not familiar enough with them to make distinctions, but generally the coffee they produce is both better and more interesting than the Kona coffees that are pooled and sold generically.

Special Categories: Maragogipe

Maragogipe is a variety of arabica that produces a very large, rather porous bean. It is a mutant that spontaneously grew in Brazil, almost as though the one-time sleeping giant of the Americas thought regular beans were too puny and produced something in its own image. It was first discovered growing near the town of Maragogipe, in the eastern state of Bahia. Subsequently it has been carried all over the world and generally adopts the flavor characteristics of the soil to which it has been transplanted.

Opinions differ about the special qualities of the Maragogipe. William H. Ukers, one of the world's great authorities on coffee, found it tasted "woody and disagreeable" in 1928. Others have called it the finest coffee known and claim it has a heavier body than a comparable arabica coffee from the same region. I've compared a Guatemalan Maragogipe with other Guatemalan arabicas and found it less acidy, lighter in body, and flatter in flavor. This last test is hardly conclusive, however, since the Maragogipe I tried may have come from lower altitudes than the arabicas. Like any other straight coffee, Maragogipes should be sold by country of origin.

Because the Maragogipe bears less fruit per tree than other arabica varieties, fewer and fewer trees of this variety are being planted, and the large beans are becoming difficult to find on the specialty market. The Maragogipe coffee of the Cobán region of Guatemala has the best reputation of those currently traded, with the even larger beans of the Nicaraguan Maragogipe also well-regarded.

Peaberry

Throughout the world, the coffee fruit occasionally produces a single, rather than a double, bean. It grows to be small and round, with a tiny crevice that splits it halfway down the middle.

According to coffee folklore, peaberry grades are superior to normal grades from the same crop, apparently on the basis that the good stuff that ordinarily goes into a double bean goes into only one bean in the case of the peaberry. Nevertheless, coffee from peaberries tends to be lighter in body and flavor than coffee from high-grade normal beans from the same trees.

Peaberry coffee should be sold by country and market name like any other coffee. If you see a sign that simply says *peaberry*, you should inquire about the origin of the coffee.

Aged Coffees

As green coffee ages, it loses acidity and, depending on how it's stored, gains body. Coffee delivered for roasting soon after harvest and processing is called *new crop*. Coffee that has been held in warehouses for a period before delivery is called *old crop*. *Mature* coffees are usually two to three years old. *Aged* or *vintage* coffees, which have been held in dry and well-ventilated warehouses for six to ten years, constitute a fourth category. Under these conditions the acidity disappears and is replaced by a peculiar syrupy richness. In general, coffees with full body and robust flavor age better than the more delicate growths.

At present, few aged coffees are available; aging coffees represents a long-term capital investment most contemporary exporters are unwilling to make. Aged Venezuelan and Colombian coffees are occasionally for sale in specialty stores, however, and aged Sumatran and Celebes are available, but are seldom sold as straight coffees. If none of your local stores carries aged coffees, Peet's Coffee & Tea in Berkeley, California, usually carries one or two unblended, aged Indonesian coffees that can be purchased through the mail (see Sending for It). You ought to try an aged coffee at least once; you will immediately note a rather dull, sweet heaviness, not at all like the more stimulating richness of a full-bodied new-crop coffee or the still-lively sweetness of a mature coffee.

If you dislike acidy coffees, you might like a straight aged coffee. These coffees are most useful, however, in blends to give body and sweetness to young, dry, sharply acid coffees.

Organic and Progressive Coffees

I decided to contribute the second (perhaps controversial) adjective to this heading in order to suggest how the aspirations that cluster around the organic coffee movement go far beyond a simple appeal to consumers who want to protect their health. It is equally a matter of wanting to protect the planet and some of the other, poorer people who live on it. The organic coffee movement is part health movement, part environmental movement, and, on occasion, part grass-roots social improvement movement.

Organic coffees are coffees whose growing conditions and processing have been certified by one of several independent monitoring and testing agencies to be free of the use of pesticides, herbicides, and other potentially harmful chemicals. The agency conducts inspections of the farms and processing facilities, tests the soil and plants, and generally monitors the progress of the coffee from tree to marketplace. This process is understandably costly.

If organic coffees existed only to protect the consumer from potentially harmful agricultural residues, there would be (and are) simpler and cheaper ways to meet the same need. As I suggested earlier, consumers could simply buy a traditional coffee grown naturally, like Yemen Mocha or Ethiopian Harrar. Or they could buy a coffee that has been subjected to independent laboratory tests to verify that it does not contain harmful chemical residues. Many such coffees are now appearing in specialty stores. Or they could simply forget about the whole issue and drink whatever coffee came along, trusting that very little harmful residue could possibly survive the cumulative rigors of processing, roasting, and brewing.

But consumers who buy a certified organic coffee are often supporting a complex set of goals and processes in which the consumer health issue is more vehicle than end in itself. Although some of the certified organic coffees emerging on the market today come from small farms or estates, many are produced by small peasant growers who have been assisted in organizing themselves into cooperatives that share processing facilities, agricultural information, and various forms of mutual assistance. Although such cooperatives are common wherever coffee is grown on small plots, the cooperatives that grow organic coffees stress the well-established procedures of organic farming: composting, organic pest control, etc.

In return, the farmers obtain a premium for their coffee. Because the coffee they grow is certified organic, they have an opportunity to bypass the usual export channels and to move their coffee into the consuming country via businesspeople who specialize in fine coffee or organic produce. Thus, farmers who a few years before might have been selling their coffee to people cruising the backroads in trucks, buying coffee at pennies a pound, now may be selling it through a cooperative to specialists in organic produce or fine coffees. The process is facilitated by a loose network of those who promote organic agriculture in the growing countries, and those importers and roasters who promote organic produce in the consuming countries.

Organic certification is the key to the success of the entire process. Its cost, and the cost of the somewhat lower yields occasioned by the organic method, are passed on to the consumer, who pays a little more for a guaranteed pure product, in the process supporting more sustainable agricultural practices and a better life for a number of small coffee growers.

Whether certified organic coffees will continue to be produced predominantly by small growers and idealistic cooperatives, or whether larger farms with less idealistic agendas will begin to certify coffees, remains to be seen.

It is also not clear whether the American certification movement will extend beyond its present focus on Hawaii and Latin America to other parts of the world that produce more unusual or distinctive coffees, like Africa or Indonesia.

Organic Coffee and Cup Quality   At this writing, there appear to be no great certified organic coffees. This does not mean that no great coffees are grown without chemicals; many undoubtedly are, but are not certified as such. Nor does it mean that great organic coffees cannot be grown deliberately and programmatically. If peasant-grown Yemen and Ethiopian coffees are as good as they are without chemicals, I fail to see why more self- conscious growers can't also produce great coffees following an organic program. The problem simply may be that the great coffees and the organic concept haven't gotten together yet.

At this writing, the most widely available certified organic coffees are from Peru or Mexico's Chiapas State. Both produce a smooth, pleasant, medium-bodied cup characteristic of those areas. A Costa Rican organic I tasted recently was not the equal of the best Costa Rican coffees, but was still excellent: full-bodied and classic. Best of all was a Guatemalan organic from the Huehuetenango district that showed many of the characteristics of finer, higher-grown coffee: heavier body and richer and more complex acidity and aroma.

It seems inevitable that the organic market niche will grow, and with it will come better and better coffees. Care always seems to pay off in the coffee business, and organic farmers are nothing if not careful and caring. In the meantime, there doubtless will be many people who will choose to drink a slightly more expensive coffee with slightly less excitement in the cup in order to support the goals and aspirations of the organic coffee movement, while assuring themselves of an absolutely pure product.

Blends and Blending Your Own

Since blending is the ultimate proof of coffee expertise, and since it gives consumers a chance to participate in the creation of their own pleasure, specialty-coffee customers often blend their own coffees. The only drawback to such a rewarding practice is impatience: Consumers may decide to begin blending coffees before they know enough to do it right, and sellers may get frustrated if they have to stop to make a blend of five coffees for a customer when there are ten more customers waiting in line. But few storekeepers will object if they feel the customer is really blending, rather than just showing off or demanding attention.

Different roasts, coffees with different caffeine contents, or straight coffees from different countries can be blended. One of the more common practices is to blend dark and light roasts, a procedure I discuss in detail in Chapter 2. Another reason to blend is to cut caffeine content. If you drink only decaffeinated coffee, you may get bored, since specialty shops carry a limited number of caffeine-free coffees. An excellent compromise is to blend a caffeine-free coffee with your favorite straight coffees, thus cutting your caffeine intake while fulfilling your sense of adventure.

The art of blending straight coffees of the same roast is a subtler business, but hardly difficult once the basic principles are understood. Blenders who work for large commercial coffee companies need to be highly skilled because their goals are more complex than our simple efforts to blend a coffee that suits us better than would a straight coffee, taken alone. The commercial blender blends to cut costs while keeping quality high, and wants to assemble a blend with consistent taste even though the straight coffees that make up the blend may differ. Certain coffees are not always available; some coffees may be cheaper than others at certain times of the year, and so on. But in an economy dominated by highly advertised brand names, the blend has to taste more or less the same every time. So blenders may find themselves amid a shifting kaleidoscope of prices and availabilities, constantly juggling coffees in an attempt to keep the taste the same and the cost down.

A good commercial blend takes a fresh, sharp, acidy, aromatic coffee such as a Colombian, Costa Rican, or Mexican and combines it with a decent grade of Brazilian coffee to cut costs. If it's a very high-priced blend, the blender might combine more than one quality coffee with the Brazilian: a rich, full-bodied coffee to balance a bright, acidy coffee, for instance. Low-cost blends might decrease the proportion of mild and Brazilian coffees and make up the difference with a very bland and inexpensive robusta. The cheapest blends eliminate the high-priced mild coffee entirely and simply combine a decent grade of Brazilian with the robustas.

With blends found in specialty-coffee stores, the blender's main goal is simply to produce a distinctive and consistent coffee, rather than to cut costs. A typical specialty roaster may have only one blend, a house blend, or as many as a half dozen for all pocketbooks, tastes, and times of day. A few larger specialty roasters, like their commercial counterparts, also may blend for price, although with less urgency and compromise.

Consumers who create their own blends have less to consider than either commercial or speciality blenders. They shouldn't have to worry about consistency, and they can't use blending to bring the price down much, since most straight coffees sold through specialty stores are already premium coffees with premium prices. Blending for price would be like trying to save money by cutting caviar with truffles. Commercial coffee concerns can save money on their blends because they are able to buy large quantities of cheap coffee at bargain prices. As I indicate in Chapter 4, a more effective way to save money would be to buy green coffee in bulk and learn to roast it yourself.

So you will be blending for taste. The way to go about this is simple: Combine coffees that complement one another with qualities the others lack. The world's oldest and most famous blend, for instance, combines Arabian Mocha and Java. Part of the reason for its fame is tradition. The blend originated when Mocha and Java were the only coffees the world knew. Nevertheless, it embodies the sound principle of balancing extremes or complements. Remember that Mocha is a mildly acidy, winy coffee with a fairly light body; Java is a heavier-bodied coffee, sweeter and deeper-toned.

Together they make a brew that is both less and more—less striking and distinctive, but more balanced and comprehensive.

The first, pleasurable task in assembling a personal blend is to learn to distinguish acidity, body, flavor, and finish in coffee, and possibly some of the more individual quirks: the dry finish of African coffees, the smoky tones of Guatemalan Antigua. You should also know what qualities you prefer in a coffee and what to blend for. You may simply want an all-around coffee with the best of all worlds, or a basically heavy, mellow coffee with only a little acidy brightness, or a brisk, light coffee with plenty of body as well.

Always proceed the same way. If you have a favorite coffee that seems to lack something, combine it with a coffee that has in extreme form what your favorite lacks.

- For brightness, snap, and acidity, add a Costa Rican, Colombian, Guatemalan, or any of the good Central American coffees.
- For body and richness, add a Sumatran Mandheling, Celebes, or New Guinea.
- For sweetness, add a Venezuelan Maracaibo or Haitian.
- For even more sweetness or to dull a bright coffee, add an aged coffee or monsooned Indian coffee.
- For flavor and aroma, add a Kenyan, Hawaiian Kona, Jamaican Blue Mountain, Sumatran, Celebes, Guatemalan, or Colombian.
- To add a winy note, make the acidy coffee an Ethiopian Harrar; to add richness as well, make it a Kenyan or Yemen Mocha.

The only real mistake you can make blending is to combine two coffees that are distinctive or extreme in the same way. Two coffees with sharp, winy acidity, such as a Kenyan and an Ethiopian Harrar, would produce a pointless blend. Better to combine an Ethiopian Harrar with a richer, low-key coffee such as a Mysore. One has to be particularly wary of the distinctive, gamey coffees of Africa, which may make a dissonant blend with other acidy coffees. On the other hand, coffees such as Mysore or most Venezuelans are so congenially understated that they get along with everything. Others, such as Mocha and the large Latin American family of coffees, are like easygoing individualists who manage to mix with almost everybody, yet still maintain their distinction.

Blending with Chicory or Fig

Dark-roast coffee is sometimes blended with chicory, particularly in northern

France and the southern United States. Chicory is an easily grown, disease-resistant relative of the dandelion. The young leaves, when used for salad, are called *endive*. The root resembles the dandelion root and, when dried, roasted, and ground, produces a deep brown, full-bodied, almost syrupy beverage that has a bitter peppery tang and doesn't taste at all like coffee. In fact, it tastes as if someone put pepper in your herbal tea mixture. It is almost impossible to drink black; sweetened with milk, it makes a fairly satisfying hot beverage, though it leaves a bitter, cloying aftertaste.

According to Heinrick Jacob in *Coffee: The Epic of a Commodity*, some Germans first exploited the use of chicory as a coffee substitute around 1770. The Germans adopted chicory because it lacked caffeine and (possibly most important) because it eluded the tariffs imposed on such foreign luxuries as coffee. Jacob describes the trademark on eighteenth-century packets of chicory: "A German farmer sowing chicory seed, and waving away ships freighted with coffee beans. Beneath was the legend: "Without you, healthy and rich." But it was under Napoleon's "Continental system," a reverse blockade aimed at cutting England off from its European markets and making conquered Europe self- sufficient, that chicory came into its own. The French developed the sugar beet to replace sugarcane, but the chicory root was the best they could come up with for coffee. It was not much of a substitute, since it has neither caffeine nor the aromatic oils of coffee. After the collapse of the Napoleonic empire, the French went back to coffee, but never totally lost their taste for chicory.

The famous New Orleans–style coffee, which came to the southern United States with the French colonists, tastes the way it does for three reasons: It has chicory in it, the beans are dark-roasted, and some cheap, naturally processed Brazilian coffee has been added to give the brew that old-time sour twist. If you like New Orleans–style coffee and want to carry your taste to more refined levels, you first need to determine which components account for what you like about the flavor: the chicory, the dark roast, or the sour beans.

I assume by now you've tried dark-roast coffee. Next, buy ground French chicory, sold at most large specialty-coffee stores. It costs a little less than coffee and goes farther, which is another reason for developing a taste for New Orleans–style coffee. Now simply experiment by varying the proportions of chicory to ground dark-roast coffee. About 10 percent chicory will barely affect flavor, but will considerably increase the body and darkness of the brew. The peppery taste clearly emerges at 20 percent, but still doesn't overpower the coffee flavor, and you can drink such a blend black with pleasure. Most New Orleans blends are 30 to 40 percent chicory. At these proportions the bitter chicory flavor at least equals the coffee flavor, and I think most people would have trouble drinking such a blend black.

If you mix chicory and dark-roast coffee and it still doesn't taste as good to you as the canned commercial New Orleans blends, then it's the cheap, naturally processed, Rioy-tasting beans you like, and you probably can't buy them unless you find a Latin American roaster who will let you have some green.

In Great Britain a blend of coffee and roast ground fig is popular. Fig has a flavor very different from the heavy peppery bite of chicory. Mixed in proportions of one part fig to seven parts ground coffee, fig adds considerable body and a delicate fruity sweetness to the cup. I much prefer it to chicory, but since it's unavailable commercially in the United States and most readers will hardly bother to roast and grind it themselves, I won't carry on about it.

Flavored Coffees

Flavored whole-bean coffees—the hazelnut cremes, Irish cremes, and chocolate raspberries of the specialty-coffee world—are neither as innovative nor as decadent as they may appear at first glance. Although this particular approach to flavoring coffee in its whole-bean form did not come on the scene until the late 1970s, the notion of adding other ingredients to coffee to complicate or enhance its natural flavor goes back to the first coffee drinkers, the Arabs of what is now Yemen, who from the very beginning added a variety of spices to coffee during brewing.

Combining chocolate with coffee was an innovation of seventeenth-century Europeans, for whom coffee and chocolate were stimulating novelties from the opposite ends of the known world. The practice of adding citrus to coffee also has a long history, as does the practice of combining spirits and coffee.

In fact, if we examine the list of best-sellers among the flavors used to enhance whole bean coffees today, we will find very little new. The leading seller over the last couple of years is hazelnut creme, also called *vanilla nut, hazelnut vanilla,* or simply *hazelnut.* The association of this flavor with coffee almost certainly rose from the long-standing association of Frangelico, a traditional Italian hazelnut-flavored liqueur, with coffee. With the second most popular flavor, Irish creme, the relationship may derive either from the liqueur of the same name, or, more likely, from one of the most popular American coffee drinks of all time, Irish coffee, with its combination of Irish whiskey, coffee, and lightly whipped cream. Most of the rest of the list of top-selling flavors can be similarly placed in a traditional context; chocolate with the tradition of the coffee-chocolate drink Mocha; cinnamon with the practice of combining cinnamon with coffee that began with the first coffee drinkers of the Middle East; amaretto with the traditional liqueur; and so on.

Thus, coffee tradition had already established the compatibility of certain flavors with coffee long before the advent of flavored whole-bean coffees. The difference, of course, is that the traditional drinks added flavoring during or after brewing the coffee, whereas the contemporary versions are flavored well before brewing.

This difference means that coffee flavorings added to the whole bean need to be considerably stronger than those added after the coffee is brewed. The whole-bean flavors need to carry through the brewing process; assert themselves in the context of the already powerful coffee flavor; give the sensation of sweetness without sugar, the sensation of creaminess without cream, the sensation of whiskey or liqueur with only a tiny addition of alcohol; and maintain their freshness in a product that is largely handled in bulk and exposed to air and oxidation for weeks.

Such extraordinary versatility and durability can be achieved only through the wonders of modern chemistry. To my knowledge, no flavoring used in whole-bean coffees is entirely natural, and many are, in the technical sense, entirely artificial. The natural flavors used in some sophisticated soft drinks and ice creams, for example, would not have the staying power to remain with the coffee during its long odyssey from roasting plant to cup.

The people who create and market flavors for the specialty-coffee trade usually provide flavors and fragrances for a variety of purposes, and draw from an extraordinary and growing body of technical and aesthetic knowledge that includes aspects of physiology, chemistry, botany, and the long cultural traditions of flavor- and fragrance-making. Thus, the flavors added to whole-bean coffees are suggested by tradition, created by chemistry, and ultimately chosen by the roaster, who may further suggest new flavors or request custom modification of the old. Consequently, one roaster may carry a creamier version of hazelnut creme and another a nuttier or less assertive version, even though both purchase their flavors from the same vendor. Some roasters work closely with the flavor chemists, building a common vocabulary of reference. So even in this relatively artificially defined arena, specialty coffees still exhibit an individualism absent in most commercial products.

Flavor specialists often divide the flavors used in flavoring whole-bean coffees into four families. The vanilla-based group includes not only the various cremes and vanillas, but all the nut flavors, including the best-selling hazelnut, amaretto (almond), and macadamia nut. The majority of the public's favorites come from this group.

Second in popularity are flavors based on chocolate. Third are flavors based on fruit (the favorite is coconut), and finally come flavors based on spice, notably cinnamon.

If you ask either flavor specialists or roasters what their goal is in flavoring coffee, they would unanimously declare that their hope is to "enhance the coffee," or achieve a "balanced marriage of coffee and flavor." This may well be their goal, but if it's a marriage, the flavoring part is definitely the spouse who does the talking. It would doubtless be possible to produce a flavored coffee in which the added flavor component is muted and understated, so evanescent that it merely whispers romantic innuendos to the unconscious, but with most flavored coffees I've tasted the flavoring pretty much shouts, if not screams and has tantrums.

Marketing people tell me that consumers prefer it that way. Perhaps. Perhaps specialty roasters have two clienteles, a clientele that is genuinely attracted to coffee and loves its subtle range of sensual experience, and another clientele that simply likes to be surprised and entertained by interesting novelties. And perhaps marketing people listen too closely to the second group. It is interesting to note that in the past two or three years hazelnut has come to the fore as the best-selling flavor for whole-bean coffee, despite the fact that it is not a flashy flavor like amaretto or piña colada, and lacks the romantic associations of flavors like macadamia nut or passion fruit. In fact, hazelnut is a rather rich, quiet flavor that marries particularly well with coffee, and allows some of the natural roast and flavor to come through. It may be that specialty-coffee consumers are ahead of the marketers, as often happens in a business that was created in part out of a rebellion against the domination of marketing over substance.

Specialty roasters themselves divide into two camps on the issue of flavored coffees. Some, usually those who sell their coffees directly through their own stores, refuse to produce flavored coffees for a variety of reasons. The most frequently cited: Flavored coffees don't taste good; their aggressive fragrances overpower other, more authentic aromas in a retail environment; and they contaminate the store grinders. Other roasters, usually wholesale roasters who need to please large retail customers like supermarkets, have little choice in the matter; they produce flavored coffees because they must in order to stay competitive.

The taste issue is easily pin-pointed: All flavorings added to whole-bean coffees leave a flat, metallic aftertaste. With some flavors this aftertaste is barely discernable; with others it is inescapable. And recall that the effect of a well-brewed cup of coffee does not stop at the point the cup is empty; the experience rings in the senses, humming just below the surface of consciousness, for minutes, perhaps even hours, mingling agreeably with the stimulation of the caffeine. However immediate the first burst of pleasure from a good flavored coffee, its aftertaste never quite delivers the same resonance the aftertaste of an unflavored coffee does.

There are doubtless other, vaguer issues that come into play when a roaster or old-time coffee lover confronts a flavored coffee. Specialty-coffee roasters and aficionados have always been the rebels and idealists of the coffee world, and I suspect that flavored coffees smack too much of commercial compromise and technological contrivance for them. There always comes a moment when dedicated coffee roasters and brokers begin talking about why they love the business, and the main point invariably seems to be there is always more to learn, more subtleties to be fathomed, more discoveries to be made. The coffee bean is an extraordinarily complex chemical system, with some 500 chemical constituents already identified and, I'm told, at least 200 more still not even known or named. It is this tiny but potent natural universe that draws one on and simultaneously both satisfies and tantalizes the senses and the mind.

However much intelligence and creativity goes into producing flavored coffees, they are still more cultural production than natural mystery. For many coffee lovers they're too predictable. If tasting natural coffees is rafting a wild river, then for coffee aficionados tasting flavored coffees is a little like taking the water slide in a suburban theme park.

There is a well-worked-out rationale among specialty roasters in regard to flavored coffees; this is the notion that they provide a comfortable transition to "real" coffees for consumers who were raised on soft drinks. The idea is that you graduate from cherry cola to hazelnut creme to Sumatran. Supporters of this idea point out that the generation raised in the 1960s rejected coffee for several reasons: First, because coffee was seen as an establishment habit indulged in by over-the-hill fossils and warmongers; second, because coffee in the 1960s had become a lousy drink anyhow, competition and cost-cutting having ruined it; and third, because bottled and canned cola drinks had become widely available as consistent and flavorful coffee substitutes. Thus, the theory runs, the continuity of the coffee-drinking tradition was broken, and subsequent generations now need to be wooed back into the coffee fold by ingratiating beverages like flavored coffees, which link high-quality coffee with more familiar and accessible flavors like chocolate, vanilla, and cinnamon.

There may be something to this theory. It would also account for the growing popularity of espresso drinks with milk, since those beverages, particularly when drunk with sugar, are much easier for the novice coffee-drinker to enjoy than a cup of black, unsweetened American-roast coffee.

At any rate, people who do enjoy flavored coffees obviously should drink them and thumb their collective nose at the purists in the roasting room. If you are trying flavored coffee for the first time, you might want to start with one of the more popular varieties: one of the variants on hazelnut, for example, or an Irish creme, or a chocolate, macadamia nut, amaretto, or one of the variants on coconut. An even more systematic approach might be to try one from each of the four flavor families I noted earlier: the vanilla and nut, the chocolate, the fruit, and the spice.

On the other hand, if you are already drinking flavored coffees and are interested in experimenting with the unadorned product, you might begin with one of the more distinctive straight coffees, particularly those that are full-bodied and rich: Sumatran, Ethiopian Yirgacheffe, or Guatemalan, for example. Or try a darker-roasted version of one of these coffees, and add a little cream or milk to your cup. Or you might go so far as to flavor the brewed coffee yourself. Rather than buy amaretto-flavored coffee, add a little actual amaretto or almond extract to your cup. Or try a drop or two of vanilla and a twist of orange peel. In a recent newsletter, Pannikin Coffee & Tea of San Diego suggests serving brewed coffee accompanied by a tray of natural flavorings: vanilla bean, nutmeg, citrus peel, cinnamon stick, etc., thus permitting your guests to add their own flavoring to the brewed coffee.

Following the same do-it-yourself line of thinking, at least three concerns have brought out flavorings specifically designed to be added to coffee after it is brewed. Flavor-Mate presents its liquid flavorings in purse-sized plastic dropper bottles with snap-on closures, so you can flavor your coffee when you're on the move. Wagners presents its flavorings in miniature glass bottles. Crystal Persuasions is a line of flavored granulated sugars. The Flavor-Mate and Wagners lines duplicate most of the currently popular whole-bean coffee flavors. If you have trouble finding these products, Pannikin in San Diego carries a good selection (see Sending for It).

A final note of warning to those who grind their own beans: Flavored coffees are liable to ruin grinders that use burrs rather than blades to take apart the coffee. The flavoring material gums up the burrs and complicates cleaning and is almost impossible to remove completely. In other words, once you grind French vanilla, you will continue to grind French vanilla for several days, whether you like it or not. And if you grind several flavored coffees in a row, you may begin to get a sort of combined, omnibus flavor out of your grinder, a one-size-fits-all flavor, no matter what you put into it. Even the little blade grinders need to be carefully cleaned after grinding a batch of flavored coffee, so as not to contaminate the next lot.

Roasting

CHAPTER

4

Roasting It
*How coffee is roasted and
how to roast your own*

Since we have come to associate the word *coffee* so absolutely with a hot, aromatic brown liquid, some may find it hard to believe that human beings fussed for several hundred years before concluding that the most effective way to get what they wanted from the coffee tree was to roast the dried kernel of the fruit, grind it, and combine the resulting powder with hot water to make a beverage. The alternative solutions are many, and some still survive as part of the cuisines of Africa and Asia. The berries can be fermented to make a wine, for example, or the leaves and flowers cured and steeped in boiling water to produce a coffee tea. In parts of Africa, people soak the raw beans in water and spices, then chew them like candy. The raw berries are also combined with bananas, crushed, and beaten to make a sort of raw coffee and banana smoothie.

The key to the success of the current mode of coffee making is the roasting process, to which we owe the delicately flavored oils that speak to the palate as eloquently as caffeine does to the nervous system. "The coffee berries are to be bought at any Druggist," says a seventeenth-century English pamphlet on coffee drinking, "about three shillings a pound; take what quantity you please and over a charcoal fire, in an old pudding pan or frying pan, keep them always stirring til they be quite black, and yet if you exceed, then do you waste the Oyl, which only make the drink; and if less, then will it not deliver its Oyl, which must make the drink."

We may disagree with the Englishman's taste in roasting ("quite black" sounds more Neapolitan than English), but he knew what counted: the breaking down of fats and carbohydrates into an aromatic, volatile, oily substance that alone produces the essential coffee flavor and aroma. Without roasting, the bean gives up its caffeine and acids, and even its protein, but not its flavor.

Roasting Overview

The chemistry of coffee roasting is complex and still not completely understood. This is owing to the variety of beans, as well as to the complexity of the coffee essence, which still defies chemists' best efforts to duplicate it in the laboratory.

Much of what happens to the bean in roasting is interesting, but irrelevant. The bean loses a good deal of its moisture, for instance, which means it weighs less after roasting than before (a fact much lamented among penny-conscious commercial roasters). It loses some protein, about 10 to 15 percent of its caffeine, and traces of other chemicals. Sugars are burned or caramelized, which contributes color and some body to the cup.

Roasting is simple in theory: The beans must be heated, kept moving so they don't burn or roast unevenly, and cooled, or quenched, when the right moment has come to stop the roasting. Coffee that is not roasted long enough or hot enough to bring out the oil has a pasty, nutty, or bread-like flavor. Coffee roasted too long or at too high a temperature is thin-bodied, burned, and industrial-flavored. Very badly burned coffee tastes like old sneakers left on the radiator. Coffee roasted too long at too low a temperature has a baked flavor.

Most roasting equipment uses a rotating drum above a heat source, usually a gas flame. Operating like a Laundromat clothes drier, the rotating drum tumbles the beans, ensuring an even roast. The air temperature inside the drum is usually controlled at about 500° F; the precise temperature depends on the intentions and philosophy of the operator. For the first five minutes, the bean merely loses "free" moisture, which is not bound up in the cellular structure of the bean. Eventually, however, the deep "bound" moisture is forced out, expanding the bean and producing a snapping or crackling noise. So far, the color of the bean has not changed appreciably (it should be a light brown), and the oil has not been volatilized. Then, when the interior temperature of the bean reaches about 400° F, the oil suddenly begins developing. This process is called *pyrolysis*, and it is marked by darkening in the color of the bean.

This is the moment of truth for the coffee roaster, because the pyrolysis, or volatilization, of the coffee essence must be stopped at precisely the right moment to obtain the flavor and roast desired. The beans cannot be allowed to cool of their own accord or they may overroast. They are quickly dumped into a metal box, where pyrolysis continues until the beans are quenched with either cold air or a light spray of cold water. Most specialty roasters air-quench their coffee.

Roasting Equipment

The exact nature of the equipment used to roast coffee depends on the ambitions of the roaster. The coffee bean, when delivered to the roaster in burlap sacks, ranges in color from light brown to whitish green. The beans are always stored green. Roasted whole beans begin to deteriorate in flavor within a week after roasting, and ground coffee may taste stale within an hour of grinding, whereas green coffee may even improve with age.

Most large commercial roasters resemble a gigantic crew rotating inside a drum. The screw works the coffee down the drum; by the time the coffee reaches the end of the drum, it is roasted and ready to be cooled by air or water. The temperature is controlled automatically, and the roaster includes equipment that monitors both the air temperature and the temperature inside the moving mass of beans to ensure uniform roast. Such roasters are called *continuous roasters* for obvious reasons and are inappropriate for specialty roasters because they cost too much, roast too much coffee at a time, don't permit direct control of the roasting process, and don't work very well for dark roasts.

The average specialty roaster uses a *batch roaster*, which is simply a rotating drum with a heat source under or to the sides of it. When the coffee is ready, the roaster dumps it into a metal box, where it is gently stirred and cooled. These batch roasters may be as large as four or five feet in diameter, or as small as a small waste can set on its side.

On page 91 you will find a picture of the simplest kind of small batch roaster. The drum (A) tumbles the roasting coffee over the gas flame (B). The fan (C) sucks the smoke and chaff out of the drum. When the beans are dumped into the cooling box (D) and ready to be quenched, the fan is reversed, and cool air is forced back through the hot beans in the box.

More sophisticated batch roasters retain the basic structure of drum, heat, and cooling box, but may use a strong current of hot air to heat the beans, so that the metal drum itself remains relatively cool. These apparatus are sometimes called *convection roasters*. Another kind of recently developed batch roaster uses radiant heat panels on either side of the drum. Some contemporary roasting apparatus, called *fluid bed roasters*, carry the hot air principle of convection roasters even further, by dispensing with the drum entirely and virtually suspending the beans on a column of hot air, much like an electric popcorn popper does with corn kernels.

In all cases, the goal of the technology is to offer the operator maximum control over the process, and to keep the beans from touching hot metal for anything longer than a split second at a time, to prevent scorching or uneven roasting. Proponents of the various styles of batch roaster all make cogent arguments in favor of their favored system and in mild deprecation of rival approaches, but to my knowledge no conclusive comparative tests have ever been conducted to validate any of these claims and counterclaims. In my observation and experience, all batch roasting apparatus, including the oldest and crankiest, can produce outstanding coffee if used with care and intelligence.

The Roasting Procedure; System and Intuition

Roasters tend to fall into two schools: those who follow a technical system, involving precisely defined and monitored variables like time and temperature, and those who depend mainly on eyes, ears, nose, and intuition. A systematic roaster might roast all coffees for the same period of time, for instance, but roast each at a different temperature depending on the desired color of roast and the bean's moisture content and hardness, or resistance to heat. These temperatures, based on tests, would be recorded. Thus, in theory, the roasting process for a given coffee could be duplicated by anyone who could read and set the dials of the roaster. Some roasters may even go so far as to monitor degree of roast by means of a specialized *spectrophotometer*, an instrument that precisely measures shades of darkness in a roasted, ground coffee without becoming confused by the other colors the human eye takes in when it looks at a coffee.

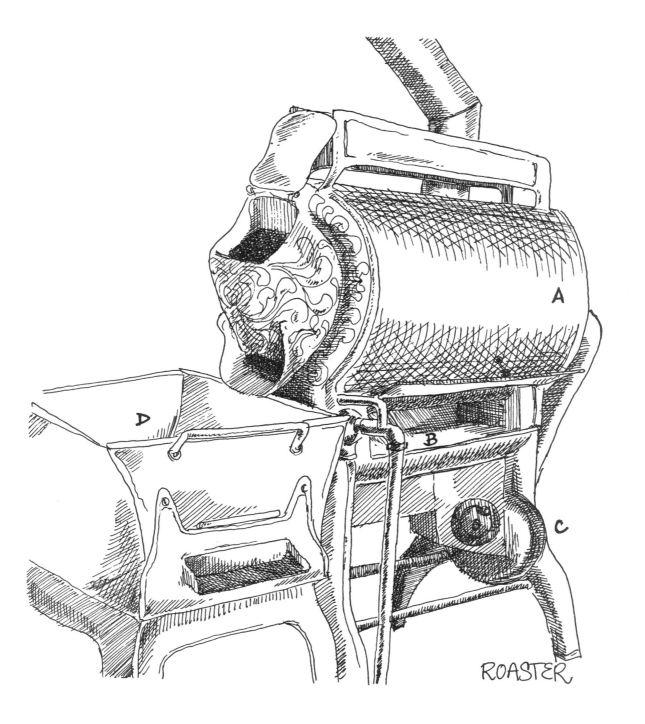

ROASTER

Most specialty roasters judge the color of a roast by looking at it, however, and judge the success of their roast simply by tasting the coffee. Technically inclined roasters may do a very good job, but if they, or roasters of any school, stop tasting and start depending on technical routine alone, the quality of the roast inevitably suffers.

As for the completely intuitive roaster, I would like to introduce a memory of the old Graffeo coffee shop in San Francisco, locally famous for its rich, sweet espresso coffee. In years past, Graffeo coffee was roasted in a small, old-fashioned batch roaster by John Repetto, the father of the present proprietor and an intuitive roaster if there ever was one.

Three open bags of green coffee stood next to the roasting machine. Two contained coffees from South and Central America, one with light and the other with heavy body. The third bag was a mix of several sharp, distinctively flavored coffees: Arabian, Mocha, Kenyan, or Ethiopian, for instance. Repetto would nonchalantly scoop almost equal parts of each into the rotating drum of the roasting machine, close the door, and turn up the flame. He then wandered around the store, waiting on customers and following this timetable, which anyone who roasts coffee at home would be wise to follow as well:

1) Coffee smells like the sack (do something else for awhile).
2) Coffee smells like bread (do something closer to the roaster).
3) The beans begin to crackle (prepare for action).

When he heard the beans crackle, Repetto knew that the oil was developing, and he began to check the color of the beans by collecting a few with a little spoon-like implement called a *trier*, which he stuck through an opening in the front of the roasting cylinder.

When the color was about medium brown (the shop sold and still sells mainly dark-roast coffee), he opened a door in the cylinder and the beans tumbled out into the box in front of the roaster. The roasting continued inside the steaming crackling beans while Repetto stirred them and studied them for color. When they were dark brown ("the color of a monk's tunic"), he tripped a lever on the side of the fan box, forcing cold air up through perforations at the bottom of the box to stop the roasting process at exactly the correct moment.

Much specialty coffee is still roasted in similarly informal fashion in similarly charming old machines. But times are changing. I recall my disappointment when I revisited the Graffeo shop and found the old roasting machine holding up plants in the store window and John's son, Luciano, wearing a white smock and watching some dials on the front of a chrome box.

I recognized this box as a *Sivitz roaster*, the creation of Michael Sivitz, a well-known technical writer on coffee who some years before had gone into the business of producing his own roasting equipment based on the fluid bed principle mentioned earlier, a principle that Sivitz pioneered. Rather than rotating the beans inside a cylinder, fluid bed machines suspend the beans in a seething mass kept moving by a powerful column of hot air. Sivitz claims that fluid bed roasters produce a more uniform roast than traditional drum roasters.

Perhaps. Coffee from the Sivitz machine tastes good, but so did coffee from the old machine. One thing is certain: Now as then, buying from the person who roasts the coffee is still your best assurance of obtaining fresh coffee, and good coffee.

Roasting at Home

Those who want to be certain their coffee is fresh—in fact, anyone who wishes to drink the best cup of coffee possible—may want to experiment with roasting coffee at home. Home roasting is very simple and very quick. It takes about as much time and skill as cooking spaghetti, and is considerably simpler than other, more fashionable back-to-basics activities, such as baking bread or making beer. Any small mistakes in the roasting process are far offset by the advantages of freshness.

Ground, roasted coffee is actually as much a convenience food as instant coffee or frozen foods are. Americans roasted their own coffee until the late nineteenth century, and many people all over the world still do. Jabez Burns, inventor of the continuous roaster, the first modern production roaster, insisted that some of the best coffee he ever tasted was roasted in a corn popper.

The physical requirements for roasting coffee correctly are very simple: The coffee needs to be kept moving in air temperatures of at least 400° F and must be cooled at the right moment.

People who roast coffee at home are usually kitchen adventurers, individualists who are convinced that their way is the only way. There are in fact many ways, the safest and most practical of which can be divided into three main approaches: 1) inside the oven; 2) on top of the stove; 3) in a small, commercially produced electric home roaster.

Roasting in the Oven

Oven roasting is, in my opinion, the best approach because you can control the roasting temperature; the persistent, oily smoke produced by roasting is contained and directed through the oven vent; and you don't have to turn a crank or hover over the roasting coffee.

The best oven technique involves spreading a thin layer of green coffee beans over a perforated surface, which allows the convection currents of the oven to flow through the beans and maintain an even roast. Several small firms have attempted to market perforated pans especially designed for this purpose but, as far as I can tell, all of these pioneers are currently out of business. An ordinary vegetable steamer, the kind that has petal-like edges and expands to fit inside a pot, works just as well. You can roast about three ounces of beans at a time in a single steamer. If you want to roast a half-pound of coffee in one session, you need three of these steamers.

Preheat the oven to about 425° F (no lower). Place the green coffee beans in the vegetable steamer and spread evenly across the bottom and up the opened sides, about two beans deep. Place the steamer in the oven and set a kitchen timer for ten minutes. Place some sample beans that have been commercially roasted to the darkness you prefer on the counter near the oven, so you can use them for a color comparison.

Soon you will hear the beans crackling, which indicates that pyrolysis has begun. A pungent odor—the smell of the roasting smoke—may escape from around the oven door. The crackling will continue. In about ten minutes from the start of roasting, or about one to two minutes after the crackling begins, check the color of the beans. Continue to check every one to two minutes until the beans in the oven have achieved a slightly lighter color than the color of the sample.

Immediately remove the beans from the oven and place them under the kitchen fan or, better yet, on the back porch. The beans will continue to roast from their internal heat for a couple of minutes, which is why you should be careful to remove them from the oven before they achieve the full color you desire. Don't be alarmed if your roast is slightly scorched or more darkly roasted in some places than in others. It should still taste much better than partly staled store-bought coffee.

Stove-Top Roasting

Some lovely, romantic stove-top coffee roasters are available, but in most cases they demand an intuitive approach to roasting, since I have been unable to figure out how to monitor the temperature inside them. I suggest a cheaper, and in some ways easier, alternative: the old-fashioned stove-top popcorn popper. A crank on top of the device rotates two vanes inside the pan, which maintain an even roast by pushing the coffee around. Stove-top popcorn poppers retail for about $20. If you buy one, make sure that the fit between the vanes and the bottom of the pan is snug, or the beans may hang up between the vanes and the bottom, making the crank hard to turn.

Assemble the following: the stove-top popcorn popper, an oven thermometer (the kind with a little metal stand), and some sample beans commercially roasted to your preference. Don't try this approach if you don't have a strong kitchen exhaust fan over the stove. Coffee smoke is oily and persistent.

First, experiment by placing the oven thermometer inside the roaster or popper and closing the lid. Check the temperature at different burner settings until you can maintain an air temperature of about 450° to 500° F inside the popper. You need to maintain a higher temperature than with the oven approach because a great deal of heat is lost every time you open the top of the popper. Make a note of the burner setting so you don't need to repeat the procedure every time you want to roast coffee. Then remove the thermometer and place about five ounces (by weight; about six fluid ounces) of green beans into the popper and close the lid. Turn the crank on top of the popper occasionally until the crackling starts, then constantly until the beans inside the popper reach a color slightly lighter than your sample beans. Start peeking inside the popper one to two minutes after the crackling begins. Immediately remove the popper from the heat and dump the beans into a bowl under your kitchen fan. Never let the beans roast unattended; excessively roasted beans are flammable.

The most common stove-top roasters are modified versions of the popcorn popper: a covered pan with a crank on top. These roasters range from rather flimsy products (around $20) to a solid cast-iron model (about $100). Because many roasters have a relatively small opening, you would need to cram an oven thermometer through the opening and examine it with a flashlight to determine how high the flame needs to be kept to maintain a proper roasting temperature of 410° to 450° F. Instead, you simply have to experiment. Start with the heat on medium-low, and if you don't see smoke and hear the beans crackling in ten minutes, turn up the heat until you do. Make a note of the burner setting and proceed as above.

Small Electric Home Roasters

There are currently two home electric roasting devices on the market. Michael Sivitz, coffee expert and hot-air roasting pioneer, markets a home roaster (about $95 including shipping) based on a heavily modified popcorn popper. The Sivitz device soups up the popper so that it will handle five to six ounces of coffee at a session. An oven thermometer enables you to monitor the degree of roast with some precision (although you'll still need to watch the color of the bean to roast precisely to your own taste), and a switch enables you to cool your beans with a blast of non-heated air. If you take time to decipher the directions and follow them carefully, the Sivitz home roaster does an excellent job. I should warn prospective buyers, however, of two drawbacks. First, the Sivitz device fills the air with chaff (you need a very powerful kitchen fan, a back porch and clement weather, or a vacuum cleaner), and second, it is a charmingly improvised object that probably would not win many design prizes in Italy. Order directly from the Sivitz Coffee Company in Corvallis, Oregon (see Sending for It). You can also order green beans (minimum order eight pounds) through Sivitz at very reasonable prices.

The *QC* (for Quality Control) *Cupping Roaster* is both more convenient and more expensive than the Sivitz device. Built in West Germany, it was designed from the beginning to roast coffee. It handles four ounces of coffee at a session, and, like the Sivitz device, uses a column of hot air to both roast and agitate the beans. However, the QC Cupping Roaster has a glass roasting chamber, enabling you to monitor roast color; an automatic cooling cycle, so you don't need to hover over the device during operation; and disposable smoke and chaff filters. It roasts slightly less coffee per session that the Sivitz roaster, and is a bit slower. The automatic roasting cycle is convenient. If you notice you are over-roasting a coffee and want to abort the cycle, you can simply advance the dial manually to initiate the cooling phase.

Overall, however, I'm impressed by the QC Cupping Roaster; it comes with clear directions, it's virtually foolproof to use, and the filter does keep chaff from flying around the kitchen. You still need a strong kitchen fan, however, because the filter only partly traps roasting smoke. The main drawback to the QC Cupping Roaster is price. This sturdy, well-made appliance sells for around $180. The disposable filters are about ten cents each; you need to install a new filter once every three roasts or so. If the QC Cupping Roaster is not available from your retailer, order directly from the Roastery Development Group, San Mateo, California (see Sending for It).

GREEN COFFEE IN STORAGE

CHAPTER 5

Grinding It
Keeping it fresh; choosing a grind and a grinder

Every step of transforming green coffee into hot brewed coffee makes the flavor essence of the bean more vulnerable to destruction. Green coffees keep for years, with only a slow, subtle change in flavor. But roasted coffees begin to lose flavor after a week, ground coffee an hour after grinding, and brewed coffee in minutes.

Traditional Arab culture still has the best solution: roast, grind, brew, and drink the coffee all in the same sitting. The process takes about a half hour, however, so I don't expect it will catch on with urban professionals. Roasting your own coffee every three or four days is an excellent compromise, but most of us are too busy to take that step either and prefer to let others do the roasting for us.

Keeping It Fresh

Roasted whole coffee beans keep fairly well. The bean itself is a protective package, albeit a fragile one. Stored in a dry, airtight container to prevent contamination or contact with moisture, roasted whole-bean coffee holds its flavor and aroma for about a week. After two weeks, it still tastes reasonably fresh, but the aroma begins to slip; after three the flavor starts to go as well. Whole-bean coffee kept past a month, though still drinkable, will strike the palate as lifeless and dead.

But if the natural packaging of the bean is broken—that is, if the coffee is ground—it goes stale in a few hours. The delicate oils are exposed and immediately begin evaporating. An airtight container helps, but not much. The oxygen and moisture shut inside with the broken coffee destroy the delicate oils, even if you never open the container again.

Canning coffee is one of the useless gestures typical of convenience foods. Essentially, the natural coffee package, the bean, is broken down and replaced with an inefficient artificial package, the can. Furthermore, canned coffee is not only preground, but pre-staled. Freshly roasted and ground coffee releases carbon dioxide gas. If the coffee were put in the cans fresh, the gas would swell even the strongest can and turn it into an egg-shaped time bomb. Various technological solutions have been found for this problem, but none is conducive to ensuring richly flavored coffee. When consumers break open the artificial package, they may find a coffee that is relatively fresh—but not for long. Since the small natural packages that make up a pound of ground coffee have already been broken, the oxygen that enters the can every time you peel off the plastic lid rapidly completes the job the canning process started.

So the easiest and most effective approach is to break down the bean as close as possible to the moment you want to use it—in other words, grind your coffee just before you brew it. Grinding coffee fresh takes very little time. Grinders are inexpensive and range from efficient electrics to picturesque replicas of old hand grinders. Grinding coffee fresh is the single best thing that you can do to improve the quality of your coffee.

The ideal coffee routine for the urban home would be as follows: Buy the coffee as whole beans, preferably a half pound at a time and preferably from a store where it is roasted on the premises. Put the beans in an airtight container in a cool, dark place, and take out only as much as you want to grind and brew immediately. *Airtight* means airtight: no recycled coffee cans or cottage cheese cartons with plastic lids; rather, a solid glass jar with a rubber gasket inside the cap that gives a good seal.

Ordering Coffee by Mail

If buying coffee in half-pound lots isn't practical because of where you live, then the airtight container and the grinder become even more important. If you order coffee by mail and you know about how much coffee you consume each month, you can put in a standing order with a coffee roaster, so your coffee comes fresh every other week, a couple of pounds at a time.

A recent marketing trend in specialty coffees is the sale of whole-bean coffee in gas-evacuated bags. A valve allows the carbon dioxide gas to escape, along with the aroma and, eventually, much of the flavor. These bags tend to appear in two sets of circumstances. In one, specialty roasters who stock supermarkets and gourmet stores may present low-volume coffees in such bags to slow staling. Fast-selling choices like Italian roast and Kenya AA may appear in bulk, but less popular coffees are stocked in bags. In other cases, roasters simply present all of their whole-bean coffees in bags.

In either case, I am suspicious of the practice, simply because the presence of the bag encourages everyone involved to handle the coffee like a canned commodity with a long shelf life, rather than like delicate produce. Buying whole-bean coffee in a sealed bag is not a bad idea if the alternative is bulk coffee that has been sitting in the store for two or three weeks. But a good specialty-coffee seller never sells coffee more than a week after it has been roasted. Who knows how long those bags with the "freshness valves," wine-label graphics, and wine-cellar prose have been sitting on the supermarket shelves, cooing gourmet romances at passersby?

Resist the sirens' song. Buy your coffee in bulk at a good specialty store. If you're isolated, put in a standing mail order with a specialty roaster (see Sending for It) or, better yet, buy a large supply of green beans and roast your own. As I indicated in the previous chapter, home roasting is simple and permits you to develop a virtual cellar of exotic coffee beans. The Sivitz Coffee Company in Corvallis, Oregon (see Sending for It) sells green coffee beans through the mail at excellent prices, as does Fante's in Philadelphia. Many of the other suppliers listed in the Sending for It section will also mail green beans if asked.

Storing Coffee

Putting beans in the refrigerator is downright disastrous, even if you use an airtight container. Moisture is the enemy of roasted coffee; the flavor "oils" in roasted coffee are not oils, but very delicate, volatile water-soluble substances that moisture immediately dilutes and odors taint. Refrigerators tend to be both damp and full of odors. Freezing is better, but only if the container is impeccably airtight, the freezer is top-notch, and you freeze only the lighter roasts. Dark-roast coffees (Italian, espresso, French) do not freeze well under any conditions. The delicate oils on the surface of the bean jell, then deteriorate when the coffee is thawed.

Store your coffee in an airtight jar in a cool, dark place. If you enjoy coffee and can't shop for it at least every other week, start roasting your own.

Grinding Your Own

There is an awesome number of coffee mills and grinders on the market. I haven't taken them all home and tested them, but I have tried enough to make some solid recommendations. Please, however, don't assume that, because I have not recommended an appliance, it is not a good choice. It simply may mean that I haven't had the opportunity to test it. If a coffee grinder comes recommended by a reliable specialty-coffee seller and you like the look of it, buy it.

First, a note on the terms *coffee mill* and *coffee grinder*. The industry is attempting to use the two terms to distinguish between, on one hand, appliances that tear the coffee apart by means of corrugated plates or burrs and, on the other, those that knock the coffee apart by means of rapidly whirling blades. Unfortunately, there is no consensus on which term applies to which group of appliances, and catalogs and retailers use the terms according to their own points of view. Consequently, I use *grinder* in these pages to describe all implements that reduce coffee beans to proportions that can be brewed. May the most persuasive designation prevail. Prices indicated are approximate retail by catalog or stores in the San Francisco Bay Area as of summer 1991.

Despite the pretensions of modern technology, there are still only four ways to grind coffee. The oldest is the mortar and pestle. The next oldest is the millstone, updated to steel burrs or corrugated plates. The next is the roller mill, which is used only in giant commercial grinders. The most recent is the electric blade grinder, which works on the same principle as the electric blender.

Mortar and Pestle

If you really want to get back to basics, the mortar and pestle may be the grinder for you. It's cheap, esthetically satisfying, builds up your wrist muscles, and satisfies the profound suspicion so many of us harbor that if it doesn't tire us out, it's not really good for us. The mortar and pestle does have drawbacks: It takes too long, you can't grind many beans at a time, and it's hard to get a uniform grind. The price is right, though (around $20).

Grinders Using Steel Plates or Burrs

The earliest coffee drinkers broke up their coffee beans with a mortar and pestle, but very early in its history coffee began to be ground between the same millstones that the early peoples of the Middle East used to reduce grain to flour. Later, the Turkish-style coffee grinder evolved, a portable, specialized device similar in size and function to the contemporary pepper mill. Small, corrugated metal plates replaced the large mill stones, creating a grinder technology that has never been improved upon. Many variations have been developed, including hitching the plates to an electric motor, but the principle remains the same.

The heart of the grinder consists of either two little corrugated metal disks, or a corrugated metal cone that fits inside a second, hollow corrugated cone. One element is stationary and the other is rotated by a handle or motor. The coffee is fed, a bean or two at a time, between the corrugated disks, where it is crushed until it drops out of the bottom of the grinder. This solution has never been improved upon because the grind is uniform, and adjusting the space between the plates regulates the fineness of the grind accurately and consistently.

Hand Grinders. The cheapest hand grinders are the wooden hand-held models. The beans are fed through a little door in the top of the box, and the ground coffee falls into a drawer at the bottom. These grinders are adjustable for any except the finest grind. Most look like something out of a Dutch genre painting but are manufactured everywhere from Japan to New Jersey, and range in price from $10 to as much as $60. For a hand grinder that works well, however, you probably need to pay $40 to $50 for one of the Zassenhaus line of grinders, which are widely available at specialty-coffee stores. They impose a clean, northern European look on the box grinder, and are technically excellent.

The box grinder has several problems: The cheaper versions will not produce a fine enough grind for many coffee brewers, owing to the small, inefficient burrs. In even the good ones, the crank may be too short for good leverage. Worst of all, the grinder tends to slide around on the table. One of the Zassenhaus designs solves this problem by introducing small indentations in opposite sides of the grinder, thus permitting you to sit and hold the grinder between your knees as you crank.

Hand grinders that can be mounted on the table or wall solve most of the problems posed by smaller hand-held box grinders. They can be screwed down, have longer handles, and usually produce more uniform grinds because the grinding plates are larger. The best, if you can find it, is a wonderful, early industrial age-looking cast iron grinder imported by the British firm Woodard & Charles (about $75). Hand grain mills with metal plates work even better, although they take more space in the kitchen. The best currently being made is the Jupiter mill (around $90). The more widely available Corona mill is cheaper by half (around $45), but the grinding burrs are tin-plated and the manufacture inconsistent. Both the Woodard & Charles grinder and the Jupiter grain mill are available by mail from Fante's in Philadelphia (see Sending for It). The Jupiter mill can also be found in some particularly well-stocked natural food stores. By the way, do not buy a grain mill with stone burrs for use with coffee; the stones get gummy and do not operate well.

Electric Burr Grinder. This brings us to the twentieth century and the age of electricity. One type of electric grinder simply powers the burrs or steel plates with electricity. The big grinders in grocery and coffee stores work on this principle, as do the somewhat smaller grinders in cafés.

Small household versions of these large machines are produced by several manufacturers, including Braun, Bosch, and Bunn. They range in price from about $50 to $80, depending on model and discount. All work the same way. A receptacle at the top of the appliance stores a supply of beans. When you activate a spring-loaded timer, beans feed automatically, a few at a time, through the burrs, which spray the ground coffee into a removable receptacle at the bottom of the appliance. The timer shuts the grinder off automatically. Although this procedure undoubtedly sounds convenient, in practice it can be trying. These machines do produce a more consistent grind than the cheaper electric blade grinders, they usually do not have to be fussed over while they grind, and they definitely don't need to be cranked by hand. You must be prepared, however, to clean the aperture for the ground coffee after every third or fourth use (some coffee stores sell a brush for this purpose; a small, stiff paintbrush works fine), and to open the grinder regularly to the coarsest setting and run it empty to clear the coffee path. If the grinder design permits, you also must periodically open the grinder and clean the burrs and housing. If you grind oily dark roasts, you may find that a brush is not enough for cleaning your grinder; you may have to literally carve the caked coffee from parts of your grinder when you carry out a major cleaning. Finally, burr grinders cannot be used successfully with flavored coffees; the flavoring liquids absorbed in the beans both gum up the burrs and taint subsequent batches of non-flavored coffees.

The warning signs that a small burr grinder needs cleaning are simple. If the coffee doesn't come out or the motor seems to be working too hard, you need to clean the aperture where the ground coffee sprays out. If the coffee beans don't feed smoothly, you need to run the grinder empty on the coarsest setting or, if it is so designed, open it up and do a thorough cleaning.

The ultimate benefit of the electric burr grinder can be gained only by spending $150 to $250 on one of the larger machines intended for use with home espresso machines. For the committed espresso fanatic, these sturdy, reliable grinders are a necessity. For the general coffee enthusiast, they can grind coffee for all brewing needs. The least expensive, if you can find it, is the Saeco 2002. The heavier Rancilio, Olympia, and Gaggia MDF espresso grinders all cost $200 or more. Jericho, an American firm,

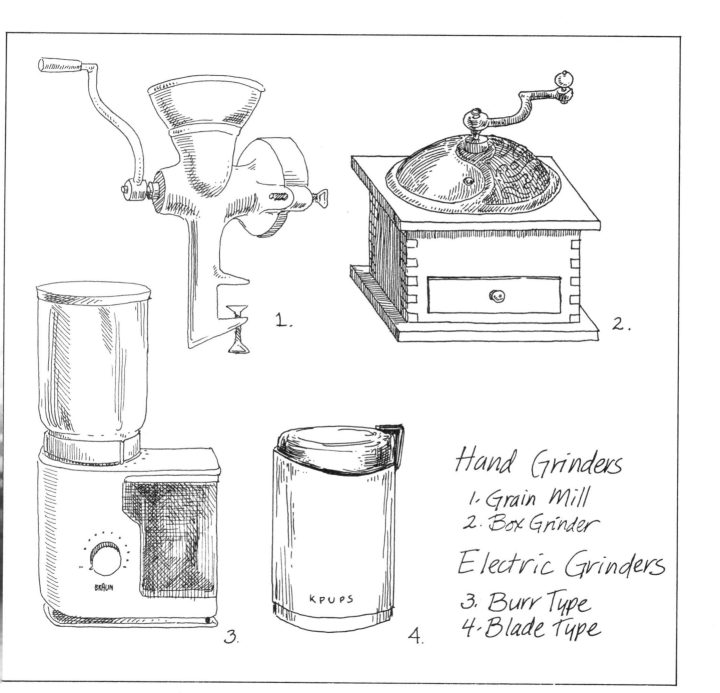

Hand Grinders
1. Grain Mill
2. Box Grinder

Electric Grinders
3. Burr Type
4. Blade Type

has introduced a smaller, home version of the old-fashioned electric store grinder for about $250. All of the machines I've tried in this class are strong, well-made appliances.

The Electric Blade Grinder

The third and most recent development in coffee grinding is original to the age of electricity. Two steel blades powered by a small electric motor whirl at extremely high speed at the bottom of a cup-like receptacle and knock the coffee beans to pieces. With the burr method the fineness of the grind is controlled by the distance between the plates, whereas with the blade method fineness is controlled by the length of time you let the blades whang away at the coffee. This makes the whole process a little hit and miss, unless you're so systematic you start timing the process.

Blade Grinder Minuses. The disadvantages of blade grinders? Above all, they grind less consistently and predictably than burr grinders do. Even the less expensive burr grinders hold their setting well, and give you the same grind, day after day. Only the most attentive and compulsive among us are capable of achieving the same consistency with a blade grinder. For brewing methods using paper filters, minor inconsistencies in grind don't much matter. For plunger-style brewing, drip-brewing, open-pot brewing, and espresso, all of which demand a more consistent grind for success, anyone who has taken the trouble to read this far will probably want the more predictable results obtainable either from the best hand grinders, like the Zassenhaus, or Woodard & Charles coffee grinders, from the Jupiter grain mill, or from a good electric burr mill like the Braun, Bosch, or Bunn. True fanatics will want to go a step further and purchase one of the specialized $150 to $250 espresso grinders mentioned

earlier. Blade grinders are also useless for Turkish- or Middle Eastern-style coffee, for which, again, you need either a good hand grinder, such as the Zassenhaus, Woodard & Charles, or Jupiter, or one of the specialized "Turkish" hand grinders that look like large pepper mills. The best electric espresso grinders usually work for Middle Eastern coffee as well, although you should ask for a demonstration.

Another minor drawback to the blade grinder is the difficulty presented in getting the coffee out from under the little blades and into a brewer. You face the same problem when you clean the grinder.

Blade Grinder Pluses. The advantages of blade grinders are more succinctly stated: They are cheap and grind quickly, and they don't take up much space in the kitchen. You also can use them to pulverize nuts and similar cooking ingredients, and, unlike burr grinders, they can be used with flavored coffees. The two models favored by most specialty coffee store buyers are the Bosch (around $25) and the Braun (around $20). In both formal and informal tests they appear to make a more uniform grind than their current rivals. The Bosch may be somewhat less durable than the Braun, however, and does not give the consumer the option of replacing the grinding blade. The Krups, Salton, and Regal blade grinders also perform well. The Regal often can be found in discount department stores for up to $10 less than its European competitors.

You should be careful not to run a blade grinder continuously for more than a few seconds, since it will begin to heat the ground coffee. If you make a fine grind, grind in spurts of about five seconds each. It also helps to bounce the bottom of the grinder gently on the counter between spurts to tumble the partly ground coffee back down around the blades.

How Fine the Grind

In general, grind coffee as fine as you can without clogging the holes of the brewer or turning the coffee to mud. The finer the grind, the more contact there will be between coffee and hot water, and the faster and more thoroughly the essential oils will be released, without activating harsher, less-soluble chemicals.

On the other hand, you don't want to grind your coffee to a powder, because completely pulverizing it destroys the essential oil, which becomes vaporized by the heat and friction of the grinding process. Nor do you want to clog the holes in a coffee maker or filter, or fill your cup with sediment. Some brewing methods have special requirements. Both Middle Eastern coffee and espresso are special cases, as are open-pot and Melior or plunger-pot coffee (see Chapters 6 and 7).

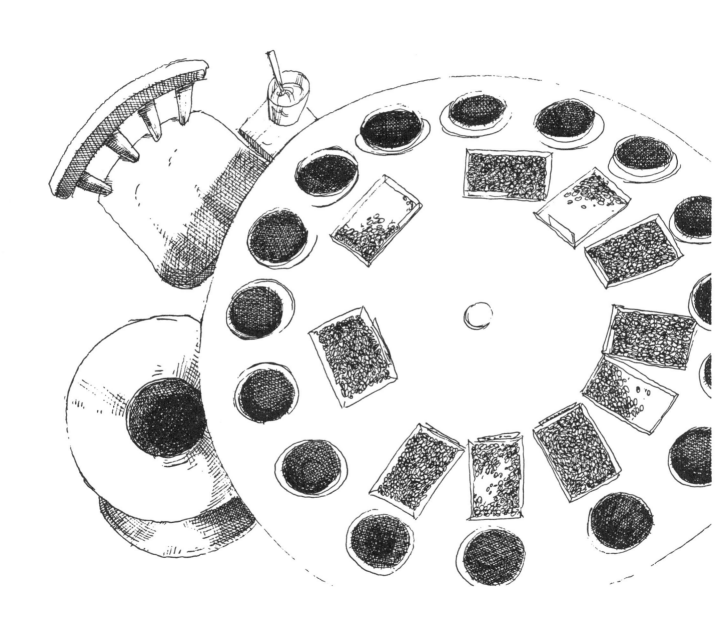

CHAPTER 6

Brewing It
Choosing a method and a machine; brewing it right

No matter what they're called, all ways of brewing coffee are basically the same: The ground coffee is soaked in the water until the water tastes good. Nobody, to my knowledge, has figured out a different way to make coffee. The only equipment you really need to make great coffee is an open pot, a flame, and, possibly, a strainer.

Three Variables, Thousands of Ideas

It's a tribute to human imagination and lust for perfection, however, that the simple act of combining hot water and ground coffee has produced so many ingenious variations and occupied so many brilliant people for uncounted hours over the past three centuries. Thousands of coffee makers have been patented in the United States and Europe, but of this multitude only a handful have had any lasting impact or embodied any genuine innovation. The few ideas to achieve greatness can be divided according to three variables: how hot one makes the water; how one gets the water to the coffee; and how one separates the spent grounds from the brewed coffee.

Water Temperature

Until the eighteenth century, coffee was almost always boiled. Boiling, however, damages coffee flavor because it vaporizes much of the coffee essence while it continues to extract other bitter-tasting chemicals. The French began steeping, as opposed to boiling, coffee in the early eighteenth century, but this innovation did not penetrate the coffee-drinking mainstream until the nineteenth century and had to wait until the twentieth to triumph. Today, all American and European methods favor hot water (around 200° F), as opposed to boiling.

If boiling water has been universally rejected, cold water has not. You can steep coffee in cold water and get substantially the same results as with hot water; the only difference is that the process takes longer (several hours longer) and makes an extremely mild brew. Since reheating destroys flavor in coffee, cold-water coffee is made concentrated and, like instant, is mixed with hot water.

Getting the Water to the Coffee

The second variable—how you get the water to the coffee—is a question of convenience. If you're not in a hurry, you might just as well heat the water in a pot and pour it over the coffee yourself. But if you want to do something else while the coffee is brewing, you might want a way to deliver the hot water to the coffee automatically. Furthermore, coffee-making requires consistent and precise timing, a virtue difficult to maintain in this age of distractions. The advantage to machines is their single-mindedness; they make coffee the same way every time, even if the phone rings.

One of the earliest efforts at automation was the pumping percolator, patented in 1827 by Frenchman Nicholas Felix Durant. The French ignored it, but the United States, the cradle of convenience, adopted it enthusiastically. The pumping percolator uses the bubble power of boiling water to force little spurts of hot water up a tube and over the top of the coffee. The hot water, having seeped back through the coffee, returns to the reservoir to mix with the slowly bubbling water at the bottom of the pot. The process continues until the coffee is brewed.

Ironically, the principle of the automatic filter-drip, which was destined to supplant the pumping percolator in the United States of the 1970s, was patented a few months earlier than the percolator. Jacques-Augustin Gandais, a Parisian jewelry manufacturer, patented a device that sent the boiling water up a tube in the handle of the brewer and, from there, over the ground coffee. Gandais's device even looks a bit like the first automatic filter-drip brewers of the 1970s. It apparently was ignored for the same reason it was later enthusiastically adopted: It sent the water through the coffee only once, rather than repeatedly, as the pumping percolator did.

Around 1840, the vacuum principle in coffee brewing was simultaneously discovered by several tinkerers, including a Scottish marine engineer, Robert Napier. Napier's original device looks more like a steam engine than a coffee maker, but, as it has evolved today, the vacuum pot consists of two glass globes that fit tightly together,

110

one above the other, with a cloth or metal filter between them. The ground coffee is placed in the upper globe, and water is brought to boil in the lower. The two globes are fitted together and the heat is lowered. Pressure develops as water vapor expands in the lower globe, forcing the water into the upper globe, where it mixes with the ground coffee. After one to three minutes, the pot is removed from the heat, and the vacuum formed in the lower globe pulls the brewed coffee back down through the filter.

The twentieth century has brought us both the automatic electric percolator and the automatic filter-drip coffee maker, an improved electric version of Gandais's 1827 device. In the automatic filter-drip coffee maker, the water is held in a reservoir above or next to the coffee, heated, and measured automatically over the ground coffee by the same bubble power that drives the percolator. The latest challenge to innovation in automated brewing is the microwave oven. The first attempts at taking advantage of its unique technology have not broken new ground, however; the solutions proposed by appliance companies are all interesting variations on time-honored technologies, ranging from microwave oven pot to microwave vacuum and filter-drip.

Separating Brewed Coffee from Grounds

Now we reach the brewing operation that has stimulated coffeepot tinkerers to their most extravagant efforts: the separation of brewed coffee from spent grounds. Again, original ideas are few, refinements endless. People in the Middle East have the simplest solution: They simply let most of the grounds settle to the bottom of the cup and drink the rest along with the brew. This is a very direct approach, like everything else about Middle Eastern coffee making. The original coffee drinkers, the Arabs of what is now Yemen, grind their beans more coarsely and strain the coffee into the cup. This is a variation of the ubiquitous open-pot method, in which coffee drinkers have an opportunity to invent their own way of separating grounds from coffee. The Arabian method was probably the earliest form of coffee brewing; the Middle Eastern or "Turkish" style was probably developed later in Egypt.

A third development took place in Vienna in 1684, after the lifting of the siege of Vienna, when Franz George Kolschitsky opened central Europe's first café, using coffee left behind by the routed Turks. Kolschitsky first tried to serve his booty Turkish style, but the Viennese wouldn't go for it. They called it "stewed soot" and continued to drink white wine and lager with breakfast. But when Kolschitsky started straining the coffee and serving it with milk and honey, his success was assured; within a few years the great café tradition of Vienna was well established. Strained or separated coffee has dominated European and American taste ever since.

A Frenchman named Jean Baptiste de Belloy is credited with inventing the world's favorite method of separating coffee from grounds, the drip pot, in 1800. Hot water is poured into an upper compartment containing the coffee and is allowed to drip through a strainer or filter into a lower compartment, leaving the coffee grounds behind. An impressive variety of refinements has been developed since, including the Neapolitan flip pot, the cloth filter, and disposable paper filters.

One other method of separation deserves mention. After the coffee is steeped, a metal filter or strainer is forced down through the coffee like a plunger, pressing the coffee grounds to the bottom of the pot and leaving the clarified coffee above. There is no accepted generic name for this sort of brewer; some call it a *plunger pot*, which I like, or *French press*, after the country where it first became popular.

General Considerations for Brewing Apparatus

Ideally, coffee brewers should be made of glass or porcelain. Stainless steel will do. If you have a choice in the matter, avoid aluminum. Food cooked in aluminum absorbs minute traces of the metal; coffee held in aluminum develops a metallic flatness. Add aluminum's tendency to pit and corrode, and I think there is ample reason to avoid this metal in a coffee maker. Tin plate may also faintly taint the flavor of coffee.

A pot should be easy to clean. Coffee is oily, and accumulated oil eventually contributes a stale taste to fresh coffee. Stubborn brown stains in the corners can be soaked out with a strong solution of baking soda or one of the commercial urn cleaners on the market. Glass and porcelain are the easiest to clean; aluminum and tin-coated metal the hardest. It is wise to avoid pots with seams or cracks, especially in the parts that come in direct contact with the brewed coffee. Check to make sure you can take the whole apparatus apart easily for an occasional thorough cleaning. In areas with alkaline, or hard, water, a lime deposit builds up even in the parts of the maker that are untouched by coffee. The universal remedy is a strong solution of vinegar. Run it through the works of the brewer, then rinse thoroughly.

Brewing Suggestions

Now for the inevitable list of brewing rules and precepts.

No matter which invention you use to brew your coffee, I urge you to do the following:

- Grind the coffee as fine as you can make it without losing any through the holes in the filter of the coffee maker. Never grind it to a powder. French

112

press, conventional (non-filter) drip, and open-pot brewing require a less fine grind.

- Use plenty of coffee: at least 2 level tablespoons or 1 standard coffee measure per 5- to 6-ounce cup. You may want to use more, but I strongly suggest you never use less unless your coffee maker explicitly instructs you to. Most mugs hold closer to 8 ounces than 6, so if you measure by the mug use 2 1/2 to 3 level tablespoons for every mug of water. Coffee brewed strong tastes better, and you can enjoy the distinctive flavor in your favorite coffee more clearly. If you brew with hard water or if you drink your coffee with milk, you should be especially careful to brew strong. If you feel that you're sensitive to caffeine, adjust the caffeine content of your coffee by adding some caffeine-free beans (see Chapter 9).
- Keep the coffee maker clean, and rinse it with hot water before you brew.
- Use fresh water, as free of impurities and alkalines as possible.
- Brew with hot water, as opposed to lukewarm or boiling water (Middle Eastern and cold-water coffees are exceptions). A temperature of 200° F is ideal, which means bringing the water to a boil and then waiting a couple of minutes before brewing. If you've done everything else right and you're in a rush, however, water that has just stopped boiling won't seriously damage a good, freshly ground coffee.
- In filter and drip systems, avoid brewing less than the brewer's full capacity. If the pot is made to brew six cups, the coffee will taste better if you brew the full six.
- Some don'ts: Don't boil coffee; it cooks off all the delicate flavoring essence and leaves the bitter chemicals. Don't percolate or reheat coffee; it has the same effect as boiling, only less so. Don't hold coffee for very long on the heat for the same reason. Don't mix old coffee with new; it's like using rotten wood to prop up a new building.

Ninety-nine percent of a cup of coffee is water, and if you use bad, really bad water, you might just as well throw away this book and buy a jar of instant. If the water isn't pleasant to drink, don't make coffee with it. Use bottled water or a filter system. Hard, or alkaline, water does not directly harm flavor and aroma, but does mute some of the natural acids in coffee and produces a blander cup without the acidy snap. Water that has been treated with softeners makes even worse coffee, however, so if you do live in an area with hard water, you might compensate by buying more acidy coffees (African, Arabian, and the best Indonesian and Central American growths) or by brewing with bottled or filtered water. Automatic drip coffee makers are beginning to appear with built-in filters. Although these integral filters are effective, they seem fussy and over specialized to me; it would be better to buy a filtration system that can be used for all of your water needs, rather than one that is irrevocably stuck inside the coffee brewer.

Brewing Methods and Machinery

About 75 percent of the coffee consumed in the United States in 1989 was brewed with paper filters, a method that produces coffee in the classic American style: clear, light-bodied, with little sediment or oil. Any other brewing method (except cold water concentrate) produces a coffee richer in oils and sediments and heavier in flavor than the typical American cup of filter coffee. Those adventurers who experiment with other brewing methods should keep this difference in mind.

Open Pot

The simplest brewing method is as good as any. You place the ground coffee in a pot of hot water, stir to break up lumps and saturate the coffee, strain or otherwise separate the grounds from the brewed coffee, and serve. Open-pot coffee is a favorite of individualists and light travelers. I had a sculptor friend who insisted on making his coffee in a pot improvised from a coffee can and a coat hanger. For such nonconformists, the challenge is separating the grounds from the coffee without stooping to the aid of decadent bourgeois inventions like strainers.

Bring the cold water to a boil and let it cool for a minute or so. Toss in the coffee. Use a moderately fine grind, about what stores call *drip*. Stir gently to break up the lumps and let the mixture steep, covered, for 2 to 4 minutes. If you are willing to compromise, obtain a very fine-mesh strainer; the best are made of nylon cloth. Strain the coffee and serve. If you consider yourself too authentic for a strainer, pour a couple of spoons of cold water over the surface of the coffee to sink whatever grounds have not already settled; in theory, at least, the cold water, which is heavier than the hot, will carry these stubbornly buoyant pieces to the bottom. If you wish to clarify the coffee further, put the shell of one egg into the pot with the coffee. The shell will absorb some of the sediment that clouds the brew.

For the lazy or less committed, some specialty stores sell a little nylon bag (about $5) that sits inside the traditional straight-sided coffeepot, supported on the outside by a plastic ring. This simple device is a modern version of the coffee Biggin, a device named after its early nineteenth-century English inventor. The coffee Biggin was extremely popular in England in the late nineteenth and early twentieth centuries. It has the added advantage of permitting a much finer grind of coffee than traditional open-pot methods. You put the ground coffee in the nylon bag, pour hot water over it, and stir lightly to break up the lumps. In 2 to 4 minutes, you simply lift the bag and grounds out of the brewed coffee.

French Press or Plunger Pot

French press is essentially open-pot coffee with a sophisticated method for separating the grounds from the brew. The pot is a narrow glass cylinder. A fine-mesh screen plunger fits tightly inside the cylinder. You put fine-ground coffee in the cylinder, pour boiling water over it, and insert the plunger in the top of the cylinder without pushing it down. After about 4 minutes, when the coffee is thoroughly steeped, you push the plunger through the coffee, clarifying it and forcing the grounds to the bottom of the pot.

The plunger pot was apparently developed in Italy during the 1930s, but found its true home in France after World War II, when it surged to prominence as a favored home-brewing method.

The growing popularity of this method in the United States has unleashed a flood of French-press brewers, most of them imposters from everywhere except France. A consumer's first decision in purchasing such a brewer is whether to spend a little money on a version that supports the glass brewing receptacle in a plastic frame ($15 to $25), or to spend considerably more on a brewer with a metal frame ($40 to the totally unreasonable). Complicating the decision is the enthusiasm with which the design community has embraced the French press; its technical simplicity and potential as an after-dinner conversation piece has provoked an orgy of self-conscious visual invention almost equaling the similar attention lavished on the designer teapot.

Among the cheaper plastic-framed brewers, for example, choices range from the simple Junior and Club models from Melior to the more expressive Bodum designs: the cheerful Coffee Presso with its angular frame and flared base, the dignified cork-based Bistro, and the aggressively post-Modern Archi.

Both Melior and Bodum produce the traditional metal-frame French-silhouette brewers. Depending on the metal used in the frames (nickle-plated brass to gold-, silver-, or rhodium-plate) these versions can range from $60 to almost $200. Less expensive renditions of the traditional metal-framed design come from China and Japan and sell for $40 to $60. Designer-look metal frame brewers vary from the cleanly classic (the

Melior Orsay), to the playfully post-Modernist (the Rialto), to the famously post-Modernist (the Michael Graves design for Alessi), to the uncategorizably post-Modernist (the Bodum Sereno, with wiggly little shapes perforating the metal sheath). These striking objects range in price from about $50 for the smallest capacity Rialto to about $150 for the largest capacity Graves-Alessi design.

In addition to obvious differences in look and finish, there are subtle differences in technical design and manufacture among these brewers. In general, the more support the frame gives the glass brewing cylinder the better. A sheath is better than a couple of skinny bands, and a deep sheath is better than a shallow sheath. The glass brewing decanter should be solid, flame-proof, and free from lines and bubbles. Finally, a stainless mesh filter is superior to a nylon mesh filter, and a metal plunger knob is superior to a plastic knob.

The plunger pot is an enthusiast's brewer; it appeals to those who like to dramatize their coffee making. With the plunger brewer, coffee is not an after-dinner option that emerges routinely from the kitchen; it is the product of a small ceremonial event that unfolds at the table.

The coffee the plunger brewer produces is heavy and densely flavored; the subtle, aromatic notes present in fresh, well-made filter coffee are overwhelmed by a deep, gritty punch. The French like such coffee; many Americans may find it muddy and flat-tasting. Those who take their coffee with milk or cream may prefer it; those who drink their coffee black may not. Some may like it after dinner but not before. It is neither better nor worse than coffee made with filter paper, just different. Its flavor and dense body are owing to the presence of sediment, oils, and minute gelatinous material that chemists call *colloids*, all of which are largely eliminated by paper filters.

Style of coffee aside, the advantages of the plunger brewer are its drama, its portability, and its elegance, all of which make it an ideal after-dinner brewer. It is more difficult to clean than most drip or filter pots, however, and the coffee must be drunk immediately, because there is no practical way of keeping the coffee hot after brewing. Small, plastic-framed plunger pots, often available for as little as $12, provide a practical one-cup brewing alternative for singles who like this style of coffee. When you brew with your plunger pot, take care to preheat it, and avoid too fine a grind unless you're feeling athletic; the plunger will become almost impossible to push down. Also be careful to press the plunger straight down; if you push from an angle, you're likely to break the glass decanter.

Drip: Flip-Drip or Neapolitan Macchinetta

The drip pot was invented by a Frenchman, de Belloy, and popularized by Benjamin Thompson, an eccentric American who became Count von Rumford of the Holy Roman Empire, married two rich widows, and spent much of his leisure time making enemies and coffee. The drip maker typically consists of two compartments, an upper and a lower, divided by a metal or ceramic filter or strainer. The ground coffee is placed in the upper compartment and hot water is poured over it. The brewed coffee trickles through the strainer into the lower compartment.

The traditional American straight-sided metal drip pot has gone out of fashion, but a very attractive French-silhouette porcelain version can be bought at most specialty stores for about $45.

Gold-plated mesh filter units that turn any appropriately sized receptacle into a drip brewer are available for $10 to $20, depending on size. Some can be purchased with a matching thermos receptacle; you drip the coffee through the gold mesh filter into the thermos. From a technical point of view, such filter-thermos sets are superior to the traditional drip pot, since keeping the coffee hot during brewing is one of the challenges of drip brewing. Make sure you preheat the thermos, however.

A popular variation of the drip pot was invented in 1819 by Morize, a French tinsmith. This is the *reversible, double,* or *flip-drip* pot, which has since been adopted by the Italians as the *Neapolitan macchinetta.* Rather than being laid loosely on top of the strainer, as in the regular drip pot, the ground coffee is secured in a two-sided strainer at the waist of the pot. The water is heated in one part of the pot, then the whole thing is flipped over, and the hot water drips through the coffee into the other, empty side. Several versions of the flip-drip pot are available. An aluminum version is the cheapest (around $8 for the smallest, up to about $10 for the largest). Since aluminum is an undesirable material for coffee brewers, however, I recommend instead one of the several attractive copper versions (around $40) or a contemporary-look stainless ($40 and up).

Use as fine a grind of coffee as possible in a drip brewer. If the coffee drips through painfully slowly or not at all, or if you find more sediment in your cup than you prefer, try a coarser grind. Even with the correct grind, you may find that you occasionally need to tap or jostle the pot to keep the coffee dripping. When you pour the hot water over the ground coffee, make certain that you saturate all of the coffee to prevent dry lumps from islanding up and getting left out of the brewing process. Cover to preserve heat. Mix the coffee lightly after it has brewed, since the first coffee to drip through is stronger and heavier than the last.

Both drip and filter coffees often cool excessively during the brewing process; it helps to preheat the bottom half of the pot with hot tap water before brewing. If that isn't enough, buy a heat-diffusing pad and keep the pot on the stove while brewing. If the coffee contains too much sediment, disposable paper filters are available to fit most drip brewers.

Pumping Percolator

Until about 15 years ago, the pop of a pumping percolator producing coffee ranked with the acceleration of a well-tuned car as one of North America's best-loved sounds. Now the pumping percolator appears to have gone the way of tail fins and bologna sandwiches. However reassuring the sensuous gurgle of a percolator is psychologically, chemically it means only one thing: You're boiling the coffee and prematurely vaporizing the delicate flavoring oils. Every pop of the percolator means another bubble of aroma and flavor is bursting at the top of the pot, bestowing its gift on your kitchen rather than on your palate.

Opinions differ as to the extent of the damage that the percolator inflicts on coffee flavor. In 1974, when the pumping percolator was still holding off the automatic filter-drip brewer, *Consumer Reports* magazine served coded cups of drip and percolator coffee both to experts and to its staff. The experts unanimously and consistently preferred the drip coffee to the perked coffee, but the staff's reaction was mixed. I find I can invariably pick out perked coffee in a similar test by the slightness of its aroma and the flat, slightly bitter edge of its flavor. However, there are more ways to ruin coffee than to put it in a good pumping percolator; stale coffee, for instance, tastes bad no matter how you brew it. Freshly opened canned coffee brewed with care in a good pumping percolator tastes better than mishandled, three-month-old Jamaican Blue Mountain put through a filter.

If you must have a pumping percolator, a good electric is probably the best choice, since the heat is automatically controlled to produce perked rather than boiled coffee, and most electrics have a thermostat that should reduce the heat at the optimum moment to prevent overextraction.

Vacuum Filter

Coffee made by the vacuum-filter method does not differ markedly from coffee made with other filter systems. Since the manipulations involved are a bit more complex than those demanded by the filter method, the vacuum pot has lost considerable

1. French Press
2. French Drip
3. Neapolitan Flip-Drip

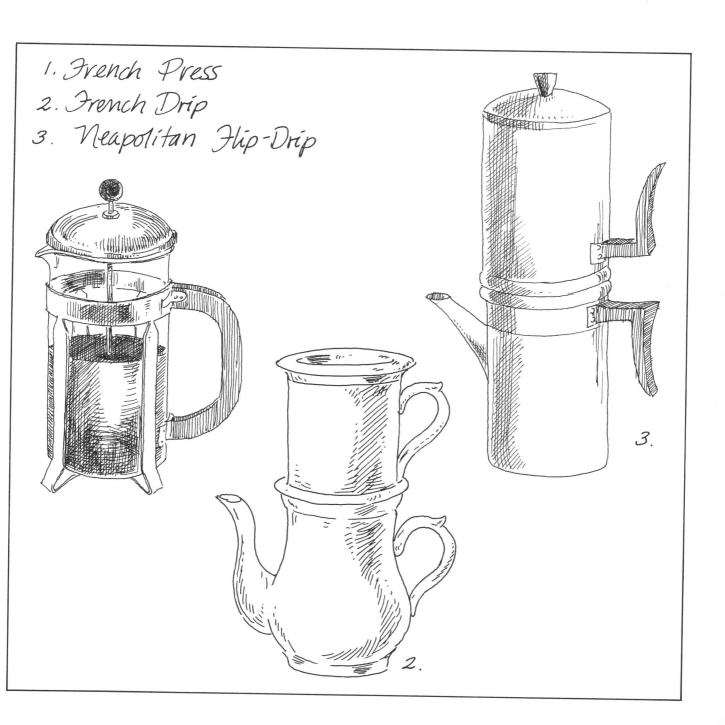

popularity since its heyday in the 1920s and 1930s. But for some, the leisurely and alchemical shifting of liquids in the two glass globes has a continuing appeal, and the coffee produced should be as good as any. Cultures that value ceremony are particularly fond of the vacuum filter. In Japan, for instance, one-cup vacuum brewers are widely used in coffeehouses to custom-brew specialty "call" coffees. Unfortunately, the charm of the gesture considerably transcends the quality of the coffee; in most of the places I went in Japan, the flame under the brewer was kept so high that the coffee was essentially boiled, losing most of its distinction and subtlety in the process.

This proves, I suppose, that making good vacuum-filter coffee requires patience. At this writing, the only vacuum brewer generally available in the United States is the simple and attractive six-cup Bodum (around $30) stove-top model. For those who wish to brew at the table, the Bodum comes with stand and spirit lamp (around $65 for the set).

The wonderfully esoteric British Cona Table model ($130 to $200 depending on model and discount) brews coffee by means of a spirit lamp only and is obviously meant to be brought out after dinner for a leisurely at-the-table ceremony. After several minutes of exquisitely complex maneuvers, it produces two to four cups of excellent coffee brewed by impeccable filter principles. The Cona is difficult to find. It can be purchased by mail from The Coffee Connection in Boston or Peet's Coffee & Tea in Berkeley (see Sending for It). The Coffee Connection also carries the even more esoteric Odette ($500), an extraordinary gold-plated object that works like something out of Captain Nemo's submarine. It automatically extinguishes the spirit lamp by means of a counterweight activated by the shifting of water from the lower receptacle to the brewing receptacle, thus initiating the final phase of the brewing process without the vulgarity of human assistance.

Filter Drip

Coffeepot tinkerers started using cloth filters around 1800; disposable paper filters came later and were never really popular until after World War II. The main objection to paper filters then and now is that they must continually be replaced. The main objection to cloth filters is that they get dirty and are difficult to clean. In this age of disposables, the paper filter has triumphed, but permanent filters, in nylon mesh or gold-plated metal, are currently making inroads. The use of permanent metal filters blurs the distinction between ordinary drip brewing and filter brewing, since they essentially turn a filter brewer into a drip brewer. The description and admonitions that follow refer to coffee brewed with paper filters, not with metal or nylon mesh filters.

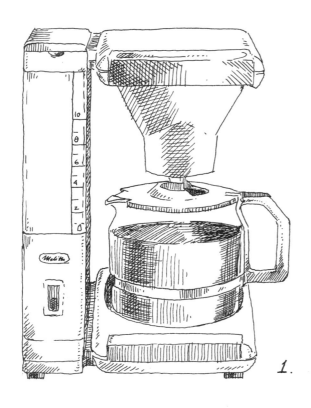

1.

1. Automatic Filter Drip
2. Cona Vacuum

2.

Nearly all filter coffee makers work the same way. A paper filter is placed in a plastic, glass, or ceramic holder; fine-ground (a fine grit just short of powdery) coffee goes in the filter, and the filter container is set atop a flameproof glass or ceramic flask. From there you proceed as you do for drip coffee.

The advantages of filter brewing: It permits you to use a very fine grind of coffee and effect a quick, thorough extraction. The paper filters make the grounds easy to dispose of and the coffee maker easy to keep clean. Because of their simplicity and popularity, coffee cones are the cheapest coffee-brewing devices on the market. Those who like a light-bodied clear coffee free of oils, colloids, and sediment will enjoy a good filter coffee; those who like a heavier, richer brew will prefer other methods.

The disadvantages: Paper filters slow the drip process to such a degree that the coffee may require warming before drinking. Furthermore, your initial investment in the cone may be small, but you'll be paying for filters for the rest of your coffee-drinking career. The first of these disadvantages can be easily circumvented. The best way to keep filter coffee hot is to brew directly into a preheated thermos. Other, more expedient methods are half submerging the brewing receptacle in a pot of hot water atop the stove or putting it on a heat-buffering device or electric warmer (both Melitta and Chemex sell warmers specially designed for this purpose). The expense of paper filters can be avoided by purchasing a reusable cloth filter available in specialty stores (about $3) but I don't recommend these compromise filters; they take too much out of the coffee and are hard to keep clean.

Filter coffee tastes best when brewed in large quantities. The big restaurant urns that take a pound of ground coffee at a time brew splendid coffee; an 8-cup filter brewer makes very good coffee; a 1-cup filter cone tends to make a weak, mediocre cup no matter what you do. This phenomenon of diminishing return in proportion to diminishing filter brewer size is well known in the coffee trade. What causes it I'm not certain, but I suspect it is the relatively greater proportion of filter paper surface to ground coffee in the smaller brewers. In a one-cup cone, the filter paper seems to eliminate too many of the flavorful oils along with the sediment.

Filter Papers. If you run water through most white filter papers and taste the hot water afterward, you will detect a papery taste. With some batches of non-brand-name papers, this taste is alarmingly distinct; with high-quality papers, such as those distributed by Filtropa, Melitta, or Chemex, the taste is faint. Whether or not you can actually detect the paper taste in a cup of filter coffee obviously depends on how strong you brew the coffee and which papers you use. It also depends on the amount of paper in the filter; Chemex makes very high-quality papers, but because they are heavier or denser than the norm and must be triple-folded on one side to fit the cone, they may produce a stronger paper taste than similarly high-quality Melitta-style pocket filters.

The papery taste derives mainly from the various chemicals used in processing the paper. Consumers overlooked the taste issue for years until one of the typical health alarms of the 1980s surfaced. We became aware that dioxin, a potent carcinogen, is one of the chemicals used in bleaching paper, including most paper employed in coffee filters.

Although tests so far indicate that no detectable amount of dioxin reaches the cup, the very possibility has provoked a total makeover of the filter industry. There are now three kinds of paper filters available: those that have been bleached with the original, suspect process; those that claim to be "oxygen-whitened" or "oxygen-cleansed," and free of both dioxin and chlorine; and those that are not bleached at all, and are cardboard brown in color. "Oxygen-whitened" has a suspiciously vague advertising ring to it, but at least one manufacturer of oxygen-treated filters, Green Mountain, offers laboratory certification that its product is free of detectable dioxin and chlorine.

I see very little point to continuing to buy the old-fashioned, conventionally whitened filters except for reasons of price. From the point of view of coffee quality, the Green Mountain filters are plainly superior. They leave almost no taste behind in hot water, whereas even the best conventionally treated filters impart a faint papery or bleachy taste. And although the unbleached brown filters do contribute a distinctly woody or cardboardy taste, I still prefer them to the conventionally whitened papers. Their low-keyed, woody sweetness seems to fit better with coffee flavor than the high, papery notes imparted by conventional filters.

If you have trouble finding alternatives to the ordinary bleached filters, you can order the certified dioxin-free Green Mountain filters directly from Green Mountain (see Sending for It), and unbleached filters from the The Vermont Country Store, Box 3000, Manchester Center, VT 05255-3000; (800) 362-2400.

Styles of Filter Brewer. There is an enormous array of filter brewers on the market in which to use your new style of filter papers. You have a choice of materials (as always, glass and ceramic are the best) and filter shape, which ranges from the simple cone to the Melitta-style pocket or wedge, to the flat-bottomed basket filters. Adherents and manufacturers of each style make cogent arguments for the technical superiority of their preferred shape. I have not, however, found much difference among coffees made with the three styles of filter. Other factors, such as coffee quality, water quality, water temperature, filter quality, and the care taken in delivering the water to the coffee, appear to be more important than filter shape.

Brewers Using Cone-Shaped Filters. Among brewers using the cone-shaped filters, the most famous in the United States is the Chemex system, the original filter brewer that was developed from, and still resembles, a well-made piece of laboratory equipment. Many find its austere design (honored by the Museum of Modern Art in New York) and authentic materials (glass and wood in the traditional models) attractive, but the single-piece hourglass shape makes cleaning difficult. The original hand-blown models with wood handles range in price from about $40 to $50 depending on capacity; the same models in machine-molded glass run from around $20 to $30. Chemex also makes versions with attractive integral glass handles for $20 to $30. If you choose not to set a Chemex brewer in a pot of water or on a stove-top diffusion pad to keep it warm while brewing, you may want to purchase the matching electric warmer (around $30). You definitely need a sturdy bottle brush for cleaning; Chemex makes its own for around $8.

Brewers Using Wedge-Shaped Filters. The Melitta company, originator of the wedge-shaped pocket filter, is the leading producer of filters and filter accessories, both in sales volume and in value for the dollar. Melitta products are consistently well made, well designed, and sensibly priced. The top of the Melitta line of pour-over coffee makers is a porcelain model with simple, rounded lines reminiscent of the traditional French-drip pot (around $35). The classic Melitta flameproof glass decanter with plastic cone costs about $14 to $20, depending on capacity. The matching Melitta electric warmer is a bargain at under $20.

The latest device in heat preservation for drip coffee is the thermos brewer. A filter cone rests on top of a thermos; the coffee is filtered directly into the preheated thermos. There are many on the market (from about $25 to $40); if you already have a thermos, Melitta probably makes a filter unit to fit it.

Permanent Filters.   A note on permanent filters: I don't recommend cloth filters, since they are difficult to keep clean. Gold-plated permanent filters, in both standard Melitta wedge and basket styles, are very popular. They are excellent products, but if you like filter coffee, you may not like coffee made with these filters as much as you like coffee brewed with paper filters. The mesh allows a good deal of sediment and colloids to enter the brewed coffee, which gives it a heavy, often gritty taste, closer in style to drip or French-press coffee. Permanent filters also require a coarser and more uniform grind to work correctly.

Suggestions for Filter Brewing. Careful brewing can make a considerable difference in the quality of filter coffee. Bring cold water to just short of boiling and pour a little over the grounds, making sure to wet all the coffee. Pour the rest of the water through and stir the coffee lightly after brewing. If you make a small quantity, less than four cups, you should use slightly more ground coffee to compensate for the flavor lost to the filter, and wet the filter before you put in the ground coffee.

Automatic Filter-Drip

In 1973 fewer than 1 million automatic filter-drip coffee makers were sold in the United States. In 1974 that figure rose to 3 million, and in 1975 doubled to 6 million. By now the automatic filter-drip brewer has virtually eliminated the electric percolator from the market. Either Americans are infatuated with a new gimmick or the American coffee drinker always considered filter coffee to be superior, but clung to the percolator because it saved time and steps.

The heart of the automatic filter-drip system is the familiar filter, receptacle, and decanter. The machine simply heats water to the optimum temperature for coffee brewing and automatically measures it into the filter. The coffee drips into the decanter, and an element under the decanter keeps the coffee hot once it is brewed. The consumer measures cold water into the top of the maker, measures coffee into the filter, presses a switch, and, in from 4 to 8 minutes, has 2 to 12 cups of coffee.

Furthermore, the manufacturers of these brewers have considerably improved their performance over the past 10 years. Most of the leading makers have resolved such problems as ground coffee floating or forming a doughnut around the edge of the filter basket, variations in water temperature, and excessively slow or fast filtering.

Some years ago, I was certain that I could make better filter coffee than any of these machines could, simply by pouring the water over the coffee myself by hand. Now I'm not so sure. Last time I tested against a line-up of Krups, Braun, and Melitta machines, I was hard put to match their quality. And the cheaper, mass-marketed machines have improved as well, with most of the egregious performers of yesteryear eliminated from the shelves.

On the high end of the price scale are the European-style brewers by Krups, Braun, Melitta, Rowenta, and, more recently, Bosch. For a plain model without clocks and special features, these machines cost between $30 and $50. They appear in black, white, or current designer colors and are sleek and reticent in profile. All are marketed primarily through upscale department stores and specialty-coffee stores, but the Braun and Melitta can be found in mass-market outlets as well.

On the low end are the mass-marketed, entry-level brewers by makers such as Proctor-Silex, Regal, and Hamilton Beach. These machines increasingly mimic the sleek look, fashionable colors, and fancy features of the high-end machines, though many still reassure the traditionalist with their brown tones, boxy contours, and no-nonsense operation—that is, you can still see the coffee dribble into the carafe, and there are no computer chips. Most also have no-nonsense prices, often discounted to as low as $15.

Special Features. As would be expected with an aggressively marketed appliance designed for convenience, an ever-increasing array of special features adds to the price (and, one hopes, to the usefulness) of the fundamental brewer found in the local discount department store:

- A pause feature enables you to temporarily interrupt the brewing cycle to pour a cup of coffee. This is a very useful feature, given that coffee drinkers are not known for their patience.
- An under-the-cabinet design saves space by allowing you to mount the machine beneath a kitchen cabinet, suspended over the counter. Obviously, only you can decide on the usefulness of this feature.
- A thermos carafe, designed to keep the coffee hot without the usual warming plate, is very helpful for those who want to hold coffee for any length of time. The sealed thermos retains flavor and some aroma, both of which tend to deteriorate rapidly when the coffee is subjected to an external heat source such as a hot plate. Naturally, the absolutely best solution is to buy a smaller-capacity brewer and brew more frequently.
- A closed system, designed to retain heat and aroma during the brewing process, accounts for the reticent look of the high-end brewers. Manufacturers such as Krups, Braun, and Melitta make a very strong case for this feature in their promotional materials. If all else is equal, a closed system undoubtedly improves flavor and aroma. However, if you let coffee sit on the hot plate of the brewer for 15 minutes before you drink it, a feature like this is rendered irrelevant.
- Timing devices enable you to set the brewer to wake you up with freshly brewed coffee. The night before, you fill the water and coffee receptacles and set the timer. The disadvantage is that the ground coffee stales all night long. Still, I wouldn't hold it against any coffee lover who bought one. The Toshiba My Cafe and Sanyo Cafe San VIP units attempt to eliminate staling by incorporating a grinder into the brewer; at the appointed time these devices not only brew coffee but grind it as well. They are discussed in detail later in this chapter.
- Some automatic brewers include permanent filters of nylon or metal mesh.

If you like the clarity and brightness of filtered coffee, you do not need this feature. Avoid buying a maker that permits you to use only the permanent filter and does not give you the option of using paper.

- The coffee-strength controls on brewers that I've tried are ineffective. The strong setting causes the coffee to be overbrewed and, consequently, harsh.
- A provision for brewing a smaller amount of coffee on some Krups and Rowenta machines appears to work. In the case of most other machines, it simply involves a smaller basket for the ground coffee.
- Built-in water filters have cartridges that must be replaced periodically (every 50 to 60 sessions). They correct for both impurities and extremely hard water. Currently, the only widely distributed brewer to incorporate this feature is the Melitta Pure Drip. The brewer has to be run at least once every three days to prevent the filter from drying out and losing its effectiveness. I give Melitta a high grade for effort, but suggest that if your water is bad, you may have a general problem that transcends coffee brewing and needs to be resolved with either bottled water or a filtration system. The independent version of the same filter system that Melitta uses (the Brita system) costs about $30; the replacement cartridges run about $7 to $10 each.
- Various technical strategies for ensuring that all of the ground coffee is thoroughly saturated and involved in the infusion process are often touted in promotional materials. I am not certain that these strategies should be called *features*, because all automatic filter brewers aim for thorough infusion of the coffee through one technical means or another. Some manufacturers may carry on about their "sprinkler head" system, for example; both Krups and Melitta have systems that release water into the filter receptacle in rhythmic pulses, surges, or gushes, depending on whose promotional literature you're reading. In all cases, the objective is to agitate the coffee, breaking up lumps or donuts of dry coffee and ensuring a thorough infusion. The Melitta literature sounds more convincing than the Krups, but both machines make outstanding coffee.
- Hot plates that turn off automatically to prevent fires and fouled carafes could be extremely useful to coffee drinkers with bad memories.
- Various means have been developed to modulate the temperature of the warming plate, so as to keep coffee hot with less loss of flavor. The latest and most innovative is the Melitta cup sensor system, which Melitta claims

senses how much coffee is left in the carafe and adjusts temperature accordingly. Other coffee makers have a manual adjustment, usually with two settings, a high setting for a full pot (or for those coffee drinkers who add milk or cream to their coffee) and a lower setting for a partial pot (or for those coffee drinkers who take their coffee black).

The loss of flavor through holding coffee on the warming plate is one of the great drawbacks to automatic filter machines; the best solution is to brew smaller amounts of coffee more frequently; the second best approach is to use a preheated thermos carafe. Anything else, no matter how innovative, is simply another expedient.

Automatic Filter Drip Recommendations

My recommendations are obviously not comprehensive, since sixty or seventy models of automatic filter drip are on the market and more appear every month. I have chosen to focus on those brewers that consumers are most likely to find in specialty-coffee and upscale cookware stores. Please don't assume that my failing to mention a brewer implies condemnation. For those interested in evaluations of less expensive, mass-marketed automatic filter drip brewers, or assessments of models not mentioned here, I suggest consulting the latest *Consumer Reports*.

Best and Most Expensive. The Krups Plus series: The high-end Coffee Time Plus unit with timer and two-cycle brewing sells for around $120, the low-end Coffee Aroma Plus unit for around $65, and an (impressive) thermos carafe version (ThermAroma Plus) for around $80. Although the Krups machines are not as stylish-looking as the Braun units, they make as good a cup of coffee as any automatic filter-drip brewer marketed and usually come out on top in various consumer magazine and consumer institute tastings. The range of features in the Plus series is as complete as in any line by any manufacturer. The two-cycle brewing feature, which enables you to brew one to three cups, is to my knowledge the most effective version of this small batch-brewing feature in the industry.

Best Value. The various Melitta lines of automatic filter-drip brewers offer most of the features of the Krups machines at considerably lower prices. Melitta has several lines of brewers; the latest and most expensive, the I.B.S. (Interval Brewing System) Super line, offers a thermos model, a model with built-in water filter, and another with an innovative warming plate that claims to reduce heat as the number of cups remaining in the carafe is reduced, thus preventing overheating and minimizing flavor loss. These appear to be excellent brewers, although the older Melitta lines offer the best bargains. The excellent 10-cup and 4-cup Trim brewers retail for as little as $20, for example. Melitta automatic brewers tend to rank high in published taste tests, but seldom at the top. My own tastings suggest that they make somewhat better coffee than the much-touted Braun brewers, and hold up well even against the redoubtable (and expensive) Krups machines.

Best Looking. The sleek Braun Aromaster line offers impressive styling with slightly fewer features than the Krups line, but at significantly lower prices ($30 to $70). The Braun Aromaster brewers topped the Krups in a 1987 *Consumer Reports* taste test, though a later test by the same magazine (1990) declined to make such fine distinctions. My own assessment puts the Krups on top, but the difference is so slight that it probably hardly matters to the average coffee drinker. Over the years there have been consistent complaints that the warming plate on the Aromaster brewers keeps coffee at too low a temperature for American tastes, but Braun now claims to have raised the temperature to the U.S. standard.

Best Thermos Brewer. The thermos is technically a better way to keep coffee hot than the usual warming plate. Many specialty-store buyers prefer the Rowenta Thermal automatic thermos brewer to the Krups ThermAroma Plus, because they claim the thermos component on the Rowenta retains heat better. Both retail for about $80.

Filter Brewers With Built-In Grinders

As noted earlier, at least three manufacturers have created automatic brewers with built-in coffee-grinding apparatus. Two of these machines have automatic timers; you load them with whole beans the night before, set the timer, and wake up to the sound and aroma of coffee being ground and brewed for you by your countertop robot.

The Toshiba My Cafe (around $100 to $130) has been available for some time; the larger-capacity Sanyo Cafe San VIP brewer ($160 to $190) is a relative newcomer. With both devices, the grinding and brewing take place virtually in the same receptacle. After a pair of blades knocks the coffee to pieces, hot water bubbles directly over it and drips through a mesh filter into the decanter below.

All coffee made with a mesh (rather than a paper) filter is rich in sediment and oils. Don't expect coffee from either the My Cafe or the Sanyo Cafe San to have the bright, clear flavor of good paper-filtered coffee. Both make a particularly heavy, silty cup, probably because blade grinders produce a dusty, uneven grind when they are not manipulated to keep the coffee circulated around the blades.

Hitachi has developed a unit that attempts to solve the silt problem by separating the grinding and brewing processes into adjacent compartments, making it possible to use a paper filter. At this writing, however, there appears to be no version of the Hitachi Mill & Drip with timer, so I fail to see much advantage in combining the two operations into one unit. You still need to hover over the machine to start the brewing process after the grinding has concluded.

If these innovative machines could improve quality and reduce price, they might find a market in the United States. As it is, I suspect that their appeal will continue to be limited to gadget enthusiasts looking for bragging rights.

Coffee in the Microwave

The popularity of the microwave oven has provided coffee tinkerers with their latest and brightest challenge: how to use the properties of the little ovens to actually brew coffee rather than simply reheat it. The special problem presented by the microwave is how to heat the brewing water without simultaneously burning, baking, or scorching the ground coffee. At this writing, several solutions have turned up, all drawing on the rich heritage of coffee invention.

The Welker just-one ($4) and the Mr. Coffee Quick Brew (around $14) protect the ground coffee from scorching simply by combining it with the water from the very beginning of the brewing operation, making both devices variations on the ubiquitous open-pot method. The Welker unit is simplicity itself: The ground coffee (coarse, open-pot grind) is contained inside a mesh cage and suspended in warm tap water. As you microwave the pot (for about two minutes) the water further heats up and the coffee brews. You then pour the brewed coffee out through the cage-like filter. The coffee has the predictably gritty, heavy style of open-pot coffee.

Although the idea behind the Welker device is simple, the actual brewing procedure is not. Since the wattage of ovens and the temperature of hot tap water differs from oven to oven and hot water tap to hot water tap, this gadget demands too much experimenting before it will work right. I don't recommend it. Consumers who want to brew small amounts of open-pot-style coffee are better off purchasing one of the small, inexpensive plunger pots described on pages 115–116.

The Mr. Coffee device uses a combination of open-pot and filter-drip methods. You put ground coffee and water together in the familiar wedge-shaped filter. The filter holder is closed at the bottom by a small metal strip. As the microwave heats the mixture of water and ground coffee to brewing temperature, it simultaneously heats the metal strip, which expands, eventually popping open to allow the brewed coffee to trickle out through the filter cone into the receiving receptacle.

The entire process takes about 4 minutes and produces an 8-ounce mug of rather good filter coffee; certainly as good as that produced by most small-capacity automatic-filter drip machines. The Quick Brew may be a good one-cup filter brewer for people with not much time and a large (minimum 7 1/2-inch- high cavity) microwave.

The Farberware MicroBrew, at around $30 the most expensive of the three brewers, is the only one that starts its operation with water and ground coffee in separate compartments. The water is contained in a pressure-sealed compartment at the top of the brewer, above the ground coffee, which is held in a wedge-shaped filter. As the microwave heats the water, expanding air pressure in the closed water chamber forces the gradually heating water up a short tube, measuring it over the ground coffee. From there the still-heating coffee percolates down through the filter into the serving carafe, which makes up the lowest third of the brewer.

Those who have read so far will recognize this system as an ingenious combination of vacuum drip (the pressure-induced mode of delivering the water) and filter drip (the filter method of separating spent grounds from brewed coffee.) The MicroBrew attempts to minimize the scorching of the dry, ground coffee by inducing a small, pressure-generated dribble of cool water over the coffee at the onset of the operation.

The MicroBrew makes up to 10 ounces of light-bodied, delicately flavored coffee. The fact that the brewing water is warmed as it's delivered to the ground coffee, rather than delivered at full brewing temperature, doubtless accounts for the light body and subtle flavor. Some people may find the MicroBrew's coffee pleasantly delicate and healthily low on acid and oils; most will probably find it listless. The device itself is a bit complicated and time-consuming to assemble, and requires a large-cavity microwave.

To summarize, the collective American brewing brain trust has so far given us open-pot microwave coffee (the Welker just-one), filter-drip microwave coffee (the Mr. Coffee Quick Brew), and vacuum filter-drip microwave coffee (the Farberware MicroBrew). My scorecard indicates one miss (the Welker attempt), one hit (the Mr. Coffee unit), and one maybe (the Farberware MicroBrew). It will be interesting to observe what ideas come marching onto the shelves next.

Brewing for One or Two

With the exception of espresso, most brewing systems produce their best coffee in larger-than-one-cup quantities. The flavor loss is particularly acute with filter coffee, since in a one-cup brewer the paper filter overpowers the coffee. So if you prefer filtered coffee and are looking for quality, you might consider buying a two- to four-cup brewer, and brewing a bit more than you need. The Krups Brewmaster Junior (around $30) is an excellent small automatic filter-drip brewer, but to get the best results you need to brew at least two cups, preferably three or four.

If you do not use a one-cup pour-over filter drip cone, like the inexpensive Melitta, make certain you preheat the cone and cup before you brew. It also helps to wet the filter paper at the same time that you preheat the cone, to mute the impact of the filter on the coffee. The little electric cup warmers sold as desktop accessories are useful for keeping your cup hot while you brew.

The Mr. Coffee Quick Brew microwave brewer described on page 131 is a good one-cup alternative for those who like coffee made with paper filters, and who own microwave ovens with at least a 7 1/2-inch-high cavity. The microwave method eliminates the need to preheat the brewing components, and the Mr. Coffee brewing decanter doubles as a travel mug, complete with drink-through lid. The paper filter seems to take less out of the coffee in this brewer than in the ordinary pour-over one-cup filter brewers. Perhaps the couple of minutes that the coffee and water sit together before brewing commences help saturate the paper, thus minimizing flavor loss.

If you enjoy denser, punchier coffee of the kind made without a paper filter, you have more options. One-cup, gold-plated metal mesh filters (around $10 to $12) make a good cup, providing you use a bit more ground coffee than usual and preheat the filter and cup.

The various two-cup plunger brewers made by Bodum and Melior also make excellent coffee in the heavier style. You can get a plastic-framed version for as little as $12. Again, make sure you preheat both the brewer and the cup.

Solo Traveling Brewers

The several self-contained electric brewing systems on the market are all designed with the traveler in mind. The Melitta system (the Coffee Survival Kit includes bag, storage containers, etc., and costs around $50) is bulky and uses paper filters; although it is manufactured with the usual Melitta quality, I don't recommend it because of the dominating effect of the filter on the coffee. The Ronde Quick Cafe system (around $35) uses permanent nylon-mesh filters, is compact and ingeniously designed, and makes a decent cup of drip-style coffee if you put the fussy strength-control dial on full. The little mesh filters are difficult to clean, however. The same manufacturer has combined the Quick Cafe model with a built-in alarm clock/calendar. When the alarm sounds, the coffee automatically starts brewing. The Ronde Quick Cafe International Coffee Maker (about $80) may be one of those eccentric gift gadgets for professionals with everything, but it's also compact and probably genuinely useful for some. Krups has introduced an excellent little automatic travel unit for around $40 that uses a gold-on-steel filter, and a system similar to the kind used by vacuum brewers to force the hot water up and over the coffee. The Krups device is compact and handsome, and makes excellent coffee in the heavier style. The Norelco Hot Stuff (around $25) and Russell Hobbs Travel Jug Kettle (about $30) are both attractive, no-nonsense, pour-the-water-yourself travel kits that use permanent mesh filters.

Concentrate Brewing

In Latin America, as well as in many other parts of the world, a very strong, concentrated coffee is brewed, stored, and added in small amounts to hot water or milk to make a sort of pre-industrial age instant. It's very easy to make your own concentrate, but pre-made liquid concentrates are beginning to appear in supermarkets and fancy food stores. The most authentic of those I've seen, Victorian House Concentrated Coffee, is a genuine, natural concentrate produced from good coffee with no additives, but, like all concentrates, it produces a light-bodied cup with little aroma. And priced by the cup, it is not cheap.

You can obtain a strong concentrate with almost any brewing method, although only one, the cold-water method, has gained much popularity in the United States.

Hot Water Concentrate

To make a hot-water concentrate, use 8 cups of water to 1 pound of finely ground coffee and brew in your customary fashion. If the coffee maker is unable to handle a pound at a time, halve the recipe or brew twice. Store the resulting concentrate in a stoppered bottle in the refrigerator; to a preheated cup, add about 1 ounce for every 5 ounces of hot water. A bartender's shot glass holds an ounce and makes a convenient measure.

Cold Water Concentrate

The cold-water concentrate method has been adopted by two manufacturers, Filtron and Toddy. Both make an excellent cold-water brewer for around $20. Both work substantially the same way: You steep 1 pound of regular-grind coffee in 8 cups of cold water for 10 to 20 hours, filter the resulting concentrate into a separate container, store it in the refrigerator, and add it to hot water in proportions of 1 ounce to 1 cup.

The result is a very mild, delicate brew, with little acidity (of either the good or bad variety), light body, a natural sweetness, and an evanescent, muted flavor. Those who take coffee weak and black and like a delicate flavor free of acid highlights and the idiosyncrasies of coffee flavor may well like the cold-water method. Those who for medical reasons require a milder brew also might find it suitable. And it is, like the hot concentrate, convenient.

Anyone who likes strong coffee, distinctive coffee, or coffee with milk would be better off brewing coffee another way. Another problem: If you combine 1 or more ounces of refrigerated concentrate with 5 ounces of hot water, you produce a mixture considerably less than scalding hot; add milk and the coffee is lukewarm.

Some people like to use cold-water concentrate in cooking, but I prefer hot-water concentrate because the coffee flavor is stronger and more distinctive; cold-water concentrate makes everything taste like storebought coffee ice cream. The same can be said for using cold-water concentrate in cold coffee drinks; it's true you need a concentrate to compensate for dilution by ice, but some (like me) prefer the more distinctive punch of hot-brewed concentrate.

You don't have to buy a cold-water brewer to enjoy cold-water coffee, although the storebought brewers are much more convenient than any expedient. To improvise, you need a glass bowl, a large coffee cone and filter, and a bottle with an airtight closure (snap-on plastic won't do) in which to refrigerate the finished concentrate. Take 1 pound of your favorite coffee, regular grind. You can use any coffee, any roast. Put it in the bowl, and add 8 cups of cold water. Poke the floating coffee down into the water so all the grounds are wet, then let the bowl stand in a cool, dark place for 10 to 20 hours, depending on how strong you want the concentrate. When the brewing period is over, use the cone to filter the concentrate into the second, airtight container, and store in the refrigerator. For hot coffee, use 1 to 2 ounces per cup.

Concentrate keeps its flavor for months if the bottle is tightly capped, but it is best to make only as much as you will drink in a week or two. Instructions for the cold-water Toddy brewer suggest freezing the concentrate, but I've found it loses some much-needed flavor, and I suggest you simply halve the recipe if you can't drink 8 cups of concentrate in two weeks.

Middle Eastern Brewing

Middle Eastern coffee is most often called *Turkish coffee* in this country, but this is a misnomer. For one thing, it is drunk all over the Middle East, not only in Turkey, and if a patriotic Greek or Armenian serves it to you, you had better not call it *Turkish* coffee. Second, according to all accounts, the method was invented in Cairo and later spread from there to Turkey. Middle Eastern coffee is unique, first, because some of the coffee grounds are deliberately drunk along with the coffee, and second, because the coffee is usually brewed *with* sugar, rather than sweetened after brewing. The tiny grains of coffee are suspended in a sweetened liquid, imparting a heavy, almost syrupy weight to the cup.

It's possible to produce good, flavorful Middle Eastern-style coffee in any pot; the investment you make in brewing equipment is more important to ritual and esthetics than to flavor. Nevertheless, ritual seems to be as significant as flavor is in the enjoyment of coffee, and you may want to be authentic. If so, you'll need a small conical pot that looks a little like an inverted megaphone, called an *ibrik* (Turkish) or *briki* (Greek). The best and most authentic are made of copper or brass, are tinned inside, and cost about $20. You should also have demitasse cups and saucers; the standard restaurant variety of brown or white porcelain is attractive and can be bought at any large restaurant-supply store.

The most important piece of functional equipment in making Middle Eastern-style coffee is the grinder. Since you drink the grounds and don't want to be picking grains of coffee from between your teeth, you need a very fine, uniform grind, a dusty powder in fact. Few home mills can produce such a grind. The Jupiter grain mill and the Zassenhaus box mills described in Chapter 5 do a decent job. Countries that take this kind of coffee drinking seriously produce attractive brass hand mills especially for this brewing method. If you purchase this style of grinder, I suggest that you buy the largest and sturdiest you can find; the cheaper ones appear to be more tourist trinkets than true grinders. Fante's in Philadelphia (see Sending for It) carries a good one for about $30. The only electric machines that I know produce a consistently good Middle Eastern-style coffee are some of the expensive specialized espresso grinders, particularly the Olympia ($225).

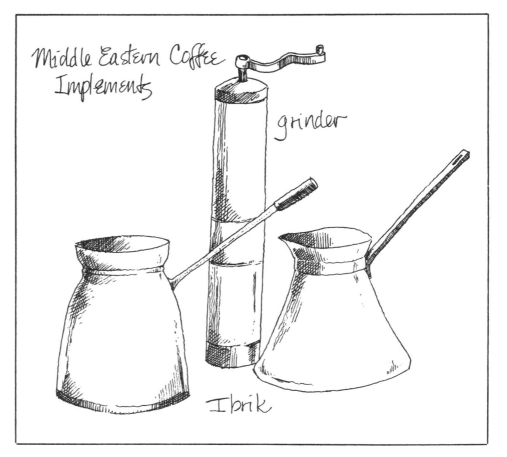

Middle Eastern Coffee Implements

grinder

Ibrik

Preground Middle Eastern coffees are available, both in cans and prewrapped, at specialty-coffee stores. Few stores can grind true Middle Eastern coffee fresh. Their grinders generally do not adjust that fine. They carry the coffee preground, which puts it in about the same class as canned coffees.

The roast you choose is a matter of taste, as is the provenance of the coffee. Most "Turkish" or Middle Eastern-style coffee sold in the United States is a fairly dark roast, the sort most stores sell as Italian. A blend of a winy coffee, such as Kenya or Mocha, some Sumatran, and a good dark French roast makes an excellent Middle Eastern coffee.

Authentic Middle Eastern coffee should have a thin head of brown foam completely covering the surface of the coffee. In Greece, this is called the *kaimaki*, and to serve coffee without it is an insult to the guest and a disgrace to the host. A Greek friend of mine tells about her mother secretly struggling in the kitchen to produce a good head of kaimaki, while the rest of the family nervously diverted the guests with small talk in the parlor. In the United States the kaimaki is usually dispensed with, for the simple reason that it's very difficult to produce. The Middle Eastern coffee that you make should taste good the first time you make it, and the foam can wait until you're an expert.

Never plan to fill the ibrik to more than one-half its capacity. You need the other half to accommodate the foam that boils up from the coffee. Start by measuring 2 level-to-rounded teaspoons of freshly ground coffee per demitasse into the ibrik. Add about 1 level teaspoon of sugar for every teaspoon of coffee. This makes a coffee a Greek would call sweet. Add 1 1/2 teaspoons of sugar per 1 teaspoon of coffee and you get heavy sweet; 1/2 teaspoon is light sweet. Omit sugar and you're serving the coffee plain, or *sketo*.

Now measure the water into the ibrik. Stir to dissolve the sugar, then turn on the heat medium to high. After a while the coffee will begin to boil gently. Let it boil, but watch it closely. Eventually the foam, which should have a darkish crust on top, starts to climb the narrow part of the ibrik. When it fills the flare at the top of the pot and is at the point of boiling over, turn off the flame. Immediately and carefully, to avoid settling the foam, pour into the cups. Fill each cup halfway first, then return to add some foam. Again, even though you may fail with the foam, the coffee is always delicious.

Middle Easterners like to add spices to their coffee. The preferred spice, and the one I suggest you try, is cardamom. Grind the cardamom seeds as finely as you grind the coffee, and add them to the water with the coffee and sugar. There are usually three seeds in a cardamom pod; start by using the equivalent of one seed (not pod) per demitasse of water, or a pinch if the cardamom is preground.

Instant Coffee

Making instant coffee is hardly brewing, but I don't have a chapter on mixing and stirring, so I'll have to include my discussion of instant coffees here, as a sort of exemplary afterthought.

I don't wish to insinuate that instant-coffee producers are terrible people who sneak around in dark clothing and limousines, stealing the public's right to a rich, fragrant cup of real coffee. Instant-coffee technologists seem passionately involved in their quest for a better coffee. At first glance (not taste), instant coffee does seem to offer many advantages: It stays fresh longer; it eliminates the mistakes that can occur when brewing regular coffee; it can be made quickly; it can be mixed by the cup to individual taste; it contains somewhat less caffeine than regularly brewed coffee. Furthermore, because the process of producing instant coffee neutralizes strong or unusual flavors, the manufacturer can use cheaper beans and pass the savings on to the consumer.

Yet few of these well-publicized advantages prove out. Instant does stay fresher, but grinding your own makes an even fresher cup. Instant is cleaner, but so are frozen dinners. True, it's hard to ruin a cup of instant, but if you've read this far, you're an expert anyhow. And if it's convenience you're looking for, the one-cup drip or plunger pot will give you much better coffee, and just as quickly. So I can't see any reasons except possibly neatness and a slight edge in price to recommend instant.

And you don't need instant coffee on backpacking or canoeing trips either—open-pot coffee works fine in the wilds and adds no more weight than instant. At five in the morning, after brushing the earwigs out of your sleeping bag and cleaning up the mess the raccoons made, you need a cup of real coffee. About the only advantage to instant is that it doesn't attract bears.

Finally, for those who like to experiment with authentic and unusual coffees, the instant coffee world offers no true alternatives. As I pointed out earlier, the "exotic" instant coffee mixes currently in the supermarkets are insipid fabrications; by comparison, freeze-dried Colombia is a superior beverage. If you crave variety, you must go back to basics.

Once we dismiss the advantages of instant, the advantages of brewed-from-scratch stand out in aromatic, taste-tingling relief. Why does instant often taste more like liquid taffy than coffee? The key, again, is the extremely volatile coffee essence, which provides the aroma and most of the flavor of fresh coffee. Remember that this oil is developed by roasting and remains sealed in little packets in the bean until liberated by grinding and brewing. Once the coffee essence hits the water, it doesn't last long, which is the reason coffee that sits for a while tastes so flat.

Instant coffee is brewed much the way a gourmet would brew coffee from beans at home: The beans are roasted, immediately ground, and brewed in gigantic percolators, filter urns really. But when that fresh, hot brew is dehydrated, what happens? Remember, to *dehydrate* means to remove the water, and with the water goes—yes, the coffee essence, the minute droplets of flavor and aroma that mean the difference between tasteless, bitter brown water and real coffee.

But here technology comes clanking over the hill to save the day. If the flavor is lost, well then, put it back in again. Coffee technologists have long known that much of the essential oil literally goes up in smoke and out the chimneys of their roasters.

So—you guessed it. The instant-coffee people condense some of the essential oil lost in roasting and put it back in the coffee just before it's packed. Clever? Also tricky—so much so that even according to industry admissions, the sharp corners of coffee flavor are neutralized. The instant process makes bad coffee beans taste better and good coffee beans taste bad.

So far I've stuck to concrete factors such as efficiency and price and fairly clear subjective factors such as flavor and aroma. But I must add that the ritual of making a true cup of coffee the right way every morning is good for the soul. It cuts down on heedless coffeeholism and helps to steady the heart for the more complex activities to come. It gets you started with the confidence that you can at least make a good cup of coffee, and it's always best to start out winning.

The Method for You

Which brewing method is best? is a naive question. Which brewing method is best for me? is a question to which it is possible to approximate an answer. Take just two variables, body and convenience. Coffee made by the Middle Eastern method is the heaviest in body, espresso the next heaviest, and cold-water coffee the lightest, with coffee made with paper filters a close second. Between them are the coffees produced by all the other methods: open pot, plunger pot, drip, and so on. Who is to say which is best?

Even the question of convenience is relative. The cold-water method is clearly the most convenient, automatic filter-drip is a close second, and Middle Eastern and open pot are last. Still, no one can tell my sculptor friend that making coffee without a strainer in a coffee can is bad because it is clumsy and inconvenient. He appreciates the inconvenience; it adds to his satisfaction and takes his mind off the obscure anxieties of his work. One of the principal reasons for drinking coffee is the esthetic satisfaction of ritual. You ought to love not only the coffee your pot makes but the pot itself and all the little things you do with it.

CHAPTER 7

Espresso
What makes espresso espresso and how to do it at home

Espresso is several things at once. It is a unique method of brewing in which hot water is forced under pressure through tightly packed coffee, a cup at a time. It is a roast of coffee, darker brown than the normal American roast but not quite black. In a larger sense, it is an entire approach to coffee cuisine, involving not only roast and brewing method, but grind and grinder, a technique of heating milk, and a traditional menu of drinks. In the largest sense of all, it is an atmosphere or mystique: The espresso brewing machine is the spiritual heart and esthetic centerpiece of the European-style café.

Elements of Café Espresso

The espresso system was developed in and for cafés. Despite advances in inexpensive home espresso systems, it is still difficult to duplicate the finest café espresso or cappuccino in your kitchen or dining room without spending a good deal of money. Even those on a budget can come close, however, and I outline the strategy for that effort in later pages. For now, I want to discuss the big, shiny café machines.

Fundamentally, they make coffee as any other brewer does: by steeping ground coffee in hot water. The difference is the pressure applied to the hot water. In normal brewing processes, the water seeps by gravity down through ground coffee, loosely spooned into a filter; in the espresso process, the water is forced under pressure through very finely ground coffee packed tightly over the filter.

A fast, yet thorough brewing makes the best coffee. If hot water and ground coffee stay in contact too long, the more unpleasant chemicals in the coffee are extracted, and the more pleasant aroma and flavor evaporate. Hence the superiority of the espresso system: The pressurized water makes almost instant contact with every grain of ground coffee and rapidly begins dribbling out into the cup. Another advantage of the espresso system is freshness. Every cup is brewed in front of you, a moment before you drink it; in most cases the coffee beans are also ground immediately before brewing. Other restaurant brewing methods make anywhere from a pot to an urn at a time from preground coffee, then let it sit, where it loses flavor and aroma to the detriment of the coffee and the advantage of the ambience.

Evolution of the Café Machine

The oldest café espresso machines and the smaller home espresso machines work on a simple principle. Water is heated to boiling inside a closed tank; a space is left at the top of the tank, where steam gathers. When a valve is opened below the water line, the pressure of the steam trapped at the top of the tank forces hot water out of the valve and down through the coffee. The idea originated in 1822 with Louis Bernard Rabaut and was first applied to a large café machine by Edward Loysel de Santais in 1843. Santais's machine wowed visitors to the Paris Exposition of 1855 by producing "two thousand cups of coffee an hour." More than likely, however, Santais's machine brewed coffee a pot at a time. It remained for several Italians at the turn of the century to modify Santais's invention, and to create the first modern espresso machine. They decreased the size of the strainer that held the coffee, but increased the number of valves, enabling these "rapid filter" machines to produce several single cups of coffee simultaneously, rather than a single big pot at a time. Then as now, the espresso operator packed a few teaspoons of very finely ground, dark-roast coffee into a little strainer. The strainer was clamped into a receptacle protruding from the side of the machine. When the operator opened the valve (or, in more modern machines, pulls a handle or pushes a button), hot water was forced through the coffee and into the cup.

The early espresso machines look like shiny steam engines pointed at the ceiling. The round water tank is set on end and bristles with picturesque spouts, valves, and pressure gauges. These shiny towers topped with an ornamental eagle dominated the European café scene until World War II. After the war, Italians wanted an even stronger cup of coffee to go with their Vespas, and they wanted it faster. The espresso-pioneering Gaggia family obliged them. The water tank was laid on its side and concealed inside a streamlined metal cabinet with lines like a Danish-modern jukebox. The simple valve of the old days was replaced with a spring-powered piston that pushed

PREPARING ESPRESSO
1. FILLING FILTER BASKET
2. TAMPING COFFEE
3. CLAMPING ON FILTER HOLDER
4. FORCING HOT WATER THROUGH COFFEE

1.   2.   3.   4.

the water through the coffee harder and faster. The operator depressed a long metal handle. The handle in turn compressed a spring-loaded piston that forced a dose of hot water slowly through the coffee as the handle majestically returned to its original erect position. The new spring-loaded machines pushed the water through the coffee at a pressure that is now accepted as ideal for espresso brewing: nine atmospheres, or nine times the ordinary pressure exerted by the earth's atmosphere. By comparison, the pre-war steam-pressure machines exerted a feeble one-and-a-half atmospheres of pressure.

In the 1960s, just when pumping the handle became the signature performance piece of espresso cafés, less dramatic and more automated means for forcing the hot water through the coffee began to appear. The earliest of these no-hands machines were built around simple hydraulic pumps. Today's versions heat water separately from the main reservoir, control water temperature and pressure with precision, and flatter the hi-tech pretensions of the late twentieth century with digital read-outs.

These push-button machines tend to carry the streamlined look to an extreme. Everything is concealed inside a single, sleek enamel and chrome housing. All have one feature in common: The operator pushes a button or trips a switch rather than pumping a long handle. Since so much of the process is automated, the push-button machines are easier for the novice to master, but do not necessarily make better espresso. Proprietors of some of the best cafés in the San Francisco Bay Area, at any rate, prefer the pump-piston machines because they give the sophisticated operator maximum control over the brewing process.

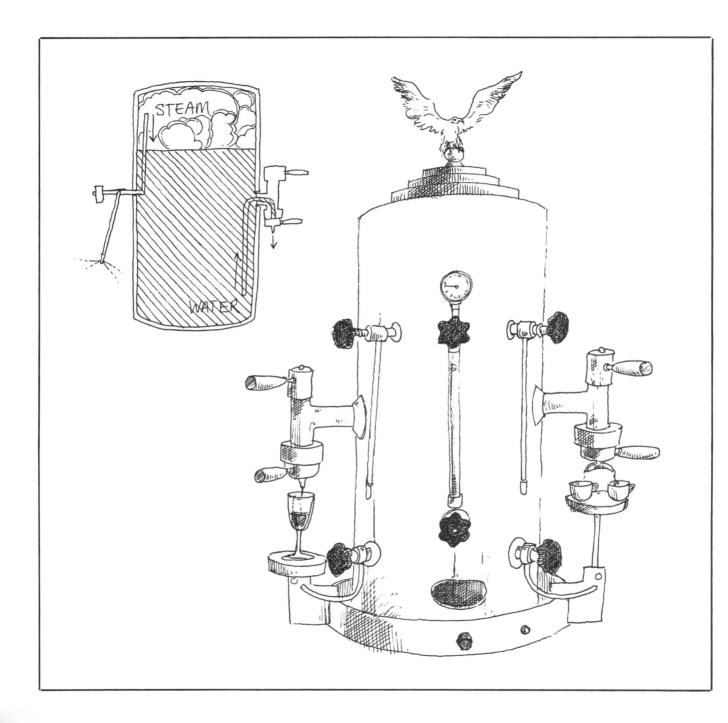

STEAM

WATER

Frothed Milk

With the long, gleaming handle perhaps going the way of the running board, the best routine left to the espresso operator is heating and frothing the milk used in drinks like cappuccino and caffè latte. Espresso is a strong, concentrated coffee, and, in accordance with European tradition, many of the drinks in espresso cuisine combine it with large quantities of milk. If the milk were unheated, it would instantly cool the coffee. Early in the history of the espresso machine, someone realized that the steam collected in the top of the tank could be used to heat milk as well as provide pressure for making coffee. A valve with a long nozzle was fed into the upper part of the tank where the steam gathers. When the valve is opened by unscrewing a knob, the compressed steam hisses out of the nozzle. The operator pours cold milk into a pitcher, inserts the nozzle into the milk, and opens the valve. The compressed steam shoots through the milk, heating it and raising an attractive head of froth or foam.

Café patrons soon discovered that steamed, frothed milk both tastes and looks better than milk heated in the ordinary way, and it became an important part of espresso cuisine. The white head of foam is decorative, can be garnished with a dash of cocoa or cinnamon, prevents a skin from forming on the surface of the milk, and insulates the hot coffee.

A Remarkable Cup of Coffee

It is difficult to say how much of the success of the espresso machine is due to its scientifically impeccable approach to coffee making, and how much to its drama and novelty, but, given European tastes, it certainly does produce a remarkable cup of coffee: freshly ground, and brewed so quickly that, as an Italian friend of mine says, you get only the absolute heart of the coffee. Nevertheless, many a mainstream American coffee lover facing espresso for the first time may take one swallow and either finish it stoically or hide the little cup behind a napkin. The distaste is understandable. This impeccable brewing system is designed to make a cup of coffee in the southern European or Latin American tradition rather than in the northern European or North American. Good espresso is rich, heavy-bodied, and almost syrupy; furthermore, it has the characteristic bittersweet bite of dark-roast coffee.

The sharp flavor and heavy body make it an ideal coffee to be drunk with milk and sugar, but hardly the sort of beverage to be consumed unsweetened or in large quantities. Most espresso drinkers outside Italy prefer cappuccino, a drink made of about one-third espresso and two-thirds hot milk and foam. The milk dilutes and mellows the strong, sharp coffee.

Classic Espresso Drinks

Southern Europeans have drunk strong, sharply flavored coffee in small cups or mixed with hot milk for generations. Consequently, most of the drinks in espresso cuisine are not original with the machine; rather, the machine brought them from promise to perfection. Here are some of the most popular drinks from the classic Italian cuisine. A few American additions to the Italian menu follow.

Espresso. About 1 1/2 ounces of espresso coffee, black, usually drunk with sugar. Properly presented, should fill about two-thirds of a demitasse. Can be flavored with a drop or two of almond or tangerine extract.

Espresso Romano. Espresso served with a twist or thin slice of lemon on the side.

Espresso Ristretto. "Restricted" or short espresso. Carries the "small is beautiful" espresso philosophy to its ultimate: The flow of espresso is cut short at about 1 ounce, producing an even denser, more perfumy cup of espresso than the norm.

Double or Doppio. Double serving, or about 4 ounces of straight espresso, made with twice the amount of ground coffee. Best drunk by veteran espresso bibbers, early in the morning, before a 12-hour workday and a long evening.

Cappuccino. (*Café crème* in France) A serving (about 1 1/2 ounces) of espresso, topped by hot milk and foam. Ideally, a good cappuccino consists of about one-third espresso, one-third milk, and one-third foam, in a heavy 6-ounce cup. Like most espresso drinks, it is usually drunk with sugar. In the United States this is the most popular, and also the most abused, espresso drink.

Some cafés drown the coffee with too much milk, others pile irrelevant whipped cream on top, and still others ruin the drink from the start by running too much water through the ground espresso, producing a bitter, watery cup.

Caffè Latte. (*Café au lait* in France; *café con leche* in Spain) One or two servings of espresso and three times as much frothed milk, in a big bowl or wide-mouthed glass. This is the favored breakfast drink of southern Europeans. Caffè latte has a greater proportion of milk to coffee than a cappuccino does and tastes weaker and milkier. Strictly speaking, the milk and coffee should be poured simultaneously, from either side of the bowl. The hot milk and coffee are often served separately in Europe. In the United States, cafés often distinguish between caffè latte (made with espresso) and café au lait, made with ordinary American coffee from the filter carafe.

Espresso Macchiato. A serving of espresso "stained"' (*macchiato*) with a small quantity of hot, frothed milk. Served in the usual espresso demitasse.

Latte Macchiato. A glass filled with hot frothed milk, into which a serving of espresso is slowly dribbled. The coffee colors, or stains, the milk in faint, graduated layers, darker at the top shading to light at the bottom, all contrasting with the layer of pure white foam at the top.

Caffè Mocha. Not to be confused with Mocha Java, a traditional American-roasted blend of Mocha and Java coffees. A mocha to an espresso drinker is about one-third espresso, one-third strong hot chocolate, and one-third hot frothed milk. The milk is added last, and the whole thing is usually served in an 8-ounce mug. With a classic mocha the hot chocolate is made very strong, so it can hold its own against the espresso, and the customer adds sugar to taste; the hot chocolate is at most lightly sweetened. Some cafés add chocolate fountain syrup to a caffè latte and call it a *mocha*. So be it. Voltaire is said to have consumed 40 cups of mocha a day at the Café de Procope.

Garnishes and Whipped Cream. Some cafés garnish the froth of cappuccino and caffè latte with a dash of unsweetened cocoa, which adds a subtle chocolate perfume to the drink. Others use cinnamon, which I don't approve of; I find the flavor too distinctive and out of harmony with the dark tones of the coffee. The practice of making both chocolate and cinnamon available and allowing patrons to administer their own garnish makes sense and saves time for the espresso operator. Straight espresso is delicious with whipped cream (*con panna*), but topping a good, foamy cappuccino with whipped cream is as pointless as putting catsup on red-sauced spaghetti.

The Classic Cuisine at Home. Detailed instructions and suggestions for brewing espresso and frothing milk with home machines are given later in this chapter, and recipes for coffee drinks from a variety of cuisines are presented in Chapter 12. When making espresso drinks at home, of course, one does as one likes with coffee and milk; the proportions for specific drinks given above are meant to help clarify and facilitate communication between American cafés and patrons, not to dictate how one enjoys espresso at home.

When making a caffè mocha at home, use an unsweetened, dark cocoa powder, available in bulk from most specialty coffee stores. This is the same powder used to garnish frothed milk in the espresso cuisine. Add about 3 heaping teaspoons to every cup of milk to produce the strong hot chocolate mix used in mochas and other espresso drinks. Combine the cocoa powder and milk while heating the milk with the steam wand; don't froth the chocolate and milk mix, just heat it. Leave it unsweetened, or mix in 1 to 2 teaspoons of brown sugar per cup of milk. Combine one part of the resulting strong hot chocolate with one part freshly brewed espresso, then top this mixture with one part hot frothed milk for the classic mocha. For plain hot chocolate use the same strong chocolate-milk mix, but top with about one part hot, freshly frothed milk to every two parts chocolate mix.

American Espresso Variations

Americans have begun to subject the classic espresso cuisine to their own brand of cultural innovation. In general, it would seem that we are frustrated by the brevity and precision of the classic cuisine, and want bigger drinks with more in them. Perhaps an ounce-and-a-half of coffee in a tiny cup does lack comfort in the middle of the Great Plains or atop the World Trade Towers. Still, I think it would be better if Americans understood and experienced the intensity and perfection of the true cuisine before immediately expanding it, watering it down, or adding ice to it. At any rate, here are some of the more honorable results of American espresso cuisine tinkering.

Double Cappuccino. (Or *double cap*, pronounced partly through the nose, as in baseball cap) If this innovation is made correctly, you should get about 3 ounces of uncompromised espresso, brewed with double the usual amount of ground coffee, topped with 3 to 5 ounces of hot milk and froth. Usually served in an 8-ounce cup or mug. If the ground coffee is not doubled, and the operator simply forces twice as much water through one serving's worth of ground coffee, you're getting a bitter, watery perversion, rather than a taller, stronger version of a good drink.

Double Caffè Latte. The same philosophy as above applied to a caffè latte; made properly, the amount of ground coffee is doubled, the amount of coffee brewed is doubled, but the proportion of hot milk and froth is maintained at about three times the volume of coffee.

Mocha Latte, Moccaccino. I ran into the latter portmanteau term in the chain of Coffee Connection stores in Boston. It appears to be another name for the more explicitly named *mocha latte*, a taller, milkier version of the classic mocha. If I were to suggest proportions for this invention, they would be one-quarter properly strong espresso, one-quarter properly strong chocolate, and one-half milk and froth. These proportions produce a drink that is milkier, taller, and more muted than the classic mocha, but still rich enough to satisfy.

Café Au Lait. In some American cafés, a drink made with about half American-roast, filter coffee, and about half hot milk and froth, served in a 10- or 12-ounce glass or bowl. The proportion of coffee to milk has to be larger than with the espresso-based caffè latte, because American filter coffee is so delicate in flavor and light in body compared to espresso.

Iced Espresso. This is usually a double espresso, poured over plenty of crushed, not cubed, ice, in a smallish fancy glass. Some cafés top the iced coffee with whipped cream. Cafés that brew and refrigerate a pitcher of espresso in advance when they feel a hot morning on the way fail to deliver the brewed-fresh perfume of true espresso, but the practice still makes a fine drink, and one that doesn't need to be iced and diluted as much as the version made with fresh espresso.

If you want to make this or other iced espresso drinks at home and your blender doesn't crush ice, you can improvise as generations of home bartenders have done before you: Put cubed ice in a towel and hammer on it with something flat and heavy. The exercise doubtless will make you enjoy the drink even more.

Iced Cappuccino. Best made with a single or double serving of freshly brewed espresso poured over crushed ice, topped with an ounce or two of cold milk, then some froth (not hot milk) from the machine to top it off. This drink should always be served in a glass. The triple contrast of coffee, milk, and froth, all bubbling around the ice, makes a pleasant sight on a hot day.

Espresso Granita. This is originally an Italian specialty, but has been adapted in the United States in ways that make it degenerately ours. Traditional Italian granitas usually involved freezing strong, unsweetened espresso, crushing it, and serving it in a parfait glass or sundae dish topped with lightly sweetened whipped cream. The latest American version blends espresso, milk, and ample sugar, and freezes the combination in special dispensing machines. It's called a *granita latte* in Seattle, where it apparently originated. The granita latte is a nice summer experience, particularly if it's made with café-brewed espresso rather than with somebody else's espresso flavoring.

To make the classic granita at home, brew several servings of full-strength espresso, freeze, then crush thoroughly before serving in a parfait or sundae dish. Top with lightly sweetened whipped cream dusted with chocolate powder.

Misunderstandings and Misrepresentations

Unfortunately, America has contributed more than innovation to the classic espresso cuisine. It has also watered it down, misunderstood it, and misrepresented it.

The art of espresso cuisine, as practiced in the best bars of Italy, is a masterpiece of coffee making, once tasted, seldom forgotten. Unfortunately, few American coffee drinkers have an opportunity to experience the aromatic perfection of the true cuisine. There are a growing number of American places where one can experience honest espresso coffee-making—Seattle, San Francisco, Santa Barbara, sophisticated enclaves in Manhattan and other large cities, and occasional outposts beyond. But even in these places, production is uneven, and you are as likely to encounter overextracted coffee drowned in scalded milk as you are a good cappuccino, for example. Good espresso cuisine demands not only a technically complete system and good intentions on the part of the café owner, but a skilled and attentive operator. And the operator, as any conscientious café owner will tell you, is the most difficult part of the equation.

The most prevalent and destructive mistake of novice espresso operators is running too much water through the coffee, often in a generous effort to provide customers with something more substantial than a little black stuff at the bottom of a demitasse. Instead of substance, of course, the customers are rewarded with a thin, bitter, watery drink that will make them wish they had ordered filter coffee or mint tea. Such overextracted coffee destroys all beverages in which it appears, including cappuccino and caffè latte.

The espresso system is so efficient that the goodness is extracted from the ground coffee almost immediately, making a small amount of intense brew, usually no more than 1 1/2 ounces per serving. Any water run through the coffee after that moment of truth contributes only bitter, flavorless chemicals to the cup. Those who want greater quantity should drink another style of coffee or order a double, which doubles both the amount of ground coffee and the amount of hot water run through it.

A less egregious error in the production of cappuccino is drowning the coffee in hot milk, which produces a weak, milky drink closer to a caffè latte than an intense, perfumy cappuccino. East Coast cafés often systematically drown otherwise well-handled espresso in eight or nine ounces of milk.

Overcompensations and Reactions

The Italian espresso industry may be having the same problem as the American in finding conscientious and skillful operators, because it has begun feverishly producing innovations essentially designed to automate the espresso brewing process to the point that the operator is reduced to irrelevant schlep or predictable button pusher. The most distressing result, which fortunately has not found much foothold in the United States, is machines that mix cappuccino and caffè latte in a device that works much like a commercial hot chocolate dispenser. The result is little more than instant coffee mixed with hot milk.

Other innovations are less sinister. There are machines that grind the coffee, load it, and brew the espresso, all at the push of a single button, for example. The operator still has to heat and froth the milk, however, although even here help is on its way. The otherwise conventional Faema café machines now offer the option of the Cappuccino Magic device, which sucks milk out of a carton, heats and froths it, and bubbles it nicely into the cup.

The simplest of these new espresso expedients are pods or (bless the advertising industry) "kisses" of preground, prepackaged espresso coffee. The pod or kiss looks like a disk-shaped tea bag filled with ground coffee. The operator simply pops one (or two for a double) of these pods into a specially designed espresso filter, clamps the filter onto the machine, pushes the button or depresses the lever, and the brewing proceeds as usual. The operator still needs to know when to stop the brewing process, but the grind and measurement of coffee remain consistent. Currently, these pods are produced in Italy and shipped to the United States in protected containers, but if they become popular I am sure American roasters will begin their own podding process.

Pod espresso is not as bad as one might expect, although hardly an Italian masterpiece. The pods may catch on, despite the fact that they currently cost two to four times as much as whole-bean espresso.

Espresso at Home

If you have experienced authentic espresso or cappuccino and you want more, you may prefer to produce your own. In this case, your first step should be deciding what you like about the encounter. If you like the pungent flavor of the espresso and are indifferent to the rich texture of the coffee or the effect of frothed milk, then you may be just as happy with dark-roast coffee brewed as you would any other coffee. Start with a half-pound of coffee roasted very dark brown but not black (variously called *espresso*, *French*, or *Italian*), ground for your regular coffee maker. But if you like the rich, syrupy body and flavor of true espresso, or if you like espresso drinks like cappuccino or caffè latte, you will need to purchase a specialized espresso brewing

Coffee ground too finely or packed too tightly— Espresso leaks out in little drops.

Coffee ground too coarsely or packed too loosely— Espresso gushes out.

Coffee ground to perfect grit and lightly but consistently tamped— Espresso dribbles out.

apparatus. Study the series of charts that appear later in this chapter describing the various options available for brewing espresso at home. To understand the capabilities of the various kinds of machine, however, you may need to review the following espresso fundamentals.

Espresso Brewing Fundamentals

Coffee and Roast. Café espresso is brewed using a coffee roasted dark brown, but not black. This roast is called *espresso*, *Italian*, or *French* in stores. Remember, however, that you can use any coffee in your espresso brewer, as long as the beans are properly ground. You may prefer a coffee darker than espresso roast (often called *dark French* or *dark Italian*), or lighter. The espresso method will produce a rich-textured and heavy-bodied beverage, no matter what coffee you choose. But only with the classic espresso roast will you achieve the sweet, rich tang of the café drinks. Always use at least as much coffee as is recommended by the manufacturer of your machine. Never use less. If in doubt, use two level tablespoons of finely ground coffee for every demitasse of espresso.

Brewing Principles. There are two requirements for making good espresso. First, you need to grind the coffee just fine enough, and tamp it down in the filter basket just hard enough, so that the barrier of ground coffee resists the pressure of the hot water sufficiently to produce a slow dribble of dark, rich liquid. Second, you need to stop the dribble at just the right moment, before the oils in the coffee are exhausted and the dark, rich dribble turns into a tasteless brown torrent.

Grind. The best grind for espresso is very fine and gritty, but not a dusty powder. If you look at the ground coffee from a foot away, you should barely be able to distinguish the particles. If you rub some between your fingers, it should feel gritty. Most canned espresso coffees, such as Medaglia D'Oro or Motta, are ground much too coarsely. Your best bet is to grind your own coffee. If you have whole beans ground at the store, ask for a fine grind for an espresso machine.

Filling and Tamping. Fill the filter basket with coffee to the indicated point (or to just below the brim if there is no indication), spread it evenly, then lightly tamp it down. Don't hammer on it. Either use the little round, flat-bottomed device called a *tamper* that may have come with your machine, or lightly press the coffee down across its entire surface with your fingertips. If you fear the grind is too coarse, press a little more heavily; if too fine, press lightly or not at all. Never use less than the minimum volume of ground coffee recommended for the machine, even if you are brewing a single cup. If the coffee gushes out rather than dribbling, compensate by using a finer grind. If it oozes out rather than dribbling steadily, use a coarser grind or go easier on the tamping.

Most stovetop espresso brewers contain the ground coffee in a largish sleeve inside the machine, rather than in a café-style filter that clamps to the front of the machine. With these stovetop devices, do not tamp the coffee. Use the same fine grind as recommended above, use plenty of it, distribute it evenly in the filter, and proceed.

Brewing. Timing is everything in espresso brewing. The richest and most flavorful coffee issues out right at the beginning; as brewing continues, the coffee becomes progressively thinner and more bitter. Consequently, collect only as much coffee as you will actually serve. If you are brewing one serving, cut off the flow of coffee after one serving has dribbled out, even if you have two servings' worth of ground coffee in the filter. If you are brewing two servings, cut off the flow after two. And no matter how many servings you're trying to make, never allow the coffee to bubble and gush into your serving carafe or cup. Such thin, overextracted coffee will taste so bad that it's better to start over than to insult your guests or palate by serving it.

Gauge when to cut off the flow of coffee by sight, not by clock or timer. The fineness of the grind may vary, as will the pressure you apply when tamping.

Consequently, the speed with which the hot water dribbles through the coffee will also vary from serving to serving. If in doubt, cut off the flow of coffee sooner rather than later. Better to experience a perfectly flavored small drink than an obnoxiously bitter large one.

If your brewer does not have a mechanism for cutting off the flow of the coffee, and if the design of the machine permits, use two separate coffee-collecting receptacles, one to catch the first rich dribbles, which you will drink, and a second to catch the pale remainder, which you will throw away. Whatever you do, don't spoil the first bloom of coffee by mixing it with the pale, bitter dregs.

Frothing the Milk

Most Americans prefer espresso blended with hot, frothed milk as cappuccino or caffè latte. Fortunately, most espresso-brewing appliances now sold in the United States have built-in steam valves and wands suitable for frothing milk. If you like espresso drinks with milk, make certain that any machine you purchase has such a mechanism.

Heating milk with an espresso machine is easy; producing a head of froth or foam is a little trickier, but, like riding a bicycle or centering clay on a potter's wheel, exquisitely simple once you've broken through and gotten the feel of it.

Steps in Making Drinks with Frothed Milk. There are three stages to making an espresso drink with frothed milk. The first is brewing the coffee; the second is frothing and heating the milk; the third is combining the two. Never froth the coffee and milk together, which would stale the fresh coffee and ruin the eye-pleasing contrast between white foam and dark coffee. Nor is it a good idea, even if your machine permits it, to simultaneously brew espresso and froth the milk. Concentrate on the brewing operation first, taking care to produce only as much coffee as you need. Then stop the brewing and turn to the frothing operation.

The Frothing Apparatus. The steam wand, also called *steam stylus, pipe,* or *nozzle,* is a little tube that protrudes from the top or side of the machine. At the tip of the wand are one to four little holes that project jets of steam downward or diagonally when the steam function is activated. Nearby you will find the knob that controls the flow of steam; it may be conveniently located next to the steam wand, or it may be a foot or so away at the side or top of the machine. While you are brewing coffee, this knob and the valve it controls are kept screwed shut.

Some machines do not have a screw knob to control the flow of steam for frothing; instead, you simply activate the steam function with a switch and take what you get. In general, it's better to purchase a machine in which the steam pressure for frothing is adjustable.

The transition between brewing and frothing in inexpensive machines is usually accomplished simply by closing the coffee brewing valve and opening the steam valve. In the more expensive, button-operated pump machines, there may be a more complex transitional procedure, which will be described in the instructions accompanying your machine.

A Dry Run. Before attempting to froth milk for the first time, practice opening and closing the steam valve with the machine on, the brewing function off or closed, and the steam function activated. Get a general sense of how many turns it takes to create an explosive jet of steam, and how many to permit a steady, powerful jet. It is the latter intensity that you will use to froth milk: not so powerful that the jet produces an overpowering roar, but powerful enough to produce a strong, steady hiss.

If you are using a stovetop machine and the steam is not producing a sturdy hiss, raise the heat slightly, and make certain that pressure is not escaping through the coffee valve. If steam explodes out of the wand at the first half turn of the knob, reduce the heat under the machine. You should be able to open the knob at least a half turn before the full force of the steam is heard and felt.

The Frothing Routine. You can froth the milk in a separate pitcher, or in each cup before you add the coffee. In either case, fill the container or cup about halfway with cold milk (the colder the better; hot milk will not produce froth). Open the steam valve for a few seconds to bleed any hot water from inside the wand. Then close the valve until just a wisp of steam appears from the tip of the wand. This is to prevent milk from being sucked back up into the wand as you immerse it into the milk.

Immerse the tip deeply into the milk. Slowly open the valve, then gradually close it until you get a strong, but not explosive, release of steam that moves the surface of the milk, but doesn't wildly churn it. Now slowly lower the milk container, thus bringing the tip of the wand closer to the surface of the milk. When the wand tip is just below the surface of the milk you will hear a hissing sound, the surface will begin to seethe, and frothy bubbles will begin to form. If the wand tip is too deep in the milk, there will be no hiss and the surface will not seethe; if it is too shallow, you will spray milk all over your apron. If it is just right, a gratifying head of froth will begin to rise from the surface of the milk. You need to follow the froth upward as it develops. Listen for the hiss; if you don't hear it, or if it turns to a dull rumble, the wand is too deep in the milk.

156

FROTHING MILK

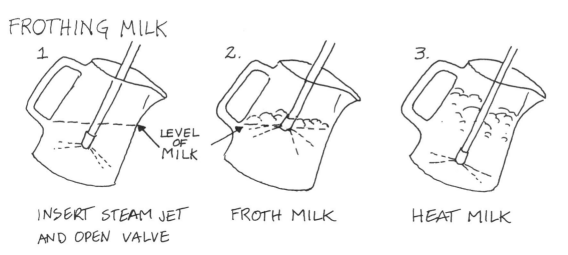

1. INSERT STEAM JET AND OPEN VALVE — LEVEL OF MILK

2. FROTH MILK

3. HEAT MILK

The first swelling of froth will be made up of largish, unstable bubbles. Periodically drop the tip of the steam wand back into the milk and hold it there for a moment, to let some of these bubbles pop and settle. Then bring the tip of the wand back to just below the surface of the milk again to rebuild the head of froth. Repeat this process until you have a creamy, dense head of froth made up of a stable matrix of tiny bubbles.

Heating the Milk. At this point, feel the sides of the milk container to see if the milk is hot. If it is not, lower the wand tip completely into the milk and keep it there until the container's sides heat up. Never heat the milk to boiling, and again, always froth the milk first, before you heat it, since cold milk froths best. If you are frothing milk for the first time and you end up with hot milk and not much froth, enjoy what you have and try again later with cold milk.

Finishing. Always conclude the frothing operation by opening the steam valve for a few seconds to clear milk residues from the holes at the tip of the wand. If you are using an inexpensive machine that utilizes steam pressure to brew the coffee, it is a good idea to let the steam valve remain open when you turn off the machine, to bleed the remaining steam from the boiler and relieve pressure on the valves and gaskets.

If you don't immediately raise an impressive head of froth, be patient. You may have to suffer through a few naked cappuccini at first, but inside a week you'll be frothing like a Milanese master.

Milk-Frothing Gadgets

Several manufacturers have attempted to simplify the milk-frothing operation by adding little gadgets to the steam wand. Some of these devices work very well; others simply complicate clean-up.

Of the devices currently marketed, the two most effective are the Faema Cappuccino Magic and the Krups Perfect Froth. The Cappuccino Magic literally sucks milk out of a container and froths it for you. With the Krups Perfect Froth you follow traditional frothing procedure, but rather than holding the tip of the wand at the surface of the milk, you immerse it completely. It introduces a jet of room-temperature air into the milk along with the steam and froths the milk from the inside, as it were, rather than from the surface. Like the Faema device, it is virtually foolproof.

The problem with these devices is twofold. First, neither gives the operator much control over the frothing operation. With the traditional technique, an experienced operator can easily control both the height and density of a head of froth, and can choose to make the milk very hot, or merely warm, depending on taste. The Faema device gives you some control over the density of the foam, but none over the temperature of the milk. The Perfect Froth makes a loose, unstable head of froth no matter what you do, and you can't choose to heat the milk rather than to froth it, as you can with the traditional technique. As long as the steam is activated and Perfect Froth is in the milk, it froths.

None of this would matter if these devices gave you the option of either using them, or ignoring them and frothing in the traditional way. In most cases, however, you're stuck with your little frothing gadget, even if you decide you've outgrown it. It's a little like buying a bicycle with training wheels that you can't take off. The Faema Amica offers no option for milk frothing other than the Cappuccino Magic device, which is a permanent part of the machine. The more expensive Faema model, the Faema Family, does allow you to remove the Cappuccino Magic device and replace it with a normally functioning steam wand.

As for the Krups Perfect Froth, it is easily removed or reattached to the steam wand of any Krups espresso machine, old or new. But the Krups machines themselves have been redesigned so that the operator no longer has the option of controlling the intensity of the steam flow. You simply activate the steam function and begin frothing. The idea seems to be that if you have Perfect Froth, you don't need an adjustable steam valve. This limitation at least partly cancels the apparent option Krups offers of either using Perfect Froth, or removing it and frothing milk in the conventional way. If Krups had kept the adjustable steam valve on its new machines, one could say with confidence that the Krups machines had something for everyone: Perfect Froth for novices and a conventional frothing system for more experienced or ambitious operators. But now I'm not so sure; I suspect that anyone who already knows how to froth milk will find the lack of an adjustable steam valve on the new Krups machines frustrating.

All the other milk-frothing gadgets I've tried still require you to froth milk in the conventional way. Some make this process a bit easier for beginners, some don't.

The Braun turbo cappuccino is a tiny plastic turbine at the end of the steam wand. The steam passes through the turbine, spinning it, which beats the milk and supposedly helps froth it. The device produces a wonderfully gratifying jet-engine whine when it's fully revved up, but it doesn't help the frothing operation much. It may even get in the way. You still need to master the trick of keeping the steam focused on the surface of the milk, and when you're finished the little turbine slobbers milk all over the counter. Nor can you take the turbo cappuccino off and simply use the steam wand in the traditional way. You're stuck with your little plastic turbine for as long as you own your machine.

Other frothing aids are essentially aerating devices that introduce additional room temperature air into the milk along with the steam. Why they don't work as dramatically as Perfect Froth does, I can't say, but all still require good traditional frothing technique. Their advantage is that they are easier to keep clean than the Krups and Braun gadgets. Sometimes these aerating devices are identified in promotional material, as is the Gaggia Turbo Frother or the pin that helps control the size of the frothing bubbles on the Cuisinart machines. In other cases, the manufacturer may simply make a vague allusion to a special something or other that makes milk frothing a snap.

I suggest that those who enjoy espresso drinks with frothed milk buy a machine without fussy attachments and learn to froth in the traditional way. As I indicated earlier, anyone with the smallest amount of patience can master the normal frothing operation, and in the process gain considerably more control over the texture and dimension of the froth than is possible even with the best of these attachments. And even if in the future someone does invent the perfect, no-miss, totally controllable milk-frothing nozzle, frothing milk the old-fashioned way may still turn out to be one of those noble, Zen-like rituals that stubbornly resist progress, like manual shifting in sports cars, wooden bats in baseball, and catching fish with dry flies.

Stand-Alone Devices for Frothing Milk

Stand-alone, stovetop milk-frothing apparatus without coffee-making capability are available for around $30. These devices work well, but are sometimes hard to find. Coffee Connection in Boston has a good one available by mail (see Sending for It). Electric countertop milk-frothing devices occasionally appear in stores, usually priced around $60. If you buy one, make certain it has a manually adjustable steam valve. Don't fall for the little $8 insert for teakettles made by Mouli, however. You can heat milk with it, but it won't froth anything, except perhaps your patience when you try to use it.

Choosing a Home Espresso Machine

If you are still tempted to acquire a home espresso machine after my fussy directions and detailed admonitions, begin by studying the charts on the following pages.

The machines represented range from those that are virtually impossible to use to make true espresso (category 1), through moderately priced machines that will make decent espresso drinks if used with care and intelligence (categories 2 through 4), to expensive machines that will make near-restaurant quality and quantities of espresso (categories 5 through 7). Note, however, that the relatively expensive machines that make up the last three categories still need to be used with care and intelligence. Espresso is an area of human endeavor, however modest, in which excellence still needs to be learned rather than purchased. Also note that acceptable espresso *can* be made with some of the moderately priced category 2 through 4 machines, although the effort demands attention and patience, and the espresso is never quite as rich as the beverage produced by the more expensive machines.

The key technical difference between the categories 1 through 4 machines and the more expensive machines in categories 5 through 7 is the degree of pressure applied to the hot water during the brewing operation. Recall that the creamy heaviness and rich flavor of espresso result from a rapid and thorough extraction of the flavor components from the coffee, achieved by forcing hot water under pressure through compacted, finely ground coffee. The espresso brewers in categories 1 through 4 generate the requisite water pressure by the simple means of trapped steam. The expanding steam needs to get out, the water is in the way, so the steam pushes the water out through the ground coffee, transforming it into espresso. A cutaway diagram of the simplest style of steam-pressure machine appears on page 144.

Those brewers in categories 5 through 7 exert considerably greater pressure on the water by means of a pump (categories 5 and 6) or a lever-controlled piston (category 7). This more vigorous, better-controlled pressure produces a richer,

160

fuller-bodied espresso, with a superior head of the attractive brown foam Italians call *crema*. But again, the espresso from these more sophisticated machines will be better only if the operator manages the process correctly. I can still make better espresso with a $35 stovetop machine than half the espresso operators in the country can make with their $5,000 café machines.

Inexpensive Machines by Category

Brewers in categories 2 and 4 are reasonable, inexpensive choices for home espresso brewing. Those in categories 1 and 3 are problematic in various ways, but I have included them because they are part of the array of choices the consumer encounters in stores and advertisements.

Category 1 Brewers. The brewers in category 1 are the simple little stovetop apparatus Italians call *caffettiere*, or coffeepots. They are so limited that they barely qualify as espresso makers. Since they lack the means to cut off the flow of coffee, you must load them with precisely the right amount of brewing water to prevent an excessive flow of water through the coffee and the production of a thin, bitter, overextracted brew. More important for the cappuccino drinker, these machines do not have a valve and wand for frothing and heating milk. The only reason I can think of to buy one is aesthetic: Some are among the most lovely of coffee apparatus. The Alessi is rightly enshrined in the collection of the Museum of Modern Art in New York, and others, like the line imported by Cuisinart, ought to be. The very expensive but exquisitely designed Bodum Verona has a glass receptacle to receive the coffee, a practical as well as aesthetic feature, since it enables you to monitor the flow of coffee into the brewing receptacle.

Categories 2 Through 4. As I indicated earlier, machines in the first four categories all work essentially the same way. Simple expanding steam pressure in a boiler forces hot water out through the ground espresso. In the category 2 through 4 machines, however, steam from the boiler is also tapped by a steam wand for use in frothing milk, a feature that distinguishes the 2 through 4 units from the simpler brewers in category 1.

The principal difference between the machines in category 2 and those in categories 3 and 4 is the heat source. Category 2 brewers are stovetop designs, whereas the brewers in categories 3 and 4 are countertop designs with built-in electric heating elements. A further difference: The category 2 stovetop designs usually hold the ground coffee in a sort of largish sleeve hidden inside the brewer, whereas the categories 3 and

4 countertop machines contain the coffee in a detachable, café-style filter holder protruding from the front of the machine.

The advantages to the category 2 stovetop designs are price (they sell for as little as one-third the price of a countertop machine with similar capabilities) and portability (they don't require you to commit counterspace). Their disadvantages: You need to learn by experiment how high to keep the heat during brewing and frothing, and they require that you brew considerably more than one serving of espresso per session, owing to the relatively large size of the internal sleeve that holds the ground coffee.

Many people find the countertop machines in categories 3 and 4 easier to use and less intimidating than the stovetop designs, because the internal heating element provides consistent, predictable steam pressure, and because the external filter holder makes loading and cleanup easier and permits brewing smaller servings.

There is a crucial difference between the countertop electric machines in category 3 and those in category 4, however. The less inexpensive category 3 brewers provide no means for shutting off the flow of coffee into the cup or carafe; it simply bubbles on until the machine is turned off or the water in the boiler is exhausted. This deficiency has two consequences: First, it makes controlling the brewing operation difficult, and second, the continually running coffee dissipates the steam pressure available to froth milk. Consequently, I recommend against any machine in category 3.

Category 2 and 4 Recommendations. All of the stovetop machines listed in category 2 can make decent espresso drinks if operated attentively, but need careful placement on the burner to facilitate the frothing process, and require loading with the full amount of ground coffee recommended by the manufacturer, even if you wish to make only one cup. The main difference among the three: The inexpensive Bialleti Graziella Caffè is made of aluminum, whereas the Via Veneto and Rapallo are constructed of stainless steel. All catch and hold the brewed coffee in cups or a carafe provided by the operator, however, so by using a ceramic container it is possible to avoid prolonged contact of aluminum and brewed coffee even with the Graziella Caffè.

Unlike the two stovetop designs, the little countertop electric machines in category 4 permit you to brew one or two servings directly into the cup.

The two most widely available, the Krups Il Primo and Braun Espresso Master, have somewhat compromised steam apparatus. The Braun turbo cappuccino device doesn't help frothing and is troublesome to clean. The solidly made Krups Il Primo comes with the Perfect Froth attachment, a gadget that actually works, and that can be removed for normal frothing. Unfortunately, Il Primo provides no means to

1 Stovetop Expresso Machines;
without Valve for Frothing and Heating Milk;
without Mechanism for Controlling Coffee Output

Brewing pressure supplied by natural build-up of steam pressure in boiler

Advantages: Some models are very inexpensive; others are very attractive.

Disadvantages: Cannot produce espresso drinks using frothed milk; require great care to produce even passable espresso; can brew only multiple servings.

Various aluminum-bodied brewers ($15-$25)
Various stainless steel-bodied brewers ($25-$40)
Designer brewers; Alessi, Cuisinart, etc. ($50-$180)
Bodum Verona ($250)
(prices approximate 1991 retail)

2 Stovetop Espresso Machines;
with Valve for Frothing and Heating Milk
with Mechanism for Controlling Coffee Output

Brewing pressure supplied by natural build-up of steam pressure in boiler

Advantages: Inexpensive; easy to store; if operated carefully can produce acceptable espresso and espresso drinks with frothed milk; can be used to froth milk or prepare hot beverages independent of the coffee-making operation.

Disadvantages: Require care to produce acceptable espresso; can brew only multiple servings.

Bialetti Graziella Caffè ($35)
Via Veneto ($65)
Rapallo ($65)
These devices come and go at the whim of importers; similar machines may be available under other names.
(prices approximate 1991 retail)

control the intensity of the steam output, which makes frothing without the Perfect Froth difficult, and pretty much commits you to using it whether you prefer to or not. The Italian-made Taylor and Ng Amore is a bit lighter in construction than the Braun and Krups machines, but has a simple, straightforward frothing apparatus, and usually sells for about $20 less than its two more widely distributed competitors. Italian-made machines similar to the Taylor and Ng occasionally show up on the shelves of department stores, bearing names of American appliance companies. These can be excellent little units, but if you buy one, make certain that it allows you to cut off the flow of water through the coffee, and that it has a screw valve controlling the steam output.

I don't find any of the category 2 and 4 machines completely satisfactory, but all are acceptable given the alternatives. If you are strapped for money, buy the little Graziella Caffè or a similar stovetop design. If you like the idea of the Perfect Froth, buy the Krups Il Primo; if you want more control of the frothing operation, try to find a Taylor and Ng Amore. If you don't like any of those options and are willing to spend $50 to $100 more, move up to a category 5 electric pump machine.

Final Reassurances and Cautions. Despite their limitations, the inexpensive machines in categories 2 or 4 will make decent espresso drinks if used with patience and attention. The espresso will lack the much admired *crema*, or brown foam, of the café beverage, and will be lighter in body, but still will exhibit the correct perfumy espresso flavor. And, if made carefully, the cappuccino and caffè latte these little machines produce will be close to indistinguishable from drinks produced on a larger machine.

All of these smaller machines have effective means to relieve trapped pressure, but there is always the danger of malfunction and a sudden release of steam pressure if you leave a machine with the power on, and both the steam valve and coffee valves closed. If you need to interrupt the frothing procedure, either turn the machine off or leave the steam valve cracked open. Not only will pressure be relieved, but the hissing will remind you that you have unfinished business in the kitchen.

More Expensive Machines by Category

With categories 5 through 7, we enter the world of the true espresso machine. These miniature versions of the café giants generate higher water pressure and hence richer espresso than the smaller machines, give the skillful operator even more control over the brewing process, and permit the making of a rapid-fire succession of drinks without interrupting the process for cool-down and refill, thus making them

3 Small Countertop Electric Espresso Machines; with Valve for Frothing and Heating Milk; without Mechanism for Controlling Coffee Output

Brewing pressure supplied by natural build-up of steam pressure in boiler

Advantages: Inexpensive; provide more predictable, stable steam pressure than stovetop models in categories 1 and 2.

Disadvantages: Lack of means of controlling coffee output makes brewing acceptable espresso extremely difficult; occupy some counter space; cannot be used to froth milk or prepare hot beverages independent of the coffee-making operation.

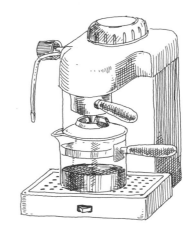

  Maxim Espres ($50)
  Salton Cappuccino Express ($60)
  Conair Cuisine ($60)
  Krups Espresso Mini ($70)
  Gaggia Fantastico II ($95)
  (prices approximate 1991 retail)

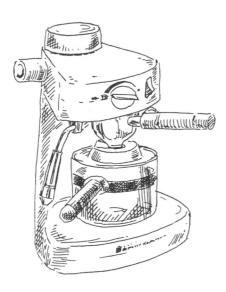

4 Small Countertop Electric Espresso Machines; with Value for Frothing and Heating Milk; with Mechanism for Controlling Coffee Output

Brewing pressure supplied by natural build-up of steam pressure in boiler

Advantages: Same as category 3, but brewing operation can be controlled with greater precision; if operated carefully can produce acceptable espresso and espresso drinks with frothed mik; can be used to froth milk or prepare hot beverages independent of the coffee-making operation.

Disadvantages: Require close attention to make acceptable espresso; occupy some counter space.

  Taylor & Ng Amore ($75)
  Krups Il Primo ($100)
  Braun Espresso Master ($100)
  (prices approximate 1991 retail)

5 Larger Countertop Electric Espresso Machines; with Valve for Frothing and Heating Milk; Switch-Activated Pump System Controls Coffee Output

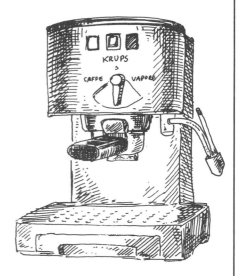

$150 to $300 (all prices approximate 1991 retail)

Advantages: Make near-café quality espresso drinks with frothed milk if used correctly; refillable reservoirs make it possible to produce any number of espresso drinks without interruption or cool-down; achieve brewing termperature relatively rapidly.

Disadvantages: Take up counter space; relatively expensive; lighter in construction than category 6 and 7 machines.

Gaggia Gran Gaggia ($150)
Excellent price; superior filter catch. Feels flimsy; knob controlling steam valve is awkwardly placed on top of machine; lower wattage and smaller capacity than most machines in class.

Bosch Espresso Cup ($180)
Unconventional centrifugal spin system produces good espresso. Poorly designed frothing apparatus; very small brewing capacity per session; feels flimsy.

Krups Espresso Novo ($200)
Thermal block heating system; adjustable steam wand; includes detachable Perfect Froth milk-frothing attachment. Steam output for frothing cannot be adjusted; ineffective filter catch.

Gaggia Espresso Gaggia ($225)
Excellent reputation; superior filter catch.

Saeco Espresso 2002 ($250)
Metal housing; very solidly constructed; cup warmer. No water-level indicator; filter catch only sporadically effective.

Krups L'Espresso Plus ($280)
Same machine as Espresso Novo, but packaged to reassure the novice; includes optional filter baskets to use with pre-ground coffee pods, sample pods, instructional videotape, and Perfect Froth attachment.

Rotel Espressomat ($280)
Thermal block heating system; very fast warm-up; variable brewing termperature control; accessory storage bin; cup warmer.

Cuisinart EMP-7 ($280)
Water softening cartridge; Super Creme Disc to intensify production of *crema*. Transition from brewing to frothing slower than most machines in class; adjustable pin in steam wand is fussy.

Faema Amica ($300)
Solidly constructed; superior filter catch. Cappuccino Magic frothing device is effective, but cannot be removed to permit conventional frothing.

DèLonghi Bar ($300)
Can use pods; filter holder catch; adjustable steam wand.

appropriate for entertaining or small offices. The charts roughly indicate the differences among the three categories.

Category 5 Machines. The machines in category 5 retailed for between $150 and $300 in 1991. All use pumps to pressure the hot water through the coffee, except the Bosch, which uses a centrifugal system. All except the eccentric Bosch employ the familiar café-style detachable filter and filter holder, which clamp onto the front of the machine, and brew multiple single or double servings of espresso. All have a largish water reservoir separate from the heating unit. Most heat the water to brewing and frothing temperature in a small aluminum boiler; the Krups and Rotel machines use a thermal block system—a long stretch of coiled pipe encased in a heating element. All machines except the Bosch can be refilled while in use. Most of the reservoirs are removable, to facilitate the refilling procedure. The listed reservoir capacity (which is always more than the actual, functional capacity) ranges from 12 to as many as 40 cups. The average is around 25. Remember, however, that because these machines separate the water reservoir and the heating function, they can be refilled at any time, making a small reservoir less an inconvenience than it would be in a machine that needs to be cooled down to be refilled.

All except the Bosch must be prepared for brewing by bleeding a little hot water from the machine to clear the system. A transitional procedure also must be followed in changing from brewing espresso to producing steam for milk-frothing. This transition is necessary because the optimum water temperature for brewing is lower than the optimum temperature for steam production. The transition tends to be simplest and fastest in the thermal block machines. The time required for the transition can be an important decision point in deciding which machine to purchase; it can range from a few seconds to as high as one minute for the Cuisinart unit, which is a lot of dead kitchen time for a type-A espresso drinker.

Most of the category 5 machines have plastic housings, aluminum boilers, and plated brass coffee fittings. The weight of the materials that go into the machines predictably increases with price; the $250 Saeco 2002 has a metal housing and a heavy, nearly commercial-weight group and filter holder; the $150 Gran Gaggia is rather flimsy all around.

Most machines have a catch that holds the filter basket inside the filter holder, enabling you to turn the filter holder upside down and knock the spent grounds into the trash without losing the filter basket in the process. Until you own an espresso machine without this feature, it is difficult to imagine how much time you can spend digging compacted grounds out of a filter basket with a spoon, or digging the filter basket itself out of the garbage, where it landed after you catapulted it there by digging, banging, or spitting on it. Some kinds of catches are more effective than others; spring-loaded rings inside the filter holder are probably the best; little plastic flaps that you need to keep a thumb on are virtually useless.

There are several design issues related to the frothing apparatus that may influence your choice of machine. Observe the positioning of the steam wand, for example. Remember that you have to manipulate a small pitcher under it. Does it give you enough room? Or is it stumpy and half-hidden under another part of the machine? Many machines have wands that are adjustable and that swing out of the way when not in use. Also look at the knob that controls the output of steam. Is it convenient to reach and adjust while you're holding a pitcher under the steam wand? Designers have become cute about where they put the knob on some machines, apparently opting for looks rather than convenience. In some machines, like the two Krups models, there is no knob; you simply activate the steam function and the steam pressure adjusts itself. Krups, so intent on making espresso brewing accessible to the impatient, deliberately took this step to make things simpler for the novice operator. Those who already know how to froth milk will find the lack of control frustrating, however.

Some machines do not provide a light or other indication that the machine has reached brewing temperature. This omission irritates some people; others don't care. Most machines have a simple window that permits you to check the water level in the reservoir without opening the lid. At least one machine (the Saeco 2002) fails to provide such a window, and another (the Krups) has it positioned at the back of the housing.

Special Features: Crema, Water-softening, Waste Trays, Frothing Aids. Several of the category 5 machines have special features. The Cuisinart EPM-7 unit provides a little device that fits into the two-serving filter holder and churns the espresso before releasing it into the cup, promoting formation of the cosmetically important crema. The Cuisinart Super Dream Disc works, but a reasonably careful operator using the right grind of fresh coffee should have no problem producing crema with any of these machines, regardless of attachment.

The Cuisinart also comes fitted with a water-softening filter inside the reservoir, intended to protect the workings of the machine from calcium build-up. If you live in an area with particularly hard water, this may be a useful feature, since the decalcifying routine for all of these machines can get old fast. Cuisinart recommends changing the filter every six months; a replacement costs around $10.

6 Larger Countertop Electric Espresso Machines; with Valve for Frothing and Heating Milk; Switch-Activated Pump System Controls Coffee Output

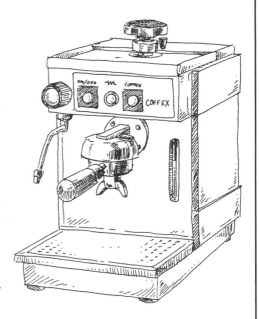

$400 to $800 (all prices approximate 1991 retail)

Advantages: Make near-café quality espresso and espresso drinks with frothed milk if used correctly; refillable reservoirs make it possible to produce any number of espresso drinks without interruption or cool-down; achieve brewing temperature relatively rapidly; sturdier in construction than category 5 machines.

Disadvantages: Take up counter space; expensive; more reticent and less romantic in appearance and operation than category 7 machines.

Saeco Rio Vapore ($425)
Excellent value; very solidly constructed; superior filter catch; self-tamping filter holder and Gran Crema feature assist in production of crema; integrated waste tray for spent grounds. Recommended.

Gaggia Baby Gaggia ($500)
Excellent reputation; superior filter catch; anti-drip system. Housing appears flimsier than most other machines in its class.

Faema Family ($500)
Very solidly constructed; superior filter catch; gives the option of using the effective Cappucino Magic frothing device or a conventional steam wand.

Rancilio Miss Audrey ($575)
Striking design; superior filter catch; integral water softening cartridge. Expensive.

Olympia Coffex or Maximatic ($800)
Outstanding reputation; all metal, very well-constructed. Only machine in its class with two boilers, one for brewing, one for frothing. No filter catch; expensive.

Some machines have little built-in drawers called *waste trays*, meant to facilitate getting rid of spent grounds when you are making multiple servings of espresso. These are handy little conveniences, but most are far too flimsy to let you nonchalantly knock the grounds out of the filter and into the drawer as café operators do. If you use your little plastic drawer to dispose of grounds, you probably will need to dig them out of the filter with a non-nonchalant spoon.

The Krups, Faema, Cuisinart, and Gaggia machines currently come with devices intended to make milk-frothing easier; I discuss these gadgets on pages 158-159.

Two of the category 5 machines are fitted for the preground, prepackaged espresso pods or kisses I mentioned earlier: the DèLonghi Bar and the Krups L'Espresso Plus, a version of the Krups Espresso Novo packaged for novices. Pods, you may recall, are little one-serving paper bags of ground espresso that fit into special filter baskets. You pop one or two pods into the special filter basket, crank the filter holder onto the machine, brew as usual, and knock the spent bags into the garbage or waste tray. Pods make the first few sessions of espresso brewing easier, and always make cleanup easier. They also spare you the need to find a good grinder to go with your machine. On the other hand, they cost considerably more than whole-bean espresso coffee, do not permit you the rather gratifying activity of making your own espresso blends, and even at their best will not produce an espresso as aromatic and fresh as can be created with good, freshly ground coffee.

You should also be aware that the special filter baskets for pods usually permit you to use only the pods recommended by the maker of the machine, so before you invest in a pod-based system you should determine how much these required pods cost, whether you like the coffee they produce, and how much trouble it will be to resupply yourself with them over the long haul. And if you do buy a machine that uses pods, make certain that filter baskets that permit you to use ordinary ground espresso are also included. Otherwise, you will be buying yourself into a corner. So far, all pod-based systems I am familiar with provide this option.

Category 5 Recommendations. To my knowledge, all of the category 5 machines produce satisfactory espresso, and there are far too many trade-offs among price, features, and quality of materials for me to make any clear-cut, overall recommendation. I would advise against the Bosch machine; its flimsiness, small capacity, and clumsy milk-frothing apparatus belie the excellent reputation of its manufacturer. If you're counting every dollar, you might look for a Gran Gaggia without the useless Turbo Frother attachment. If you can't find one in your local stores, you can order one by mail from Peet's Coffee & Tea in Berkeley (see Sending for It). If you're an impatient sort, you might like the Perfect Froth milk-frothing device and fast thermal block technology of the Krups Espresso Novo. If you prefer a machine with conventional frothing apparatus that warms up even faster than the Krups, the Rotel Espressomat, also a thermal block machine, is ready to brew 35 seconds after you turn it on, and has several other small but thoughtful features, like built-in storage for accessories, adjustable brewing temperature, and a cup warmer. For those who like the water-softening cartridge feature, the Cuisinart unit might be a good choice. Finally, if you simply want a sturdy, dependable machine with solid components and a metal housing at a good price, the Saeco 2002 can't be beat.

Even More Expensive Machines by Category

The machines in categories 6 and 7 started at about $400 in 1991; they are somewhat larger, heavier machines made to stand up to more intense use than the category 5 units. Most have brass, rather than aluminum, boilers and heavier forged brass components. Some are impressive, even romantic in appearance. These are cost-is-no-object appliances for those who entertain regularly and have large kitchens with plenty of counter space. They are also a good choice for small offices with upscale tastes; it's hard to imagine a design office in the 1990s without one.

Category 6 Machines. The category 6 brewing apparatus are bigger, sturdier versions of the category 5 machines, manufactured with better materials and more attention to detail. They work about the same as the category 5 machines, however, and offer a similar range of features.

The Olympia Coffex (also sold as Maximatic) is an expensive but proven performer. Its gleaming metal housing and solid brass components inspire confidence; many argue that its double boilers (one for brewing water, one for steam production) make it technically superior to any of its competitors, which use the same heating apparatus for both functions. The Baby Gaggia is a famous, respected machine that has been imported for years, although the latest model shows some signs of corner-cutting; the once metal housing is now made of plastic, for example. Still, this is a fine machine; like the Olympia it requires no waiting for the transition between brewing and frothing, and the components that handle the coffee are as solid as any. The Saeco Rio Vapore may be the best buy in its class; it is heavy, very well made, and has an unusual and effective self-tamping filter holder and a built-in waste tray for spent grounds. Its manufacturer will warrant it for commercial use, making it a low-cost alternative for small restaurants.

7 Larger Countertop Electric Espresso Machines; with Valve for Frothing and Heating Milk; Hand-Operated Piston Controls Coffee Output

$400 to $750 (all prices approximate 1991 retail)

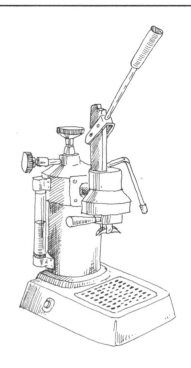

Advantages: Make near-café quality espresso and espresso drinks with frothed milk if used correctly; sturdier in construction than category 5 machines; more conversation-provoking in appearance and operation than category 6 machines; offer more finely tuned control of brewing pressure than category 5 and 6 machines.

Disadvantages: Take up counter space; expensive; slower to warm up than category 5 and 6 machines; must be turned off and bled of steam pressure before refilling; boiler is exposed in most machines, and hot to the touch.

La Pavoni Europiccola ($425)
Least expensive in class; well-made; handsome. Smaller capacity than other machines in class; if allowed to stay on for long periods must be watched carefully; no filter catch.

Riviera Baby Riviera ($475)
Solid and well-made; handsome; can safely be left on for long periods; effective filter catch.

Olympia Cremina ($540)
Solid and well made; can safely be left on for long periods; only machine in class to protect boiler with a housing, making it desirable for households with small children. Some find its boxy housing charming, others find it institutional; no filter catch.

La Pavoni Professional ($590)
Solid and well made; handsome; can safely be left on for long periods. No filter catch.

Riviera Espresso ($750)
Café-style, spring-loaded piston exerts greater brewing pressure than manual piston in other machines in class; can be plumbed directly to water line for easy refill, but does not need to be; romantically handsome, with chrome and brass finish and an eagle atop the boiler; can safely be left on for long periods: superior filter catch. Expensive.

The Faema Family is a very well-made machine with heavy components and a solid metal body. It offers the option of using either the no-miss Cappuccino Magic frothing device, or a conventional steam wand. The Rancilio Miss Audrey has a rakishly post-Modern look, together with a very practical water-softening cartridge in the reservoir to protect the pump and other components from calcium build-up.

Category 7 Machines. The category 7 units look like the traditional pump-piston café machines, but most work differently. The café machines push water through the coffee with a spring-loaded piston; when you pull down the handle you compress a spring, and the spring propels the water through the coffee while the handle rises. With most of these smaller home machines, there is a direct relationship between handle and piston. As you pull down on the handle, the piston directly forces the hot water through the coffee. You supply the power, not a spring. Only the top-of-the-class Riviera Espresso has a spring-loaded, café-style piston. Many espresso aficionados prefer the manual piston machines, because they permit greater control over water pressure during brewing than do either electric pump systems or spring-loaded machines like the Riviera Espresso.

Regardless of how the piston works, the machines in this category all are heavy, extremely well made, and redolent with café nostalgia. But since they heat up an entire reservoir of water at a time, they are much slower to achieve brewing temperature than the category 5 and 6 pump machines; most take around ten minutes. And because the entire tank of water is heated, these machines must be turned off and the steam pressure relieved before being refilled.

I suppose that, from a get-on-with-it, 1990s point of view, a quick-to-warm-up, cheaper pump machine is preferable to these relics of an earlier era. But from the point of view of romance, durability, and maximum control over the brewing process, you can't do better. All have been imported for years without significant change in design or construction. The Olympia Cremina has a charming early 1950s look to it, and the La Pavoni and Riviera machines have elegant pre-World-War-II silhouettes, in the case of the Riviera Espresso complete with eagle atop the boiler. And this is honest romance, based on genuine relationship of form to function, unlike some contemporary pump machines that manufacturers have tarted up with phony turn-of-the-century copper sheathing and irrelevant pipes and gew-gaws.

Categories 6 and 7 Recommendations. As was the case with the category 5 machines, there are too many trade-offs related to personal sensibility for me to make any firm recommendations among the high-end category 6 and 7 machines. All make excellent espresso drinks if used properly. Patient romantics may opt for the shiny lever machines, while efficiency-minded realists may prefer one of the quick, solid pump machines. Skim through the discussion of features and design options for the category 5 machines before you shop for these more expensive apparatus, since many of the same cautions and observations apply.

If you have trouble locating any of these larger machines, consult the Sending for It section at the end of the book; all can be purchased through the mails from vendors whom I know personally to be reliable and helpful. Obviously, however, the best approach to purchasing any complex, expensive appliance is to deal with a knowledgeable merchant in your town with a good assortment of machines, someone who is willing to demonstrate them to you and talk you through their strengths and weaknesses, and who is close by in case something goes wrong with your purchase.

Even with the sophisticated pump and piston machines of categories 4 through 6, you must be sure to follow correct espresso brewing procedure: Obtain the correct grind of coffee, fill the receptacle to the point indicated, spread and tamp the

coffee consistently, and stop the brewing process at the correct moment. Since these machines are rather large, complex appliances, they do not automatically transfer heat to the components that hold the coffee: the filter, the filter holder, and the group. Consequently, these components should be preheated by running hot water through them at the start of a brewing session. In addition, every machine has its own, often idiosyncratic, procedures, all of which need to be known and studied.

The ultimate espresso fanatic can opt for the ultimate solution: For about the cost of a desktop computer system, you can install the Carmali Uno commercial espresso maker in your kitchen. It's only 10 1/2 inches wide, costs around $2,700, and is available from (among others) Fante's in Philadelphia.

Espresso Grinders

As you may have gathered by my obsessive carrying on about the importance of the correct grind of coffee in brewing espresso, the grinder is as important a piece of equipment as the espresso brewer. With grinders, as with the brewing machines, the more you pay, the less you need to know. A simple blade grinder such as the Bosch or Braun recommended on page 107 ($20 to $25) produces an acceptable espresso grind if you use it properly—that is, if you don't load it with too many beans; if you grind in short spurts, occasionally bouncing the grinder to knock large pieces of coffee down around the blades; and if you stop grinding when you have a grit just short of powder. At the other extreme, the $150-and-up specialized espresso grinders maintain the setting for the correct grind session after session, usually include dosing mechanisms that measure portions of coffee suitable for one serving at the flick of a lever, and may provide an attached tamper designed to make tamping the coffee an easy, one-handed operation. Between these extremes are the less-expensive, general-purpose burr-style mills, such as the Braun and Bosch described on page 104 ($50 to $80). They maintain a fairly consistent grind, but need to be cleaned regularly and generally babied.

Espresso Bar Systems

As I indicated at the beginning this chapter, espresso is a complete system of coffee-making, involving both grinding and brewing apparatus. Several manufacturers provide the espresso fanatic the opportunity of owning a complete home espresso bar system, including matched, scaled-down versions of all of the components of a café setup: machine, grinder with doser, waste tray, and accessories. One has a choice of modular systems, with separate but complementary machine, grinder, and base, or integral systems, in which everything is built into a single unit. The Gaggia line is a good example of a modular system; the Gaggia base unit neatly complements any Gaggia home espresso machine or Gaggia grinder, from the cheapest to the most expensive. Thus, the aficionado can put together a combination of components ranging in total price from as little as $350 to as much as $800. The impressive Faema Family bar system, which includes a bar unit with art moderne curves, one of the best home grinders available, and the excellent Faema Family machine, can be purchased by mail from Pannikin in San Diego for under $700.

All-in-one systems range from the Cuisinart EPM-5 unit, which integrates a higher-capacity version of the EPM-7 machine discussed earlier with grinder, doser, tamper, and tray ($450), through the sturdier Saeco Rio Profi (equivalent of the Rio Vapore brewer discussed earlier plus grinder and accessories, around $600), to the Rancilio Miss Lucy, which combines a machine similar to the Miss Audrey and a very highly rated grinder and doser for a stiff $1,250. The integral systems are neither over-priced nor bargains, by the way. The components usually would cost about the same if purchased separately, and the brewing machines and grinders have about the same capability and features as comparable stand-alone models by the same manufacturer.

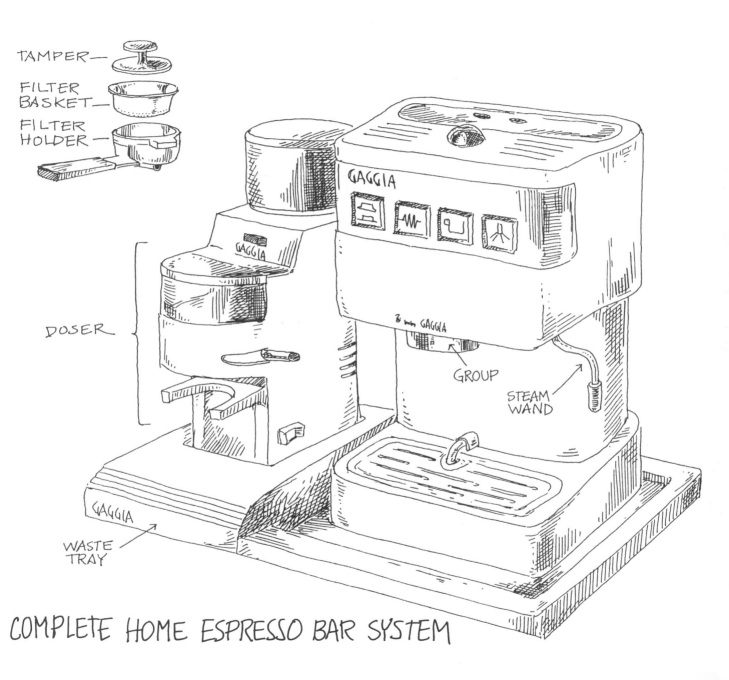

TAMPER—

FILTER
BASKET—

FILTER
HOLDER—

GAGGIA

GAGGIA

GAGGIA

DOSER

GROUP

STEAM
WAND

GAGGIA

WASTE
TRAY

COMPLETE HOME ESPRESSO BAR SYSTEM

A Concise Espresso Glossary

Bar system: A complete home espresso system, including brewing and milk-frothing apparatus, specialized grinder and doser, accessories, and waste tray.

Boiler: The tank in which water is heated for brewing and steam production in most espresso brewing apparatus.

Crema: The pale brown froth covering the surface of a well-brewed cup of espresso. Italians tend to diagnose espresso by the look of the *crema*; if the *crema* is too brown the espresso has been packed too finely in the filter basket; if too pale the espresso has been ground too coarsely or packed too loosely, and so on. This preoccupation with the *crema* can become obsessive; sometimes Italians spend more time examining the *crema* than tasting the espresso. If your espresso has thin *crema* but still tastes good, enjoy the flavor and forget the *crema*.

Doser: A spring-loaded device on some specialized espresso grinders that dispenses one serving of ground coffee per pull. These devices are mainly useful for those who entertain a good deal, or those who wish to master the full espresso procedure with café-quality flair.

Drip tray: A tray under the group designed to catch the overflow from the brewing process.

Filter holder or porta-filter: The metal device with plastic handle that holds the coffee filter, and clamps onto the group.

Filter or filter basket: The perforated stainless-steel receptacle that holds the ground coffee during the brewing operation. It fits inside the filter holder or porta-filter, which in turn clamps onto the group. Larger machines usually provide two filter baskets, one for brewing a single serving and one for brewing a double serving.

Group or delivery group (from Italian *gruppo*, or unit): The fixture protruding from the front of most espresso machines into which the filter holder clamps.

Pump machine or electric pump machine: Espresso brewing apparatus in which the required water pressure for espresso brewing is provided by an electric pump, rather than by trapped steam or a manually operated piston.

Reservoir: In larger, pump-activated brewing machines, the (usually removable) tank that holds the water at room temperature before it is distributed to the boiler or thermal block unit for heating.

Steam wand, nozzle, pipe, or stylus: All names for the little pipe that protrudes from the side of most espresso machines, and provides live steam for the milk-frothing operation. *Wand* seems to be the currently prevailing designation.

Tamper: A little device, usually made of black plastic, that is used to distribute and compress the coffee inside the filter basket before beginning the brewing operation. Some tampers are little hand-held accessories that you lose in drawers just when you need them, and others are attached permanently to the front of larger espresso grinders, or to the machine itself. These attached tampers enable you to handle the tamping operation with one-handed flair. A tamper is not a necessity, by the way. You can carry out this operation with your fingertips.

Thermal block: A system that heats water for espresso brewing in batches by running it through loops of pipe enclosed in a heating element.

Waste tray: A small drawer in the base of the espresso machine or bar unit designed to facilitate the disposal of spent grounds during the brewing of multiple cups of espresso.

ARAB COFFEE SHOP

CHAPTER 8

Serving It
The social sacrament;
from Arabian coffee
ceremony to thermos jug

Ritual often chooses for its vehicle consciousness-altering substances such as alcohol, hashish, or coffee. People in many cultures frequently assume a bit of God resides in these substances, because through using them they are separated for a moment from the ordinariness of things and somehow can seize their reality more clearly. This is why a ritual is not only a gesture of hospitality and reassurance, but a celebration of a break in routine, a moment when the human drive for survival lets up and people can simply be together. This last aspect is to me the fundamental meaning of the coffee break, the coffee klatch, the happy hour, and the after-dinner coffee. These are secular rituals that, in unobtrusive but essential ways, help maintain humanness in ourselves and with one another.

In many cultures, the ritual aspects of drinking tea or coffee are given semi-religious status. The most famous of such rituals is the Japanese tea ceremony, in which powdered green tea is whipped in a traditional bowl to form a rich frothy drink, then is ceremonially passed, in complete silence, from one participant to the next. The tea ceremony is consciously structured as a communal meditation devoted to contemplating the presence of eternity in the moment. Doubtless the caffeine in the tea aids in such psychic enterprise.

Allowed to degenerate, however, such rituals simply become excuses to display our ancient tea bowls, deco martini pitchers, or ingenious new espresso machines. The whiff of the eternal in the present, appreciated alone or shared with others, is what ultimately justifies all this fancy gear.

Coffee has long been a sacramental substance. In Africa, for instance, it is used in witchcraft and fertility rites. Frederick Wellman, in *Coffee: Botany, Cultivation, and Utilization*, describes an African blood-brother ceremony in which "blood of the two pledging parties is mixed and put between the twin seeds of a coffee fruit and the whole swallowed."

Coffee in its modern form, as a hot, black beverage, was first used as a medicine, next as an aid to prayer and meditation by Arabian monastics, much as green tea is used by Zen monks in Japan to celebrate and fortify. Pilgrims to Mecca carried coffee all over the Moslem world. It became secularized, but the religious association remained. Some Christians at first were wont to brand coffee as "that blacke bitter invention of Satan," as opposed to good Christian wine, but in the sixteenth century Pope Clement VIII is said to have sampled coffee and given it his official blessing.

For Moslems, however, and particularly for Arabs, coffee has maintained its religious connotations, and the ritual aspects remain conscious and refined. There is, in fact, an Arabian coffee ceremony. If American intellectuals had turned to Arabia rather than to Japan for a modern philosophy of art, the coffee ceremony might rival the tea ceremony in influence. Though less formal, the Arabian ritual is very similar to the Japanese and, when properly performed, is doubtless as beautiful.

On a less conscious level, a multitude of coffee ceremonies take place simultaneously all over the world: in office lunchrooms, in espresso bars, in Swedish parlors, in Japanese coffeehouses, wherever coffee drinkers gather to stare into space, to read a newspaper, or to share a moment, outside time and obligation, with their friends. Ritual is further wrapped up in the smell and taste of coffee. Certain aromas, flavors, movements, and sounds combine to symbolize coffee and suggest a mood of contemplation

or well-being in an entire culture. This, I'm convinced, was the reason for the persistence of the pumping percolator in American culture. To Americans in 1950, its sound and smell signified *coffee* and made them feel good before they even lifted a cup.

Other cultures have similar associations. To people from the Middle East, the foam that gathers in the pot when cooking coffee is an indispensable part of the drink, not only because it tastes good but because it symbolizes the meditative glow that comes with brewing and consuming coffee. Italian and other espresso aficionados put a comparable, if somewhat less ceremonial, emphasis on foam. An Italian will not take a cup of espresso seriously if it isn't topped with a layer of what to a filter-coffee drinker may look like brown scum. Yet the foam, or *crema*, is what marks espresso as the real thing. Similar satisfaction resides in the milk froth that tops such drinks as caffè latte and cappuccino. The foam has almost no flavor, but a cappuccino is not a cappuccino without it.

Ritual is what gives validity to the extraordinary variety of cups, pots, and paraphernalia that human beings have developed to transport coffee from the pot to the palate. Practical issues are involved, notably keeping the coffee hot on the way, but most variations are refinements that answer the need for the satisfaction of ritual. Of course, there is nothing to stop people from buying new gadgets or fancy pots as Christmas presents or to make an impression, but purchases made for the wrong reasons usually carry a roundabout retribution. Call it *garage-sale karma*. If you don't really care about espresso, for example, your new machine may end up in your driveway some Sunday selling for $5.

Keeping It Hot

The only practical contribution that serving paraphernalia can make to coffee-drinking pleasure is keeping the coffee hot. You can do this two ways: provide a heat source for the coffee container or keep the coffee in a container that retains heat. A continuing heat source is virtually indispensable with Melitta, Chemex, and other pour-over filter brewers, since the brewing process takes so long. Most filter brewers should not be put directly on the burner; if they are, you risk boiling or overheating the coffee anyhow. The heat needs to be buffered with either a heat-reducing pad or a hot-water bath. If you are not concerned with esthetics, you can simply immerse the lower portion of the filter coffee maker in a pot of hot water. Chemex makes a heat-diffusing grid, and a Mouli Radiant Heat plate, another buffering device, can usually be found in any cookware shop for around $5.

If you want to keep filter coffee warm at the table, you can choose from among an adjustable electric warmer, a candle warmer, or a warmer especially made for coffee makers, such as the Melitta (around $20) or Chemex (around $25). Little electric warmers for a single cup of coffee are particularly useful devices for anyone who brews coffee directly into a cup with a single-serving drip cone or filter, since keeping coffee hot is the biggest challenge in this kind of brewing.

Serving Paraphernalia

Covered serving pots have been in vogue since the Arabs started drinking coffee. At import stores you can find the traditional Arabian serving pot, with its *S*-shaped spout, Aladdin's lamp pedestal, and pointed cover. You can also occasionally find an *ibrik*, or Middle Eastern coffee maker, with an embossed cover for keeping coffee hot. The changes in English coffeepot design are fascinating. On one hand stands the severe, straight-sided pewter pot of the seventeenth century, which suggests a Puritan in a stiff collar; on the other, the silver coffeepot of the romantic period, which takes the original Arabian design and makes it seethe with exotic squiggles and flourishes.

Coffee-server design has continued to swing between these extremes. Although in the past two decades the coffeepot and matching sugar dish and creamer have been out of fashion, they are making a modest comeback, right next to the martini pitcher and cocktail shaker. Always favored by an esoteric few, the Continental-style coffee server is an excellent choice for the coffee ritualist. Smaller than the English-style pot, it has a straight handle that protrudes from the body of the pot. The French often serve the coffee portion of the café au lait in this kind of pot and put the hot milk in a small, open-topped pitcher. You pick up the coffee with one hand, the milk with the other, and pour both into the bowl or cup simultaneously, in a single smooth gesture. The straight handle, which points toward you and allows you to pour by simply twisting your wrist, facilitates this important operation. These pots are available in copper for around $25.

The coffee thermos, the space-age contribution to coffee serving, works like the old thermos jug but has design pretensions. The serving thermos keeps coffee hot for hours, and though the aroma dissipates quickly, the flavor holds well. A family that eats breakfast in shifts or anyone who likes to keep coffee hot for an hour or more might want to purchase a serving thermos. It is much easier on flavor than reheating. The cheapest (about $15 to $20) are plastic and have a bright, aggressive contemporary chic. Contemporary-look stainless steel models (around $25), and traditional-look brass or silver plate ($60 and up) are also available. Covered thermal mugs make drinking coffee on the way to work in the morning a little less desperate; the Nissan vacuum mug (around $20) is a good-looking, high-tech version of the genre.

Coffee is probably best served in ceramic mugs that have been warmed first with a little hot water. There are many stylistic directions to take: fancy china, deco and moderne revivals, new-wave whimsy, hand-thrown earthenware, inexpensive machine-made mugs that look hand-thrown, classic mugs and cups from restaurant suppliers, and contemporary imported restaurant ware from Europe. I prefer the restaurant-supply cup; it looks solid, feels authentic, reflects the hearty democratic tradition of coffee, and bounces when you drop it.

Straight espresso, after-dinner coffees brewed double strength, and Middle Eastern coffees are traditionally served in a half-size cup, or demitasse. It seems appropriate to drink such intense, aromatic coffee from small cups rather than from ingratiatingly generous mugs. You should have the small demitasse spoons that go with the cups; an ordinary spoon looks like a shovel next to a demitasse. You can save considerable money on such gear at restaurant-supply stores.

Nearly every traditional espresso specialty has its specialized style of cup, mug, or glass: unadorned espresso, a heavy demitasse cup and saucer; cappuccino, a heavy 6-ounce cup and saucer; mocha, a substantial mug; caffè latte, a 12- or 16-ounce glass or bowl; latte macchiato, an 8- or 10-ounce glass.

German and Scandinavian tradition calls for paper-thin porcelain cups for the water-thin coffee served at the traditional *Kaffeeklatsch*. Andres Uribe, in his book *Brown Gold*, claims that women at the original German Kaffeeklatsch called their coffee *Blumenkaffee*, "flower-coffee," after the little painted flowers that the thin, tealike beverage permitted them to see at the bottom of their Dresden cups.

Milk and Sugar

When I was a teenager in the Midwest circa 1955, drinking coffee any other way than black was suspect. People would leer patronizingly at you and tell you that you couldn't possibly like coffee if you had to add cream and sugar to it. I assume they didn't like beef, because most of them ate it cooked and seasoned. Perhaps the 1940s and 1950s preference for thin, black coffee went along with an equivalent love of characterless white wines, dry martinis, and lager beer. It was as though to admit to liking sweet, heavy drinks was tantamount to confessing some unpardonable moral weakness.

One reason for the prejudice in the United States against milk in coffee may be the prevailing character of coffee. If you add anything to the average cup of thin, under-flavored liquid served in many restaurants, you eliminate what little taste there was in the first place. On the other hand, dark-roast European-style coffees and all the great rich, full-bodied coffees of the world, brewed correctly, carry their flavor through

nearly any reasonable amount of milk. Too much milk, of course, cools the coffee, unless you heat it or, better yet, heat and froth it with steam the way European-style cafés do. Anyone who enjoys milk in coffee might consider purchasing a milk steamer like those described in Chapter 7 (see pages 159–160).

The debate over sugar in coffee has raged almost as long as the caffeine controversy, though with considerably less rancor. The inhabitants of the Arabian peninsula, the first recorded coffee drinkers, apparently drank their coffee black and unsweetened, adding only spices. The Egyptians are given credit for having first added sugar to coffee, around 1625, and for having devised the traditional Middle Eastern mode of coffee brewing, in which powdered coffee is brought to a boil together with sugar to produce a sweet, syrupy beverage. The dairy-shy Egyptians still did not think to add milk to their sweetened coffee, however. Although the Dutch ambassador to China first experimented with milk in his coffee in 1660, this innovation did not become widely accepted until Franz George Kolschitsky opened the first Viennese café in 1684 and lured people away from their beer and wine by adding both milk and honey to strained coffee.

Now that granulated sugar is a dietary villain in many circles, people who like to sweeten coffee have begun to look for alternatives. Artificial sweeteners are inadequate; coffee exaggerates their flat, metallic flavor. To my taste, honey fades away in coffee. On the other hand, the molasses in dark brown and turbinado sugars actually reinforces the rich, dark tones of coffee flavor. You're still consuming sugar, but you are adding some iron and B vitamins. The Japanese recognize the flavor symbiosis of raw sugar and coffee by calling the former *coffee sugar*.

CHAPTER 9

Coffee and Health
How to stay healthy drinking it

When Sir William Harvey, the seventeenth-century physician credited with discovering the circulation of the blood, was on his deathbed, he allegedly called his lawyer to his side and held up a coffee bean. "This little Fruit," he whispered, eyes doubtless still bright from his morning cup, "is the source of happiness and wit!" Sir William then bequeathed his entire supply of coffee, 56 pounds, to the London College of Physicians, directing them to commemorate the day of his death every month with a morning round of coffee.

To some of a puritan or suspicious nature, this anecdote may strike a sinister note. Did Sir William die young? How *much* coffee did he drink, and did he have any enemies in the College of Physicians?

Contradictions run throughout the history of coffee. Coffee was first consumed as medicine, and graduated to serving simultaneous roles as panacea and poison. Early in its history, coffee was adopted by Arabian dervishes to fortify religious meditation. Yet no more than 50 years later, in Mecca, it was the subject of vehement religious persecution on the grounds that it encouraged mirth and chess playing among the faithful. Religion still can't make up its mind about coffee; Mormons and some fundamentalists reject it, whereas most Moslems and many Christians consider it a sober and wholesome alternative to wine and spirits.

In seventeenth-century Europe, as religion began to give way to science and priests to doctors, the debate continued. One physician claimed coffee relieved dropsy, gravel, gout, migraine, hypochondria, and cured scurvy outright, whereas another declared that coffee drunk with milk caused leprosy. "The lovers of coffee used the physicians very ill when they met together," says one wonderfully detached French observer, "and the physicians on their side threatened the coffee drinkers with all sorts of diseases."

One of the most famous accusations leveled against coffee came in a tale by a seventeenth-century German traveler, Adam Oelshlazer, in his *Relation of a Voyage to Muscovie, Tartary, and Persia*. The story concerns the king of Persia, who "had become so habituated to the use of coffee that he took a dislike for women." One day the queen saw a stallion being emasculated; upon asking the reason she was told the animal was too spirited and was being gelded to tame it. Whereupon the queen suggested a simpler solution would be to feed it coffee every morning. This story, when introduced into southern France, was said to have virtually ruined the coffee trade there for 50 years. On the other hand, a tale from a Persian saga reports that after the prophet Mohammed had his first cup of coffee (delivered by the angel Gabriel), he "felt able to unseat forty horsemen and possess fifty women."

It was in England of the seventeenth century that coffee's career as medicine reached its apex and, possibly, its nadir. The most extravagant claims were launched for its medicinal value, and the most extraordinary accusations were leveled against it. One Englishman named Walter Rumsey invented an "electuary" of coffee, to be applied internally with the aid of an instrument called a *provang*. The "electuary" was prescribed for intestinal disorders and hysteria. First one prepared the electuary, which consisted of heated butter, salad oil, honey, and ground coffee. Next one introduced the provang, a thin bone rod about a yard long with a little button on the end, into the intestinal tract by way of the rectum, and manipulated it vigorously. Finally, one swallowed the electuary, and concluded the treatment with a second energetic application of the provang. I feel that it was at this point in history that tea began to replace coffee as England's favorite beverage.

Out of all this confusion and debate came the world's first scientific analysis of coffee. In 1685 Dr. Philippe Sylvestre Dufour described the chemical constituents of coffee with some accuracy, and apparently through numerous experiments on human beings arrived at the same conclusion every other researcher has come to since: Some people can drink coffee comfortably and some can't. Dufour even found a few who slept better after drinking coffee than they had before, probably because, in Dufour's words, the coffee "relieved their disquiet, and removed their feeling of anxiety."

Dufour also helped the critics of coffee identify for the first time their true enemy: the odorless, bitter alkaloid called *caffeine*. The average cup of American-style coffee contains about 100 milligrams of caffeine; a demitasse of espresso may have up to twice as much. The average cup of tea delivers about 70 milligrams; the average chocolate bar about 80. A 12-ounce bottle of cola drink contains up to 100 milligrams, about as much as a cup of coffee.

The current conclusions about the short-term psychological and physiological effects of caffeine are not so different from the first conjectures by Arab physicians or the findings arrived at by Dufour in the seventeenth century. But the long-term effects are not nearly so well understood and remain the subject of a vigorous, confusing, and thus far inconclusive medical debate.

Short-Term Effects

The short-term effects of caffeine are well agreed upon and widely documented. A good summary appears in *The Pharmacological Basis of Therapeutics* by Dr. J. Murdoch Ritchie. On the positive side, caffeine produces "a more rapid and clearer flow of thought," and allays "drowsiness and fatigue. After taking caffeine one is capable of greater sustained intellectual effort and a more perfect association of ideas. There is also a keener appreciation of sensory stimuli, and motor activity is increased; typists, for example, work faster and with fewer errors."

Such effects are produced by caffeine equivalent to the amount contained in one to two cups of coffee. According to Dr. Ritchie the same dosage stimulates the body in a variety of other ways: heart rate increases, blood vessels dilate; movement of fluid and solid wastes through the body is promoted. All this adds up to the beloved "lift."

On the negative side are the medical descriptions of the familiar "coffee nerves." The heavy coffee drinker may suffer from chronic anxiety, a sort of "coffee come-down," and may be restless and irritable. Insomnia and even twitching muscles and diarrhea may be among the effects. Very large doses of caffeine, the equivalent of about 10 cups of strong coffee drunk in a row, produce toxic effects: vomiting, fever, chills, and mental confusion. In enormous doses caffeine is, quite literally, deadly. The lethal dose of caffeine in humans is estimated at about 10 grams, or the equivalent of 100 cups of coffee. One would have to drink the 100 cups in one sitting, however, which doubtless accounts for the unpopularity of caffeine as a means of taking one's own life.

It would seem that the resolution to the caffeine debate, at least in terms of short-term effects, is simple moderation. Drunk to excess, coffee literally verges on poison; drunk in moderation, it is still the beloved tonic of tradition, a gentle aid to thought, labor, and conversation.

But just how much is enough and how much is too much? No study will commit itself. I can only offer an estimate based on inference. I have never found a study reporting negative effects from doses of caffeine under 300 milligrams a day. Since the average cup of coffee contains about 100 milligrams of caffeine, we could infer from this evidence that anyone should be able to drink about three cups of coffee a day and enjoy the benefits of caffeine with none of the drawbacks. Such a figure assumes, of course, that one doesn't also consume quantities of cola drinks, chocolate bars, and headache pills. This is a conservative estimate, however. One could infer from other studies that five cups a day is safe for most people. Furthermore, reaction to caffeine varies greatly from individual to individual; some people can't consume any amount comfortably.

Long-Term Effects

So much for the short-term effects. Researchers in the last 15 years or so have tried to implicate coffee, specifically the caffeine in coffee, in heart disease, birth defects, pancreatic cancer, and a half-dozen other less publicized health problems. So far, the evidence is at most inconclusive. Clinical reports and studies continue to generate far more questions than answers, and for every report tentatively claiming a link between caffeine and disease, there are several others contradicting it.

One example is the purported connection between heavy caffeine intake by pregnant women and birth defects. In the mid-1970s, experiments indicated that the equivalent of 12 to 24 cups of coffee (or bottles of cola) per day may cause birth defects—in rats. Although human beings metabolize caffeine differently from rats (and other researchers had questioned some of the conditions of the experiments), the United States Food and Drug Administration issued a widely publicized warning about the possible ill effects of caffeine on the fetus. Subsequently, an analysis by Harvard researchers of coffee drinking among 12,000 women early in their pregnancies failed to find a significant link between coffee intake and birth defects. The upshot of the debate? The official position, if there is one, came from a committee of the National Academy of Sciences, which recommended what common sense dictates, what this book recommends, and what coffee lovers through the ages have argued: Pregnant women, according to the NAS committee, should exercise "moderation" in their intake of caffeine.

Similar controversies have accompanied the purported links between coffee and fibrocystic breast disease, high blood pressure, and pancreatic and lung cancer. On the positive side, an 11-year study of nearly 17,000 Norwegian men and women found that, once the effect of smoking had been eliminated from the data, people who drank coffee had lower than normal rates of cancers of the colon, kidney, and skin. Norwegian researcher Erik Bjelke's report to the 13th International Cancer Congress concluded, "While we cannot exclude the possibility that high coffee intakes may enhance carcinogenesis under special circumstances, overall, the results are reassuring."

Two similar long-term studies of large samples of individuals, the kind of studies medical researchers call "population" studies, recently indicated no consistent association between coffee-drinking and blood cholesterol levels (a study of 6,000 men and women reported by the Framingham Heart Study researchers), or between caffeine intake and heart attacks and stroke (a study of 45,000 men ages 40 to 75 by Dr. Walter Willett and colleagues of the Harvard School of Public Health).

Nevertheless, anyone who drinks regular caffeinated coffee and also is pregnant—or takes tranquilizers, or suffers from ulcers, high blood pressure, or heart complaints, or is experiencing benign breast lumps (fibrocystic breast disease)—should certainly bring his or her coffee-drinking habits to the attention of a physician for evaluation.

In light of the continuing conflicts in the medical evidence, why are so many people so eager to pin blame on coffee? Partly, I think, because of the frustrations of dealing with degenerative diseases with multiple causes, such as heart failure.

There is a tendency in the face of our impotence before certain diseases to cast about for dietary scapegoats. Coffee is ideal for such a role, not only because it has no food value, but because it makes us feel good for no reason when we drink it. When we get sick, I suspect we tend to fix the blame on something we already feel guilty about: coffee, wine, chocolate cake, or whatever.

The ease with which the early persecutions of coffee on religious grounds modulated into condemnations on medical grounds makes the motivation behind the recent popular attacks on the healthfulness of coffee doubly suspect. Every culture or religion has its dietary taboos as well as its sacraments. Certain foods are holy, and others are forbidden. A group that wishes to define its own identity must establish taboos.

In the late 1960s, for example, an entire generation was busy trying to define itself as a culture distinct from the larger Western tradition. It was natural that coffee, as a social drug firmly identified with the establishment, should come under attack. I recall, for instance, visiting a commune where in the late 1960's ingesting caffeine was a spiritual and dietary sin almost as bad as closing the door to undress. Yet these same puritans, so critical of caffeine, regularly reduced themselves to monosyllabic incoherence with marijuana. Caffeine was taboo; marijuana was close to holy.

Dietary choices, particularly of nonnutritive, mood-altering frills like coffee, are arbitary choices driven by culture and habit rather than by reason. But since we live in an ostensibly rational society, no one feels comfortable justifying dietary prejudices on religious or cultural grounds. Instead we elevate some very tentative medical evidence into dogma which we then defend as "scientific." Once upon a time foods were bad for the soul; now they're bad for our health.

Virtually every element in our diet is currently suspect on some medical grounds or another. At a time when the average glass of drinking water is suspected of harboring carcinogens, a once country-pure herbal tea like sassafras has been taken off the market because it contains a proven carcinogen, and large doses of vitamin C are suspected in birth defects, I see little medical reason for not drinking moderate amounts of a beverage against which nothing concrete has been proven, which has been consumed for centuries without decimating the population, and which is one of the few widely consumed modern foods that contains no multisyllabic preservatives, additives, or other adulterants.

For the ordinary coffee drinker, I think the real solution to the health dilemma is to start treating coffee with the love and attention it deserves. If you pay attention to what you're doing when you buy and make coffee and take a moment to appreciate the results, many of the supposed negative effects of coffee drinking might vanish. If anyone suffers from coffee, it is the unconscious coffeeholic who wanders around all day holding a half-filled cup of cold, tasteless liquid. I doubt whether someone who genuinely loves coffee will abuse it, any more than someone who really loves automobiles will drive recklessly.

Decaffeinated Coffees

Technology is always trying to give us back the garden without the snake. So you like coffee and not caffeine? Well, then, we'll take out the caffeine and leave you your pleasure, intact.

Decaffeinated coffee is indeed without venom; it contains, at most, one fortieth of the amount of caffeine in untreated beans. Nor should the removal of caffeine alter the taste of coffee. Isolated, caffeine is a crystalline substance lacking aroma and possessing only the slightest bitter taste. Its flavor is lost in the heady perfumes of fresh coffee. So if you hear people say, "Coffee doesn't taste like coffee without the caffeine," they're wrong. The only real problem is how to take out the caffeine without ruining the rest of what does influence coffee flavor. But technology has triumphed, more or less. The best decaffeinated coffee, freshly roasted and ground and carefully brewed, can taste so nearly the equal of a similar untreated coffee that only a tasting involving direct comparison reveals the difference.

Unfortunately, fine decaffeinated coffees are the exception rather than the norm. Decaffeinated beans are notoriously difficult to roast, so even the best decaffeinated beans may produce a thin-bodied, spiritless cup once they're roasted. Still, for the coffee devotee, it's better than mint tea, and you can always compromise and spruce up a listless caffeine-free coffee by adding a little full-bodied caffeinated coffee before grinding it, or by creating your own low-caffeine blend.

Most caffeine-free coffee sold in specialty stores is shipped from the growing countries to decaffeinating plants in Europe or Canada, treated to remove the caffeine, then redried and shipped to the United States. The extracted caffeine, by the way, is hardly disposed of as toxic waste. It promptly reappears on grocery shelves as a component of soft drinks and medicine.

Decaffeination Methods

Coffee is decaffeinated in its green state, before the delicate oils are developed through roasting. Hundreds of patents exist for decaffeination processes, but only a few are actually used. In the original processes, the beans were first steamed to open their pores, then soaked in an organic solvent that selectively dissolved the caffeine. The beans were steamed again to remove the solvent residues, dried, and roasted like any other green coffee.

This process has an obvious drawback: Minute quantities of the solvent may remain in the bean, spoiling the flavor and ruining the day of any health-conscious consumer who finds out about it.

A more recent process—we might call it the *solvent/water process*, although speciality-coffee sellers use euphemisms like *European process*—starts by soaking green beans in near-boiling water for several hours. The water is transferred to another tank, where it is combined with a solvent that selectively absorbs most of the caffeine. The caffeine-laden solvent is then separated from the water. The solvent is much easier to remove from water than from beans, because the solvent is lighter than water and never really mixes with it, whereas certain oils in the beans may selectively combine with the solvent, making it impossible to remove entirely. The water, now free of both caffeine and solvent, still contains oils and other materials important to flavor. In order to return these substances to the beans, the water is returned to the first tank, where the beans reabsorb the flavor-bearing substances from the water.

The joker in the process is still the solvent. People concerned about the effects of coffee on their health obviously are not going to feel comfortable purchasing a product containing even minute traces of solvent. Their worst fears were confirmed when one of the most widely used solvents, trichloroethylene, was named a probable cause of cancer in a "Cancer Alert" issued in 1975 by the National Cancer Institute. The alert addressed the potential health hazards trichloroethylene poses to people who work around it rather than to consumers of decaffeinated coffee, since only extremely minute traces of the solvent remain in coffee. The United States Food and Drug Administration, for example, permits the solvent in quantities up to 10 parts per million in ground coffee. By comparison, the doses that the National Cancer Institute administered to laboratory animals were gargantuan. To match them in equivalent terms, a human being would have to drink 20 million cups of decaffeinated coffee a day over a lifetime. Also, no one knows how much of the solvent residue—if any—is retained in the brewing process and ends up in the cup. Given the volatility of the solvent and the relatively minuscule amount left in the bean after roasting, I suspect that none whatsoever ends up in the coffee we ultimately consume.

Nevertheless, the news that the caffeine we feared caused heart disease was being replaced by a solvent that actually did cause cancer provoked understandable consternation among health-conscious consumers. The coffee industry promptly responded by replacing trichloroethylene with methylene chloride, a solvent not implicated in the National Cancer Institute study. So far tests of methylene chloride have not linked it to any known disease, and given its volatility (it vaporizes at 104° F; coffee is roasted at over 400° F for at least 15 minutes, then brewed at 200° F) it seems hardly possible that any of the 1 part per million occasionally found in the green beans could end up in the consumer's cup or stomach.

Nevertheless, a solvent-free decaffeination process became a priority for the coffee industry. The first breakthrough came from Coffex S.A., a Swiss firm with plants in several European countries. Coffex announced that it had developed a decaffeination process using water only—no solvents whatsoever. As in the solvent/water process described earlier, the various chemical constituents of the green coffee, including the caffeine, are first removed by soaking the beans in very hot water. In the Swiss Water Process, however, the water is stripped of its caffeine, not by a solvent, but by percolation through activated charcoal. (It really ought to be called the Swiss Charcoal Process.) The beans are returned to the hot water, where they reabsorb the remaining, caffeine-free flavor constituents from the water. This process is more costly than the solvent process because the separated caffeine cannot be recovered from the charcoal and sold separately, as it is with the solvent method.

There is also some controversy about the quality of the final product. Coffex has publicized tastings by coffee professionals who claim that water-only decaffeinated coffees taste fresher and better than those decaffeinated by the solvent/water process. Most specialty coffee people I know disagree, however, and my tastings, admittedly limited, suggest that the water-only coffees have less flavor, although possibly more body, than the solvent/water-processed coffees. People who like a sweet, mild cup might prefer a Swiss Water Processed decaffeinated. Conclusive comparisons are difficult to make, because it is impossible to obtain identical coffee samples that have been decaffeinated by the two methods.

The two most recent solvent-free decaffeination processes to appear in the trade journals are even more promising than the water-only method, but at this writing neither has become established in the specialty market. One uses coffee oil to extract the caffeine; I have no details on this method, but I expect that more information will be available if it becomes an option in the specialty trade.

In the other method, the most promising approach of all, the beans are bathed in a highly compressed form of carbon dioxide (CO_2), the same naturally occurring substance that plants consume and human beings produce. In its compressed form the carbon dioxide behaves partly like a gas and partly like a liquid, and has the property of combining selectively with the caffeine in the bean itself, thus eliminating the need for an intermediate step involving soaking the bean in water. The caffeine is removed from the carbon dioxide through charcoal filtering, just as it is in the water-only process, but the flavor components remain in the bean throughout the process, rather than being soaked out and then put back in again, as they are in both the water-only and the solvent/water processes.

The equipment needed for this operation is costly, but a large commercial foods concern has established a plant in the United States utilizing this method, and plans are underway for a large CO_2 process decaffeination plant in the San Francisco Bay Area that will serve the needs of specialty importers and roasters. It seems inevitable that coffees decaffeinated by the carbon dioxide method eventually will appear in specialty stores. According to one technical expert who has reviewed the process, it should provoke considerably less flavor and aroma loss than other methods. Perhaps. Many coffee roasters I've spoken to have not been impressed by the first samples they've tasted, but the fault could be in the quality of the green coffees submitted to the process rather than in the process itself.

Now a final development: Critics of the use of solvents in decaffeination have

Coffee Health Concerns

Concern	Where discussed	Comments	Possible Responses
Caffeine	Pages 190–200	Studies of long-term health risks associated with caffeine are contradictory and, for the most part, inconclusive.	Drink less coffee and enjoy it more; drink less coffee and drink dark-roasted, high quality coffee; drink coffee brewed by the cold concentrate method; drink decaffeinated coffee.
Fears that solvent residues from some decaffeination processes may contaminate brewed coffee	Pages 195–199	Amounts of residue detected in green coffee decaffeinated by current solvent methods are so low they hardly bear consideration. That any residue whatsoever survives the roasting and brewing processes is highly unlikely.	Stop worrying and enjoy your decaffeinated coffee; go back to caffeinated coffees and practice one or more of the expedients listed above; drink water-only or "Swiss Process" decaffeinated coffees.
Fears that residues of dioxin used in bleaching filter papers may contaminate brewed coffee	Pages 123, 201	No detectable amounts of dioxin have been turned up in coffee brewed by the filter method; however, "oxygen-whitened" and unbleached filter papers work just as well, taste better, and are environmentally more sound.	Switch to a brewing method that does not use paper filters; switch to "oxygen-whitened" filter papers; switch to unbleached filter papers.
Fears that residues of agricultural chemicals used in growing coffee may contaminate brewed coffee	Pages 65, 75–77, 202–204	Given the cumulative impact of the roasting and brewing processes, it is extremely unlikely that any of the small amounts of residues legally allowable in green coffee ever reach the cup. Environmental concerns may be considerably more significant than health concerns.	Drink traditionally grown coffees from Yemen or Ethiopia; drink coffees certified free of harmful chemicals by independent laboratory test; drink coffees certified organic by relevant international monitoring agencies.
Fears that propylene glycol used in flavored coffees is not natural, and may pose a health threat	Pages 204–205	Propylene glycol has long been on the generally recognized as safe list of the U.S. Food and Drug Administration; it is used in numerous other foods.	Stop drinking flavored coffees and experiment with dark-roasted coffees or distinctive-tasting straight coffees like Sumatran or Yemen Mocha; flavor your own coffee.

long pointed out that, regardless of how minor the health risk for coffee drinkers, we still should not encourage the use of powerful solvents like methylene chloride in any circumstances, given their potentially destructive effect on the environment. This position has been validated by the European Economic Community's recent decision to prohibit use of methylene chloride in decaffeination processes because it is suspected to contribute to the depletion of the ozone layer. The changeover to still another, environmentally safer solvent, probably ethyl acetate, will take place over the next three to five years. Since the current administration in the United States leans toward scepticism on the ozone issue, no similar rules are likely to be forthcoming here, but that hardly matters for the specialty trade, because nearly all specialty coffees decaffeinated by the solvent/water method are treated in Europe. Many European decaffeination plants have already switched to ethyl acetate. The fact that this substance is derived from fruit has led some enthusiasts to call processes using it "natural," and you may see them so advertised.

I suggest that you buy the decaffeinated coffee that tastes good to you, regardless of process. If you're willing to drink coffee decaffeinated by the solvent/water process, you have a greater variety of coffees to choose from, at better prices. Given the temperature at which all currently used solvents evaporate, I do not think that enough of the chemical could possibly survive the roasting and brewing processes to be anything more than the tiniest pea under the health-conscious consumer's mattress. And with the European Community's switch to ethyl acetate, environmental concerns should also be satisfied.

Other Alternatives for Caffeine-Shy Consumers

Of course, if you simply want to cut down on your caffeine intake, rather than eliminating caffeine from your diet completely, there are alternatives other than decaffeinated coffees.

One is to drink less coffee while focusing on enjoying it more. This is a good tactic for people who consume too much coffee at work out of habit or reflex. Rather than drinking the coffee from the automatic coffee maker or urn, for example, make your own coffee carefully in a small plunger pot, focusing your attention on the act of brewing and drinking.

You can also buy coffees that are naturally low in caffeine. As I indicated earlier, specialty and other high-quality coffees contain considerably less caffeine than cheaper commercial coffees. Most inexpensive commercial blends are based on robusta coffees, which contain between 30 and 40 percent more caffeine than arabica. Dark-roasting also burns off considerable amounts of caffeine. So if you drink a dark roasted specialty coffee, you are probably consuming something like 50 percent less caffeine than if you were drinking a cheap canned coffee.

Or you can brew your coffee differently. The cold water concentrate method (see pages 134–135) reduces caffeine, acidity, and fats. Unfortunately, it also reduces flavor. Coffee made with paper filters probably has less caffeine than coffee made by other methods, and definitely has less fatty oil, which may contribute to high blood cholesterol in some individuals.

Lastly, you can have fun making low-caffeine blends by combining decaffeinated coffees with varying amounts of distinctive, full-bodied untreated coffees. Kenya, Mocha, Sumatra, and Guatemala, for example, all pack enough flavor and body to spruce up even the drabbest of decaffeinated beans.

Another Suspect: Acid

Caffeine is only one of the villains in the coffee controversy. Another is certain chemicals often lumped together under the term acid. Some people don't like the acid or sour note in coffee and claim it upsets their stomachs. Others say it causes jitters. I suggest that you experiment. Does that sourness in coffee make your tongue or stomach feel uncomfortable? Then what you may want is not coffee with the acid taken out (such coffees do exist), but either a good dark-roast coffee or a blend incorporating aged coffee. Dark roasting burns out most of the chemicals that cause the acid sensation, and aging mutes them. If you do your own blending, adding an aged coffee to your favorite straight coffee will produce a flavorful but very low-acid brew. Many coffees—some Venezuelan and most Mysore, for example—are naturally low in acid.

Pesticides, Filter Papers, and Flavorings

We have met the enemy, and he is us, the famous comic strip possum declared. Coffee is one of the few widely consumed contemporary foods that contains absolutely no additives, adulterants, or preservatives. Unfortunately, we haven't been able to leave well enough alone. Through our own fussing with coffee we have added a few more health-related issues to the heap.

One is the solvent used in some decaffeination processes, which I discussed earlier in this chapter. Another is the dioxin and chlorine used in bleaching some pa-

per filters, which is discussed in Chapter 6. A third consists of health and environmental issues raised by the use of pesticides, fungicides, herbicides, and chemical fertilizers in growing coffee. Finally, some consumers have questioned the healthfulness of the chemical agents used in flavoring whole-bean coffees.

All of the various health issues raised in relationship to coffee are summarized in a sort of rogue's gallery of suspects on page 198. Most of the accusations appear unfounded or overstated, but in a world where newly identified multisyllabic health threats rear their carcinogenic heads out of newspaper headlines almost daily, concern seems justified. Since I treat the other suspects elsewhere, I am confining my final remarks in this chapter to the agricultural-chemical and coffee-flavoring issues.

Agricultural Chemicals and Organic Coffees

The concerns raised by those apprehensive about the use of agricultural chemicals in coffee growing are twofold. First is the health issue for the consumer: whether harmful chemical residues may reach our systems when we drink coffee. Second are the related environmental and social issues: whether buying coffees that may be grown with the help of potentially harmful chemicals does not contribute to the destruction of the environment and threaten the health of the rural poor who raise coffee.

The consumer health issue is simplest to address. Coffee is not eaten raw like lettuce or apples. The bean is the seed of a fruit. The flesh of this fruit is discarded.

Along the way the seed is soaked, fermented, and subject to a thorough drying process. Later it is roasted at 500° F, and finally broken apart and soaked in near boiling water. This savage history concludes when we consume *only the water* in which the previously soaked, fermented, dried, roasted, and infused seed was immersed. Given this history of relentless attrition, it hardly seems possible that much if any of the small amounts of pesticide residue permitted by law in green coffee ever make it into the cup.

The environmental and social issues merit more attention. It would seem that only someone exceedingly isolated or stubborn could fail to grasp how dangerous the widespread use of agricultural poisons has become, both to our environment and to the workers who handle these substances. Coffee drinkers concerned about the impact of agricultural chemicals on environment and society, and those unwilling to accept my reassurances on the consumer health issue expressed in the previous paragraph, have essentially three alternatives:

- Buy a traditional coffee, grown as coffee was grown from its inception, before agricultural chemicals were invented. Both Yemen Mocha and Ethiopian Harrar are such coffees, and very fine coffees as well.
- Buy a coffee that an independent laboratory has certified to be free of agricultural chemicals. Such tests are usually commissioned by coffee exporters, brokers, or large roasters. Retailers who carry such coffees are happy to make the results of these tests available to their customers. Of course, the fact that no residues of harmful agricultural chemicals can be detected in a coffee does not give absolute assurance that chemicals were not used in its cultivation. But the buyer at least might feel reassured in regard to the consumer health issue, and also might feel confident that any use of chemicals by the grower was limited and careful.
- Buy a certified organic coffee. Certified organic coffees are coffees whose growing conditions and processing have been thoroughly monitored by independent agencies and found to be free of pesticides, herbicides, fungicides, chemical fertilizers, and other potentially harmful chemicals. The monitoring agencies visit the farm and verify that no chemicals have been used on the farm for several years, and then follow every step of the processing, preparing, and transporting. Such careful monitoring is of course expensive, which is one reason certified organic coffees cost more than similar uncertified coffees. Many such certified organic coffees are the product of socially and environmentally progressive cooperatives.

At this writing, there probably are no great certified organic coffees, but there are many good ones, and more are coming on the market every month. I discuss certified organic coffees in detail on pages 75–77.

Artificial Flavorings and Flavored Coffees

It seems odd to me that some consumers who choose to buy an obviously artificial product like chocolate mint- or French vanilla-flavored coffee should also want it to be a *natural* chocolate mint- or French vanilla-flavored coffee, but some do. Unfortunately, there is no such thing as a naturally-flavored whole-bean coffee, and probably won't be for quite awhile. Not only are many of the flavoring components artificial by Food and Drug Administration definition, but the substance that carries the flavorings into the pores of the bean and maintains their integrity throughout the stress of storing, transporting and brewing is another substance with a spooky multisyllabic name and is technically classified as a solvent. But propylene glycol is a solvent only in the sense that it dissolves flavorings and preserves them. It is *not* a solvent in the sense that it dissolves stomachs or any other part of the anatomy. Nor is it antifreeze; that's ethylene glycol. Propylene glycol has long been on the Food and Drug Administration's GRAS (Generally Recognized as Safe) list, and is used in many other food products.

If you don't like consuming flavors that are technically artificial and that use propylene glycol as a medium, then you probably will have to stop drinking flavored whole-bean coffees. Add your own natural ingredients after you brew your coffee—natural vanilla or almond extract, for example, or citrus peel. Various brands of coffee flavoring specifically designed to be added to brewed coffee are described in Chapter 3 (see pages 81–83). In most cases these products use naturally derived flavoring components in an alcohol and glycerin base, although a few flavors may contain propylene glycol. Completely natural flavorings presented without propylene glycol or alcohol are available in some natural food stores. The Frontier brand of natural flavorings is a good one, although only the berry and brandy flavors seem to work well with coffee. I also give a selection of more elaborate recipes for naturally spiced and flavored coffees in Chapter 12. Of course, you could always try an unflavored coffee with low acid and a distinctive taste; a Sumatran or Ethiopian Yirgacheffe, for example. Or try a good dark-roasted coffee, and add a couple of drops of vanilla extract after you brew it.

By now you may be ready to switch to mint tea, if only you were sure it didn't cause obscure diseases in yaks. I can only urge you to treat coffee with love and respect, and hope that those who drink a lot of coffee without thinking about it will examine their habit, while those who worry too much about drinking moderate amounts of coffee will relax and enjoy their cup.

CHAPTER 10

Growing It
How coffee is grown, processed, and graded

To imagine a coffee tree, think of a camellia bush with flowers that resemble jasmine. The leaves are broad, shiny, and shaped like an arrow or spearhead. They are three to six inches long and line up in pairs on either side of a central stem. The flowers—small, white, star-shaped blossoms borne in clusters at the base of the leaves—produce an exquisite, slightly pungent scent. The white color and nocturnal aroma of the flowers may suggest that the coffee plant is pollinated by moths or other night-flying insects, but in fact the plant largely pollinates itself. In freshly roasted coffee, a hint of the flowers' fragrance seems to shimmer delicately within the darker perfumes of the brew. The arabica plant is an evergreen. In the wild it grows to a height of 14 to 20 feet, but when cultivated it is usually kept pruned to about 6 feet to facilitate picking the beans and to encourage heavy bearing.

In such regions as Brazil, where one or two rainy seasons each year are followed by dry seasons, the hills of the plantations whiten with blossoms all at once. In areas with even rainfall the year around, blossoms, ripening berries, and ripe berries cohabit the trees simultaneously. The scent of an entire coffee plantation in bloom can be so intense that sailors have reported smelling the perfume two or three miles out to sea. Such glory is short-lived, however; three or four days later, the petals are strewn on the ground and the small coffee berries, or *cherries* as they are called in the trade, begin to form clusters at the base of the leaves.

In six or seven months, the berries have matured; they are oval, about the color and size of a small cherry. Inside the skin and pulp are nestled two coffee beans with their flat sides together. Occasionally, there are three seeds in one berry, but a more common aberration is a berry with just one seed, which grows small and round, and is sold in the trade as peaberry coffee. Each tree can produce between one and twelve pounds of coffee per year, depending on soil, climate, and other factors. The plants are propagated either from seed or from cuttings. If propagated from seed, a tree takes about three years to bear and six to mature.

Coffea arabica grows wild in the mountain rain forests of Ethiopia, where it inhabits the middle tier of the forest, halfway between the ground cover and the taller trees. It grows best wherever similar conditions prevail: no frost, but no hot extremes; fertile, well-watered but well-drained soil (soil of volcanic origin seems best). Heavy rainfall causes the trees to produce too much too fast and exhaust themselves; inadequate rain prevents the trees from flowering or bearing fruit. The tree requires some but not too much direct sunlight; two hours a day seems ideal. The lacy leaves of the upper levels of the rain forest originally shaded the coffee tree. Today some growers plant shade trees; others make protective trellises or plant the crop on hillsides that receive sun for only part of the day. In some fortunate regions, such as the Kona coast of Hawaii, a light cloud cover forms regularly for part of the day, providing a kind of automatic shade.

Whereas arabica trees planted at low altitudes in the tropics overbear, weaken, and fall prey to disease, trees grown at higher altitudes, 3,000 to 6,000 feet, usually produce coffee with a "hard bean." The colder climate encourages a slower-maturing berry, which in turn produces a smaller, denser, less porous bean with less moisture and more flavor. Beware, however, of easy distinctions. Some of the greatest coffees are soft bean, particularly Sumatran Mandheling and Celebes.

Researchers working in the growing countries continue to develop new varieties of arabica that begin to bear fruit more quickly after planting than traditional varieties of arabica, bear more fruit, and are more disease-resistant. These varieties often do perform as intended, but many brokers and roasters feel that this performance is at the cost of cup quality. They attribute the fall-off in quality of Colombian coffees in recent years to the efforts of the Colombian government to replace "old arabicas," mostly of the respected bourbon variety, with the newer, faster- and heavier-bearing coturra variety.

The best coffees of the world are grown either on small- to medium-sized farms, called *estates*, or on peasant plots. Processing of estate coffees is usually done on the farm itself or by consignment. The best peasant-grown coffees are generally processed through cooperatives. The farmer grows food crops for subsistence and some coffee for exchange. The cooperatives, often government sponsored, attempt to maintain and improve growing practices and grading standards.

Most Brazilian coffees are grown on vast privately owned plantations, called *fazendas*, and processed (carelessly in most cases) on the plantation. The poorest coffees

DRYING COFFEE BERRIES

of the world are peasant-grown or -gathered coffees, either robusta species or low-grown arabicas, that are not properly picked or handled. In these cases the governments involved usually have failed to provide leadership in encouraging quality and establishing cooperative processing facilities.

Harvesting and Preparation

Harvesting is one of the most important factors in how coffee tastes. Coffee berries do not ripen uniformly. The same branch may simultaneously display ripe red berries, unripe green berries, and overripe black berries. Conscientious growers go over the trees again and again, selecting only the ripe berries. Carelessly harvested coffee is stripped from the tree in one picking, and ripe, unripe, and overripe berries are all processed together.

Machines have been developed that selectively pick ripe berries by vibrating the tree at a rate that is just vigorous enough to knock loose the ripe berries, while leaving the unripe fruit still attached to the tree. Such machines are not much used at this point, however, and almost all fine coffee is still picked by hand.

Once coffee is picked, it can be prepared either by the dry method, which produces what is called *natural coffee*, or by the wet method, which produces what is termed *washed coffee*. In the older, more primitive dry method, the berries are dried, either by exposure to the sun or in a mechanical dryer, before the fruit is removed from the bean. The hard, shriveled husk is later stripped off the bean by machine, by soaking and washing with hot water, or with a grindstone or mortar and pestle.

In the wet method, most of the covering is removed from the bean before it is dried. Since the moist bean is liable to damage if treated roughly, the covering must be taken off gingerly, layer by layer. First the skin and pulp are gently stripped off by machine. This leaves the beans covered with a sticky substance, which, if removed mechanically, would damage the bean. Instead, the beans are soaked in water, which allows natural enzymes to digest this slimy layer from the bean. This step is called *fermentation*.

Next, the coffee is gently washed and then dried, either by the sun in open terraces, where it is periodically turned and stirred by workers, or in large mechanical driers. This leaves a last thin skin covering the bean, called the *parchment* or *pergamino*. If all has gone well, the parchment is thoroughly dry and crumbly and as easy to remove as the skin from a peanut. Some coffee is sold and shipped in its parchment cover, *en pergamino*, but most often a machine called a *huller* is used to rub it off before shipping. The huller is also designed to polish the coffee, giving the flinty, dry beans a clean, glossy look important to specialty roasters, who sell whole-bean coffee.

There are many moments of truth in wet-processing coffee, and many moments when expedience might tempt the grower to cut corners. The fermentation must be ended at exactly the right moment, for example. Coffee dried too quickly or at too high a temperature will be damaged. After processing, coffee must be "rested" in wooden (not metal) bins, because metal will heat the coffee.

The wet method is not widely used in countries such as Brazil, where the coffee berries ripen nearly all at once, since the labor and machinery necessary to wet-process a single gigantic crop of coffee is prohibitive. In other parts of the world, Colombia for instance, rainfall is plentiful the year around, and coffee ripens and can be processed continuously. Consequently, fewer workers process more coffee and do it better.

Washed coffee is not necessarily better than dry-processed, or natural coffee. In some cases natural coffee may have a more distinctive flavor and more body, apparently due to certain enzymes that remain in close contact with the bean throughout the drying process. Nevertheless, much more can go wrong with natural coffee than with washed coffee. Since drying the entire berry takes so much longer than drying washed beans, green berries mixed with the ripe have more opportunity to rot and impart a foul taste to the rest of the berries. More important, most natural coffee is also strip-picked, which means there will always be some contamination of flavor by green or overripe berries. Most natural coffee is also dried carelessly. Processed with care, however, natural coffees can be as good as washed coffees, if not better. They often display odd, distinctive flavor notes that are particularly valued by roasters and sophisticated consumers.

Most coffees carried by specialty-coffee stores are washed coffees. The important exceptions are Yemen Mocha, Ethiopian Harrar, and the great Sumatran and Celebes coffees, which, despite simple methods, are picked and handled with care, and are the equal of the best washed coffees.

The last step in processing is cleaning. With most high-quality coffees, the beans are placed on conveyor belts or trays and examined by workers who handpick defective beans, sticks, dirt, and other debris from the sound beans. The very best coffees may be cleaned twice. There are some fine coffees that are cleaned by sophisticated machine; most Kenya coffee is electronically cleaned, for example. Commercial coffees are also cleaned by machine, but usually much less meticulously than coffee intended for the whole-bean market. By the time a stick or bad bean reaches the consumer, it is ground or freeze-dried anyhow, so only the taste buds know. Coffee that has been cleaned by hand is usually called *European preparation;* most specialty coffees, since they are whole bean and consumers see what they get, are European preparation.

Before marketing, coffee must be graded. Approaches differ from country to country, but there are four main criteria: how big the bean is, where and at what altitude it was grown, how it was prepared and picked, and how good it tastes, or its cup quality. In some instances coffees are also graded by the number of imperfections (defective and broken beans, pebbles, sticks, etc.) per kilogram. More information on grading by country can be found in Chapter 3.

Growers of some estate coffees may impose a quality control that goes well beyond conventionally defined grading criteria, because they want their coffee to command the price that goes with recognition and consistent quality. More typically, the government of the growing country imposes grading standards to encourage and support quality and to attract and reassure foreign buyers. The most successful coffee-growing countries, like Kenya, simultaneously promote high standards through imposing strict grading criteria and growers by providing a wide range of agricultural and social assistance. In some cases, governments may extend their support efforts to the consuming countries, where they promote their growers' coffees either behind the scenes or directly through media campaigns, like the famous and successful Colombian effort featuring Juan Valdez and his donkey.

Coffees may be subject to still another grading or sorting after they reach the United States. The San Francisco broker Mark Mountanos runs several already premium coffees through additional sophisticated machine sortings to further eliminate defects and sells these ultra-selected beans for a premium as "San Francisco Preparation" coffees. A coffee-handling facility in the port of New Orleans provides a similar service. As sorting devices increase in sophistication and decrease in price, there will probably be more such regrading of coffees in the consuming countries.

Organic Coffees

I discuss the issues surrounding coffee and chemical-free or organic agriculture in Chapter 3. A good deal of the coffee appearing in specialty stores is probably close to chemical-free, simply because the small peasant farmers who grow it can't afford to purchase chemicals. They raise vegetables, keep some chickens and goats, and grow coffee to supply (a little) cash. The certified Latin American organic coffees now appearing in specialty-coffee stores may have been raised in chemical-free conditions for years; the certification process simply identifies them for the consumer, while helping the growers understand, systematize, and improve their traditional agricultural processes. The certification movement has thus far reached only Latin America. I am certain, however, that many coffees raised in Africa, India, and Indonesia are also grown by traditional means, without chemicals.

Growing Your Own

Some enthusiastic readers may want to begin growing their own coffee. Unfortunately, this is a dream that is difficult to realize. A true devotee would need a commercial-size greenhouse or a large backyard in or near the tropics. The environment must be frost-free, which eliminates most yards in the United States. Then assume that one mature tree trimmed to about six feet will produce an average of two to four pounds of coffee a year. Obviously, a very substantial coffee orchard, a dozen trees at least, would be needed to keep the average coffee lover happy.

If you want just a small specimen, the *Coffea arabica* is easy to grow indoors, makes a very attractive houseplant, and may bear flowers and berries. You can start a coffee plant in any one of three ways. The easiest is to buy a seedling. Although the arabica is not an extremely popular houseplant, indoor nurseries occasionally carry it. The next-easiest method is to take a clipping from a friend's plant and root it. Finally, you can plant some green coffee beans and wait for them to sprout in about three or four weeks. Obviously, the green beans that reach the coffee store are at least a couple of months old, and most will never germinate at all, but if you plant enough beans you should eventually be rewarded with a sprout.

Beans should be planted a little over 1/2 inch deep in good, well-drained potting soil, and kept moist at all times, but not wet. Once the plant has sprouted, treat it as you would a camellia. Keep the soil moist but never wet, and provide plenty of bright indirect or diffused sunlight. Fertilize every other month. If something goes wrong, look up *camellia* in a good gardening manual for the appropriate advice.

If you live in a frost-free area, you might want to plant some arabica in your yard. Temperatures should not be lower than 60° F normally or lower than 50° F for short periods only. Parts of Hawaii are unsurpassed for coffee. It has long been held that coffee could be grown commercially along the Southern California coast, but this has never been tried because of high labor costs. Remember, however, that you need to duplicate the conditions of the Ethiopian rain forest: moist, fertile, well-drained soil and partial shade. This last condition is especially important during the long summers in Southern California. For more advice on growing, pruning (very important if you wish your tree to produce more coffee), and caring for coffee trees, read A. E. Haarer's *Coffee Growing* in the Oxford Tropical Handbooks series, published by Oxford University Press.

CHAPTER 11

Celebrating It
Public ceremonies and ritual conviviality

Every social lubricant has its home away from home, its church, as it were, where its effects are celebrated in public ceremonies and ritual conviviality. The café or coffeehouse is as old as the beverage itself. The first people to enjoy coffee as a beverage rather than to use it as a medicine or an aid to meditation did so in coffeehouses in Mecca in the late fifteenth century. The nature of the coffeehouse was established early in history and has changed remarkably little in 500 years.

Early History and Character

Jean de Thévenot describes a Turkish coffeehouse of 1664 in *Relation d'un voyage fait au Levant.*:

> There are public coffeehouses where the drink is prepared in very big pots for the numerous guests. At these places guests mingle without distinction of rank or creed; nor does anyone think it amiss to enter such places, where people go to pass their leisure time. In front of the coffeehouses are benches with small mats, where those sit who would rather remain in the fresh air and amuse themselves by watching the passersby. Sometimes the coffeehouse keeper engages flute players and violin players, and also singers, to entertain his guests.

The "very big pots" of de Thévenot's café became the espresso machines or coffee urns of today; the "benches with small mats," outdoor terraces. And although the café shares many qualities with the bar, saloon, and boîte beloved of drinkers of spirits, it has maintained a subtly unique identity.

The milieu of the café appears to be intimately connected to the effect of coffee and caffeine on mind and body. Coffee stimulates conscious mental associations, whereas alcohol, for instance, provokes instinctual responses. In other words, alcohol typically makes us want to eat, fight, make love, dance, and sleep, whereas coffee encourages us to think, talk, read, write, or work. Wine is consumed to relax, and coffee to drive home. For the Moslems, the world's first coffee drinkers, coffee was the "wine of Apollo," the beverage of thought, dream, and dialectic, "the milk of thinkers and chess players." For the faithful Moslem it was the answer to the Christian and pagan wine of Dionysus and ecstasy.

From the inception of the coffeehouse in Mecca to the present, customers in cafés tend to talk and read rather than dance, play chess rather than gamble, and listen contemplatively to music rather than sing. The café usually opens to the street and sun, unlike bars or saloons, whose dark interiors protect the drinker from the encroachment of the sober, workaday world. The coffee drinker wants not a subterranean refuge but a comfortable corner in which to read a newspaper and observe the world as it slips by, just beyond the edge of the table.

The café is connected with work (the truck stop, the coffee break) and with a special brand of informal study. A customer buried in reading matter is a common sight in even the most lowbrow café. The Turks called their cafés "schools of the wise." In seventeenth-century England, coffeehouses were often called "penny universities." For the price of entry—one penny; coffee cost two, which included newspapers—one could participate in a floating seminar that might include such notables as Joseph Addison and Sir Richard Steele.

As a matter of fact, aside from the Romanticists, who temporarily switched to *plein-air*, it's hard to find too many intellectuals of the eighteenth and nineteenth centuries who didn't spend the better part of their days in cafés or coffeehouses. Recall that the Renaissance not only gave Europe a new world view, but coffee and tea as well. It must have been considerably easier revolutionizing Western thought after morning coffee than after the typical medieval breakfast of beer and herring.

Coffeehouses and Politics

The ideas that have issued from the cafés of history have usually advocated change rather than maintenance of the status quo. Both the French and American revolutions are said to have been nurtured in cafés. The speech that led to the storming of the Bastille took place in the Café Foy, and Daniel Webster called the Green Dragon, a famous Boston coffeehouse, "the headquarters of the Revolution." Since physiologists tell us coffee literally stimulates thought, coffee could be considered a radical beverage, because thinking tends to invidious comparisons between what is and what could be.

The first persecutions of coffee and cafés were undertaken on religious grounds, but subsequent attacks were more explicitly political. In 1511, the governor of Mecca tried to repress the very first coffeehouses because "in these places men and women meet and play violins, tambourines ... chess ... and do other things contrary to our sacred law." Similar attempts followed in Cairo, and the Grand Vizier of Constantinople ordered the coffeehouses of that city closed in the 1600s because he said they encouraged sedition. He let the saloons stay open, however. Caught drinking your first illegal cup of coffee, you got beaten with a stick; for the second, you got sewn in a leather bag and dumped in the Bosphorus. Even such rigor didn't stop the coffee drinkers. Floating coffeehouses developed; enterprising people carried pots of the brew to serve secretly in alleys and behind buildings.

In 1675, King Charles II of England published an edict closing coffeehouses. The apparent pretext was an extraordinary document titled "The Women's Petition Against Coffee, representing to public consideration the grand inconveniences accruing to their sex from the excessive use of the drying and enfeebling Liquor." Conscientiously supporting their thesis with abundant examples and plentiful details, the authors contended that since becoming coffee drinkers, men had become "as unfruitful as the deserts from whence that unhappy berry is said to be brought," and that as a consequence "the whole race is in danger of extinction." The men rose to the occasion, however, with "The Men's Answer to the Women's Petition ... vindicating their liquor from the undeserved aspersion lately cast upon them, in their scandalous pamphlet."

However concerned he may have been with questions of virility, Charles II revealed his true preoccupation in the wording of his proclamation: "... in such Houses ... divers False, Malicious and Scandalous Reports devised and spread abroad, to the Defamation of his Majestie's Government, and to the Disturbance of the Peace and Quiet of the Realm." The reaction among coffee-lovers was pronounced and immediate, and only 11 days later Charles II published a second edict withdrawing his first, "An Additional Proclamation Concerning Coffee Houses," which declared that he had decided to allow cafés to stay open out of "royal compassion." Some observers cite this turnaround as a record for the most words eaten in the shortest time by any ruler of a major nation, unsurpassed until modern times.

A World-Wide Tradition

The tradition of the coffeehouse has spread worldwide. Australia is paved with Italian-style cafés and Japan has evolved its *kisatens*, an elegant interpretation of American 1950s-style coffee shops and coffeehouses. In Great Britain, the espresso-bar craze of the 1950s came and went, but shows signs of mounting a modest comeback. Other parts of Europe and the Middle East have their own ongoing traditions. In Vienna, the home of the first European coffeehouses, the café tradition is undergoing a renaissance.

In the United States, the 1930s and 1940s brought the classic diner, and the 1950s and 1960s the vinyl-boothed coffee shop, together with the coffeehouse—haunt of rebels, poets, beboppers, and beatniks. All of these incarnations are still with us. The classic diner is enjoying a revival, countless coffee shops still minister to the bottomless cup, and I'm told that in Los Angeles there are at least a dozen new coffeehouses, all catering to a new generation of rebels, and complete with funky furniture, radical posters, and folksingers.

But the 1970s and 1980s appear to have produced still another North American café tradition. Classic Italian-American cafés of the 1950s, like Caffè Reggio in Manhattan and Caffè Trieste in San Francisco, appear to have influenced the development of a style of café that takes as its starting point an immigrant's nostalgic vision of the lost and gracious cafés of prewar Italy. From that vision come the light and spacious interiors of the new North American urban café, together with the open seating, the simple and straightforward furnishing, and an atmosphere formal enough to discourage customers from swaggering around and putting their feet on chairs, yet informal enough to mix students doing homework and executives having business meetings. Add an espresso machine and some light new American cuisine, and the latest version of the American café is defined.

CHAPTER 12

Coffee Drinks
Fancy, fortified, cold, and flaming coffees

This is a chapter of recipes, limited, however, to liquid recipes. They are divided into three groups: hot coffee drinks, coffee drinks fortified with spirits, and iced coffee drinks.

Ingredients and Methods

Cocoa

Use unsweetened powdered cocoa, as dark and perfumy as you can find. Many of the instant hot chocolate mixes on the market contain sugar and powdered milk. They are not concentrated enough to give the powerful penetration of chocolate that a good mocha or other coffee-chocolate drink requires. Specialty-coffee stores usually carry such unsweetened cocoa in bulk, as do many whole-food stores, but if you can't find it, try Van Houten's unsweetened powdered chocolate. It is not as intense and flavorful as some bulk cocoas, but it is pure and widely available.

For drinks topped with frothed milk or whipped cream, keep unsweetened cocoa powder in a shaker next to the milk-frothing apparatus or coffeepot. Garnish the froth or cream with a few shakes. Powdered cocoa on frothed milk melts and forms a delicate crust.

For mochas and other drinks that call for cocoa, add 2 to 3 heaping teaspoons of cocoa powder, brown sugar to taste, and a little grated vanilla bean to 1 cup of milk; heat gently or steam with a milk-frothing apparatus while stirring. This is an excellent hot chocolate drink, and 1/3 cup of the mixture combined with espresso and topped with frothed milk makes a fine mocha.

Orange and Lemon Peel

Most commercially grown oranges and lemons have been exposed to agricultural chemicals; even if these chemicals are safe, the skin may retain a slight chemical taste. Since the skin, not the juice or pulp, is used in coffee drinks for its intensely flavored oils, it is best to use untreated, or organic, oranges and lemons from a natural food store.

Heating and Frothing Milk

The Italian, or espresso, method of heating and frothing milk and the devices used for that process are described in Chapter 7 (see pages 158–159). Rather than heating milk from the bottom, over a heat source, espresso machines and milk-frothing devices employ a pipe, or wand, with small holes on the end. The wand is inserted into the milk, and the tiny, powerful jets of steam issuing from the holes at the end of the wand gently heat the milk without imparting a boiled or heated taste. If you care to, you can also raise a head of froth or foam on top of the milk. Coffee drinks made with hot milk do not taste quite right unless the milk has been heated with steam rather than on the stove.

Extra- and Double-Strength Coffee

Some recipes call for coffee made stronger than usual. For recipes using extra-strength coffee, make it one-and-a-half times stronger than you would normally: 3 level tablespoons ground coffee per 6-ounce cup. For double-strength, brew it twice as strong: 4 level tablespoons per 6-ounce cup. If you have an espresso machine, you can substitute coffee brewed by the espresso method at the point a recipe calls for double-strength coffee.

Caffeine

Remember that all of the drinks in this chapter can be made with decaffeinated coffee, should you wish to revel in flavor alone and go to bed early.

Hot Coffee Drinks

All over the world people like to combine large amounts of hot milk with coffee. Fill a tall glass or small bowl with equal parts extra- to double-strength coffee and hot milk, heated and frothed by the espresso method, if possible. Top with a dash of cocoa powder, ground nutmeg or grated orange peel, and granulated sugar. If you make the coffee with regular or Viennese roast, it is *Kaffee Milch* (German). Made with espresso or Italian roast, it is *Caffè Latte* (Italian); with dark French roast coffee, *Café au Lait* (French) or *Café con Leche* (Spanish).

Latin Americans like to make their coffee very, very strong and heat it with a very, very large portion of milk. *New Orleans Coffee* participates in this tradition. Use a dark-roast or chicory-blend coffee, brewed double-strength. Combine 1 part coffee with 2 parts hot milk, steamed if possible, in a tall glass or small bowl. What some people call *Mexican Coffee* is simply 1 part double-strength dark-roast coffee combined with 3 parts hot milk.

Hot Coffee and Whipped Cream

Any coffee tastes good with whipped cream. Brew the coffee a little stronger than usual, and serve it in 5- or 6-ounce stemmed glasses, the rather thick variety that taper outward at the top and are used for Irish coffee and other fortified beverages. The glass permits you to enjoy the contrast between white cream and dark coffee. Use genuine whipped cream. Canned whipped cream is too light; it melts in hot coffee as fast as you spray it on. You can also top coffee with partially whipped cream, in the style of Irish coffee. Whip the cold cream so it is thick but not stiff. If you want to sweeten the coffee, do it before you add the cream. Then slide the half-whipped cream onto the coffee so it floats on the surface; sip the coffee through the cold, thick cream.

To garnish drinks made with lighter roasts of coffee, top the whipped cream with ground cinnamon, nutmeg, or cloves. For drinks made with darker roasts, use cocoa powder or grated orange peel and granulated sugar. Made with a light- or moderate-roast coffee, this drink is often called *Viennese Coffee*; whipped cream also turns up in *Espresso con Panna* (Italian: espresso with whipped cream) and *Kaffee mit Schlag* (German: medium-roast coffee with whipped cream).

Hot Coffee and Whipped Egg Whites

Whipped egg whites also make an excellent topping for hot coffee. Beat 1 egg white and 1/4 teaspoon vanilla extract until stiff. Put 2 generously heaping teaspoons of this mixture in each cup, then add 1/2 cup medium- or dark-roast coffee, brewed extra-strength, and 2 tablespoons half-and-half, heated. The egg white will float to the top of the cup, stained with swirls of brown. If you have an espresso brewer, try this recipe with espresso; decrease the amount of coffee and substitute milk for the half-and-half.

Hot Spiced Coffees

My favorite combination for spiced coffee is clove and orange peel, with a little lemon peel to develop the flavor of the orange. I don't like cinnamon; it seems to go flat when combined with coffee and citrus. Nutmeg, allspice, and cardamom are also good with coffee, but use cardamom sparingly. For every cup of *Simple Spiced Coffee*, place 1 large strip orange peel, 1 small strip lemon peel, and 10 whole cloves in the lower receptacle of a drip or filter coffeepot. Drip the coffee as usual. Sweeten to taste with brown sugar. Use regular or Viennese rather than dark-roast coffee. A heavy-bodied coffee such as Sumatran or Celebes tastes best.

Coffee Grog is a pleasant winter notion; you can make the grog mix in advance, store it indefinitely in the refrigerator, and add it to freshly brewed coffee by the cup. *For the grog mix assemble:*

2 tablespoons butter
1 cup brown sugar
dash salt
1/4 teaspoon each ground cloves and nutmeg

Cream the butter, add the other ingredients, and combine thoroughly. Store in an airtight jar in the refrigerator. When you're ready to enjoy the grog, make a heavy-bodied coffee, like a Sumatran or Kenyan, extra-strength. Use a regular, not a dark, roast. *Assemble for each cup:*

1 to 2 teaspoons grog mix
1 large strip orange peel
1 small strip lemon peel
2 tablespoons heavy cream, heated or steamed
1/2 cup hot brewed coffee, made extra-strength.

Combine the ingredients in a preheated mug, adding the coffee last.

Fortified Coffee Drinks

Spirits and coffee contradict yet complement one another, like hot fudge and vanilla ice cream. They relax and invigorate in a single enjoyable operation. The most traditional fortified drink is brandy and coffee, but almost all spirits go well with coffee, including most liqueurs and several wines. Some possibilities are brandy, grappa, Calvados (apple brandy), Irish whiskey, Scotch whiskey, light and dark rum, kümmel, anisette, orange-flavored liqueur or cognac, kirsch, crème de cacao, sherry, tawny port, and sweet vermouth. Remember that you can add spirits to any coffee drink recipe that does not include it. Brandy is excellent in a cappuccino; brandy, rum, or sherry go nicely in a mocha.

Café Royal or *Café Gloria* is dark-roast (French or Italian) coffee, served with a little sugar (about 1 teaspoon per glass) and a jigger of brandy. Fortify it with Calvados, or apple brandy, and it becomes *Normandy Coffee.*

Café Royal flames the brandy. Partly dissolve a sugar cube on a warmed silver spoon of brandy. Hold over the coffee and ignite the brandy. Contemplate the effect, then stir into the coffee.

Irish Coffee belongs to a family of coffee drinks, all of which add a head of lightly whipped cream to sweetened, fortified coffee in a stemmed glass. Put a tea-spoon, more or less, of sugar in the glass, fill half-way to the top with hot coffee (not a dark roast; use American or Viennese), and add an ounce or so of Irish whiskey (Scotch works too); then top with whipping cream that has been beaten until it's partly stiff, but still pours. It should be soft enough to float with an even line on the surface of the coffee, rather than bob around in lumps. If the cream tends to sink or mix with the coffee, pour it into a teaspoon held just at the surface of the coffee. Irish coffee should not be stirred; sip the hot coffee and whiskey through the cool whipped cream.

You can follow the same procedure with any of your favorite coffees and li-quors; if you add brandy instead of Irish whiskey and use a darker-roast coffee you have made *Venetian Coffee.* If you make the same drink with crème de cacao it be-comes *Café Cacao.* Beyond that point, make up your own names.

Complex Fortified Coffee Drinks

The more complicated and dramatic fortified coffee drinks require advance planning and, in some cases, rehearsal. There are two main kinds: those that use light rum as the main fortifying ingredient and those that use brandy. The brandy drinks usually are made flaming, which is why I suggest a rehearsal. Such drinks have to be concocted in the evening with the lights dim, however; in sunlight the flame becomes virtually invisible and the drama negligible.

Café Brûlot Diabolique, *Café Brûlot*, *Café Diable*, and *Café Flambé* are all names for a drink in which a spiced brandy mixture is heated, ignited, and combined with a strong after-dinner coffee. A richly flavored coffee is best, such as a Kenyan, Sumatran, or Yemen Mocha. Use a regular, rather than dark, roast. *Assemble for each cup:*

> *1 teaspoon granulated or brown sugar, or less, to taste*
> *1 1/2 jiggers brandy*
> *10 whole cloves*
> *1 large strip orange peel*
> *1 small strip lemon peel*
> *1 cup hot coffee, brewed extra-strength*

Warm the sugar, brandy, cloves, and orange and lemon peels in a chafing dish. Stir gently to dissolve the sugar. Fill the glasses or cups two-thirds full of coffee, and place around the chafing dish. When the brandy mixture has been gently warmed (you should be able to smell the brandy very clearly from 3 feet away if it's ready), pass a lighted match over the chafing dish. The brandy should ignite. If it doesn't, it probably is not warm enough. Let the brandy burn for as long as you get a reaction from your audience (but not over half a minute), then ladle over the coffee. The flame will usually die when the brandy is ladled into the glasses. Don't let the brandy burn too long, or the flame will consume all of the alcohol.

If you don't have a chafing dish, put the sugar in each glass before you add the coffee; heat the brandy, cloves, and citrus on the stove. When the fumes are rising, pour into a fancy bowl and bring to the table. Carefully lay an ounce or two of the brandy mixture atop each glass of coffee; if you pour the brandy gently it will float on the surface of the coffee. To ignite the brandy, pass a match over each glass; to douse the flame, mix the brandy and coffee.

If you have trouble getting the brandy to float, try holding a teaspoon on the surface of the coffee, and pouring the brandy mixture onto the spoon, letting it spread from there over the coffee. Also remember to add the sugar to the coffee, not to the brandy mixture, or the sugar will make the brandy too heavy to float. If you're serving only one or two cups, you can simply heat the brandy mixture right in the ladle.

The same drink can be made with light rum. Follow the preceding instructions, substituting rum for brandy and omitting the flaming process. Another possibility is to use half rum and half brandy.

The best rum recipes, however, combine butter and brown sugar with rum and coffee, and are called *Coffee-Rum Grog*, or similarly nautically nuanced titles. Here's a good one: Return to the recipe for *Coffee Grog* described earlier; fortify it with a jigger of rum, brandy, or a mixture of both. Make sure that your coffee is hot and your mugs preheated, since the cream, spirits, and grog mix will rapidly cool lukewarm coffee.

And here is a recipe for *Quick Coffee-Rum Grog. For each cup assemble:*

1/2 jigger each rum and brandy, or a whole jigger of either
1 large strip orange peel
1 small strip lemon peel
10 whole cloves
pinch of ground cinnamon or a bit of stick cinnamon
1/2 cup hot brewed coffee
1 teaspoon brown sugar, or less, to taste
butter, as needed
heavy cream to taste (optional)

Rub the inside of the mugs with butter. Combine the ingredients in a saucepan or chafing dish. Heat gently just short of boiling; pour into the buttered mugs, and add a half-jigger or so of warmed heavy cream. Or, if you prefer, drink your grog black.

Coffee Liqueur

Styles of coffee liqueurs differ. Before making your own, I suggest you determine which style you prefer: Kahlua, for example, is heavy-bodied and based on a dark-roast coffee; others, like Tía María or liqueurs based on Kona coffee, use a somewhat lighter roast. If you prefer Kahlua, use a dark-roasted coffee and go a little heavier on the vanilla and (if you use it) glycerin in the recipe that follows; if you prefer one of the liqueurs based on a lighter roast, use a medium-roast, acidy coffee, like a Costa Rican or Colombian, and go a little lighter on the vanilla and glycerin. Your liqueur will never taste quite like the best commercial products, but you may end up liking it as well or better. Store your liqueur in tightly capped bottles in the refrigerator.

Assemble:

> *1 part water*
> *1 part finely ground coffee*
> *1 part brown sugar*
> *1 part 90 to 100 proof vodka*
> *1 inch fresh vanilla bean per cup of ground coffee*
> *1 teaspoon glycerin per cup of ground coffee (optional)*

Use a filter cone or pot to make the coffee. Slit the vanilla bean and add it to the water; bring the water just to boiling and simmer for 15 minutes, covered. Remove the vanilla bean and reserve. Pour the hot water over the coffee slowly, making sure to wet all the grounds. Pour the resulting concentrated coffee through the grounds a second time. Immediately dissolve the sugar in the hot concentrate. Add the vodka and the reserved vanilla bean, and refrigerate in a sterilized, stoppered bottle for a few days. Taste; when you can begin to distinguish the vanilla flavor, discard the vanilla bean and store the liqueur in a second bottle, or pour and serve. If you're impatient, substitute vanilla extract for the bean. Add 2 or 3 drops per cup of vodka any time after you've brewed the coffee. If you want your liqueur to have the very heavy body of the commercial product, add the glycerine before refrigerating. Variations: Substitute light rum for the vodka, or add a dash of tequila to every cup of rum or vodka.

The simple addition of chocolate turns coffee liqueur into *Mocha Liqueur.* Thoroughly mix one part hot water and one part unsweetened cocoa powder. Add 1/2 tablespoon of this mixture to every cup of the finished coffee liqueur, and mix thoroughly.

Iced Coffee Drinks

The trick to iced coffee drinks is to make the coffee extra-strength, at least one-and-one-half again as strong as usual, so when the ice melts your coffee won't taste watery. *Café Mazagran* is double-strength French-roast coffee poured over ice, served with club soda on the side. Sweeten and add the soda to taste. This classic drink was named after a fortress in Algeria where Foreign Legionnaires supposedly invented it. To experience it at its most North African, serve the soda in a syphon and the coffee and ice in tall glasses. If you like, add cream or half-and-half, to taste.

If you dissolve about two teaspoons of granulated sugar in a double serving of espresso, chill, and add to club soda and ice, you will be approximating the classic New York coffee soft drink called *Manhattan Special.* Add some milk with the espresso, and you have something that could be called an *Espresso Egg Cream,* after the

228

fountain speciality that tastes so good, but mysteriously has no egg or cream in it.

For ideas for iced espresso drinks based on the traditional espresso cuisine, see Chapter 7, page 150.

Spiced Iced Coffee is an excellent idea. For each cup, put 1 large strip orange peel, 1 small strip lemon peel, and 5 whole cloves in the bottom of your drip or filter brewer. Use 1 1/2 times as much ground coffee as usual; a regular roast Kenyan or Sumatran is particularly good. Brew the coffee spice mixture and chill it in a closed jar; refrigeration will make coffee even spicier. Pour over ice in tall glasses. Add half-and-half and brown sugar, to taste, or sweeten first and top with whipped cream and cinnamon garnish.

Blended Iced Coffees

Coffee, ice, and other ingredients can be blended in a variety of gratifying ways. There is no tradition behind blended coffee drinks, so feel free to invent your own names if you don't care for mine. Assemble for each serving of *Creamy Iced Coffee:*

1 cup chilled coffee, brewed double-strength

2 rounded tablespoons confectioners' sugar, or less, to taste

3 cups chopped ice

Combine all ingredients and blend until creamy. For *Creamy Café au Lait* add half-and-half to taste. For a European version use espresso or any dark-roast coffee, brewed double-strength. For a soda fountain effect add 2 rounded teaspoons malt powder, plain or chocolate. You can, of course, add ice cream as well as whipped cream to strong iced coffee. I'm sure your imagination is up to it (cherries? nuts?), but in case you're blocked, here is a simple suggestion from the Caffe Mediterraneum in Berkeley; they call it a *Berliner*. Fill a tall glass halfway with chilled Viennese (or any roast) coffee. Add a large scoop of chocolate ice cream, and top with whipped cream and a dash of cocoa powder

Finally, you can either add spirits to many of these cold drinks or chill one of the hot drinks before you add the spirits. The café cacao described earlier makes an excellent cold drink. Brew a dark-roast coffee in advance and chill; mix a jigger of crème de cacao and a few ounces of the chilled coffee in a stemmed glass and top with whipped cream. Dust with cocoa powder or grated orange peel and sugar: *Chilled Café Cacao.*

Or return to the recipe for creamy *Café Au Lait.* Add 2 jiggers Cointreau or Grand Marnier and 1/4 teaspoon grated orange peel, then blend: *Creamy Café Cointreau.* Cold, fortified coffee drinks are easy to invent, and a good outlet when it's too hot to be creative about anything more important.

Sending for It
A list of resources

The best place to buy coffee and brewing gear is at your neighborhood specialty-coffee store. Look in the yellow pages under "Coffee Dealers–Retail."

If that fails, consult the following selection of suppliers that sell coffee and accessories through the mail. *This list represents a minimal selection only, for the convenience of the isolated aficionado.* There is not space enough to even note the many other roasters across the United States who offer similarly outstanding specialty coffees, or who carry equally impressive arrays of coffee paraphernalia. Nor can this list include the many superb wholesale roasters who supply their excellent coffee only to the retail trade.

Coffee Suppliers

The listed establishments that sell coffee welcome mail orders and promise prompt service and freshly roasted beans. Virtually all supply a brochure describing their selection of coffees.

If you buy a grinder, keep your whole-bean coffees in an airtight container in a cool, dry place,

and grind a little at a time just before brewing. You can order up to about three weeks' supply at a time and always have reasonably fresh coffee.

Ground coffees will not keep well, however, even in the freezer, so if there is no specialty coffee store nearby and you don't buy a grinder, you might as well stash this book between your college political science text and last year's best seller and buy some canned coffee.

Many suppliers are happy to ship a standing order for coffee to you automatically on any periodic basis you specify. This service is often called a *coffee club* or *coffee subscription* service. Many such services also give you the option of receiving a rotating selection of coffees chosen on your behalf, guided by whatever parameters you specify (roast, growing region, decaffeination state, etc.). Another alternative for the isolated coffee lover is buying green coffee, which keeps almost indefinitely, and roasting it at home as described in Chapter 4. Virtually every supplier I list will provide you with green coffee; some may ask you to order in more quantity than their usual minimum (say 5 pounds or more). Two establishments that particularly invite orders for green coffee are indicated.

Equipment, General and Espresso

Again, the best source for coffee-making equipment is your local specialty coffee store. Large metropolitan department stores now carry a decent selection of coffee accessories, though you usually won't find higher-end espresso machines, espresso grinders, roasting apparatus, or similar exotica. The one-story, suburban style of discount department store generally carries blade-style grinders and an assortment of the less expensive automatic-filter and filter-brewers.

Of the suppliers I list, Brown & Jenkins in Vermont, The Coffee Connection in Boston, Pannikin in San Diego, and Zabar's in New York City all provide brochure-catalogs. Zabar's catalog is the most extensive. Fante's in Philadelphia, Peet's Coffee & Tea in Berkeley, and (for espresso equipment) Thomas Cara in San Francisco do not print catalogs, but do provide very well-informed phone response and a substantial array of equipment. All of the high-end espresso brewers described in Chapter 7 are carried by at least one of the listed suppliers. Cara, Fante's, and Pannikin all service their high-end espresso machines on the premises, which means that you can obtain particularly knowledgeable phone support.

Brown & Jenkins Trading Company
P.O. Box 1570
Burlington, VT 05402
(800) 456-5282

Coffee: Brown & Jenkins offers a wide range of straight coffees, including an unusual Mexican Maragogipe, several blends, an attractive assortment of flavored coffees, and a comprehensive selection of nine Swiss Water Process decaffeinated coffees. Brown & Jenkins roasts in a darker style than most East Coast roasters. Standing orders ("Coffee Club") accepted.

Equipment: Brown & Jenkins' attractive catalog describes a small but well-chosen selection of coffee gear.

Thomas Cara
517 Pacific Avenue
San Francisco, CA 94133
(415) 781-0383

Equipment: Thomas Cara specializes in traditional manual piston home espresso machines, including the Riviera, Pavoni, and Olympia lines, and high-end electric pump machines like the Rancilio. Cara often has reconditioned machines available at excellent prices, and he services all the machines he carries on the premises.

Caravali Coffee Company
P.O. Box 2502
Seattle, WA 98111
(800) 423-9004

Coffee: Caravali Coffee Company is a well-established, influential wholesale roaster that has recently begun offering its coffees by mail. Caravali currently carries 50 coffee selections, including straight coffees, blends, flavored coffees, decaffeinated coffees, and two certified organic coffees. Caravali roasts in a darker West Coast style.

The Coffee Connection
119 Braintree Street
Boston, MA 02134
(800) 284-5282
(617) 254-1459 in Massachusetts

Coffee: Coffee Connection offers an impressive range of coffees described in an unusually detailed brochure. The Coffee Connection roasts in a lighter, East Coast style.

Equipment: The Coffee Connection brochure also presents° a well-selected range of equipment, including some hard-to-find products like the Rotel Espressomat pump espresso machine, the Jericho electric grinder, and a stovetop milk frother.

Coffee Kids
174 Wickenden Street
Providence, RI 02903
(401) 331-9099

Coffee Kids is a non-profit organization dedicated to improving the quality of life for children and families who live in the often impoverished areas of the world where coffee is grown. It seeks to harness some of the goodwill of the specialty coffee world to help those whose lives are devoted to producing coffee, but who experience few if any of the financial benefits of that devotion. Projects are usually undertaken in cooperation with other international agencies, and emphasize community development by promoting independence and self-sufficiency. Coffee Kids welcomes support and inquiries at the above address.

Fante's
1006 South Ninth Street
Philadelphia, PA 19147
(800) 878-5557

Coffee: Fante's offers nearly 30 straight coffees (including an aged, or vintage, Colombian Supremo), three straight dark roasts, three dark-roasted blends, six regular blends, and will make and record custom blends. If you have trouble finding a rare coffee, Fante's will do its best to obtain a minimum 5-pound order for you within a week, and will supply it either roasted or green. Standing orders accepted; no minimum order for coffees in stock. Fante's roasts in a lighter, East Coast style.

Equipment: Fante's stocks a staggering array of coffee apparatus, including hard-to-find items like the Jupiter grain mill and the Rapallo stovetop espresso machine. The impressive selection of fully supported home espresso machines includes many of those discussed in Chapter 7.

Green Mountain Coffee Roasters
33 Coffee Lane
Waterbury, VT 05676
(800) 432-3402

Coffee: Green Mountain Coffee Roasters offers nearly 40 coffees, including a good range of decaffeinated and flavored coffees, and one certified organic coffee. Standing orders ("Coffee Club") accepted. Minimum order 1 pound.

Filters and Equipment: Green Mountain is the developer and distributor of the Green Mountain coffee filter, an "oxygen-whitened," certified dioxin- and chlorine-free filter. In addition to its line of filters, Green Mountain also sells a range of coffee brewing equipment.

Pannikin
675 G Street
San Diego, CA 92101
(619) 239-1257
(800) 232-6482

Coffee: Pannikin sells over 20 straight coffees, including an organic Peruvian, seven blends, including an unusual dark-roasted combination of Indonesian coffees called *Indo-Noir,* and eight caffeine-free coffees. Standing orders are accepted via a "Coffee and Tea of the Month Club."

Flavorings: Pannikin is a proponent of flavorings that are added to coffee after it is brewed, rather than mixed with the whole beans. It offers the Flavor-Mate, Wagners, and Crystal Persuasion lines of flavorings.

Equipment: The attractive Pannikin newsletter-brochure lists a small selection of the gear carried at the Pannikin stores, including the Faema line of high-end espresso brewers.

Peet's Coffee & Tea, Inc.
Box 8247
Emeryville, CA 94662
(800) 999-2132

Coffee: One of the oldest specialty-coffee roasters in the San Francisco Bay Area, Peet's roasts in a darker West-Coast style, and specializes in full-bodied blends such as the locally famous Major Dickason's. Peet's currently offers 15 superb straight coffees, including an aged Java; ten blends; and seven decaffeinated coffees, including a decaffeinated aged Indonesian coffee. One-pound minimum order.

Equipment: Peet's carries many of the higher-priced home espresso machines mentioned in Chapter 7, as well as a wide range of grinders and other brewers, including one of the country's largest selections of French press or plunger pot devices. Since Peet's does not have a catalog, you must call for availability and prices.

Polly's Gourmet Coffee
4606 East Second Street
Long Beach, CA 90803
(213) 433-2996

Coffee: Polly's offers a substantial selection of coffees and will custom-roast your choice of straight coffee or blend for orders of 5 pounds or more.

Roastery Development Group
245 South Railroad
San Mateo, CA 94401
(800) 999-1600

Equipment: Primarily a consultant, outfitter, and developer for specialty roasters and coffee retailers, Roastery Development Group also is the importer and a mail order source for the QC Cupping Roaster described in Chapter 5 (See page 97).

Starbucks Coffee
2010 Airport Way South
Seattle, WA 98134
(800) 445-3428

Coffee: One of the largest specialty coffee roasters in the country, Starbucks roasts in the darker style preferred by coffee drinkers of the Northwest, and offers an excellent selection of straight coffees and blends, including decaffeinated. Minimum order 2 pounds. Standing orders ("Personal Coffee Service") accepted.

Sivitz Coffee Company
349 S.W. 4th Street
Corvallis, OR 97333
(503) 753-9713

Coffee: Sivitz Coffee is a proponent of home roasting, and supplies a variety of green coffees in 8-pound minimum lots at very attractive prices.

Equipment: Although best known for his larger roasters and roasting development activities, Sivitz is also the source for the Sivitz home roaster described in Chapter 5 (See page 101).

M. E. Swing Co., Inc.
437 Eleventh Street NW
Washington, DC 20004-1302
(202) 628-7601

Coffee: A small roaster with a tradition that stretches back 75 years, Swing offers an excellent selection of coffees at low prices with an emphasis on freshness. No minimum order.

Thanksgiving Coffee Company
P.O. Box 1918
Fort Bragg, CA 95437
(800) 648-6491

Coffee: Despite the danger of loading this list with too many Northern West Coast roasters, I decided to add Thanksgiving Coffee because it offers, along with an excellent array of conventionally presented coffees, an interesting selection of organic coffees and coffees that represent social and environmental concerns. There is a coffee from an association of small farmer cooperatives in Mexico, for example, a certified organic estate coffee from Kona, and coffees that donate a portion of their purchase price to support causes ranging from a locally based ocean ecology organization ("Ocean Sanctuary-Islands Blend") to a new baseball diamond for local kids ("Grand Slam Coffee"). Standing orders ("Coffee Subscription Club") accepted.

Zabar's
2245 Broadway
New York, NY 10024
(212) 496-1234

Coffee: Zabar's offers a small selection of excellent straight and blended coffees, at good prices, roasted in the lighter East Coast style. Minimum order is 5 pounds.

Accessories: Zabar's cookware catalog offers an exceptionally wide range of coffee-making equipment, including many of the pump espresso machines mentioned in Chapter 7, all at very reasonable prices.

Words for It
A Glossary

AA　Capitalized letters are grade indicators usually describing the size of the bean. In Peru, for example, AAA is the largest bean; in Kenya, Tanzania, and New Guinea, AA is the largest; in India, A is the largest.

Acidity, Acidy, Acid　Usually, the pleasant tartness of a fine coffee. Acidity, along with flavor, aroma, and body, is one of the principal categories used by professional tasters in judging coffee. When not used to describe cup characteristics, the term *acid* may refer to certain specific chemicals present in coffee, including some that ostensibly produce indigestion or nervousness in certain individuals.

After-Dinner Roast　See *Espresso Roast.*

Aged Coffee, Vintage Coffee　Coffee held in special warehouses for several years in order to reduce acidity and increase body. Aged coffee has been held longer than either old crop coffee or mature coffee.

Alajuela　One of the better coffees of Costa Rica.

Altura　"Heights" in Spanish; describes Mexican coffee that has been high- or mountain-grown.

American Roast　Coffee roasted to standard American taste: medium brown.

Ankola　One of the best coffees of Sumatra.

Antigua　One of the best coffees of Guatemala.

Arabian Mocha, Yemen, Yemen Mocha, Mocha　See *Yemen.*

Arabica, Coffea Arabica　The earliest cultivated species of coffee tree and still the most widely grown. All fine, specialty, and fancy coffees come from Coffea arabica trees.

Armenia　One of the better coffees of Colombia.

Aroma　The fragrance produced by hot, freshly brewed coffee. Aroma, along with flavor, acidity, and body, is one of the principal categories used by professional tasters in judging coffee.

Arusha　Coffee from the slopes of Mt. Meru in Tanzania.

Automatic Filter-Drip Coffee Makers　Coffee brewers that automatically heat and measure water into a filter and filter receptacle containing the ground coffee.

Balance　Tasting term applied to coffees for which no single characteristic overwhelms others, but that display sufficient complexity to be interesting.

Bandeirante　A good estate-grown Santos coffee of Brazil.

Baní　A good, low-acid coffee of the Dominican public.

Barahona　Considered by many to be the best coffee of the Dominican Republic.

Batch Roaster　Apparatus that roasts a given quantity (a batch) of coffee at a time.

Blend　A mixture of two or more straight, or varietal coffees.

Body　The sense of heaviness, richness, or thickness when one tastes coffee. Body, along with flavor, acidity, and aroma, is one of the principal categories used by professional tasters in judging coffee.

Bogotá　One of the best coffees of Colombia.

Bourbon Santos, Santos　See *Santos.*

Bourbon   A botanical variety of *Coffea arabica*—var. *bourbon*—that first appeared on the island of Bourbon, now Réunion. Some of the best Mexican and Brazilian coffees, among others, are from Bourbon stock.

Brazilian   Straight coffee from Brazil. Most Brazilian coffee is carelessly picked and primitively processed, and is not a factor in the specialty trade. The best washed Brazilian coffee (usually Bourbon Santos) is a good but undistinguished Latin American-style coffee: smoothly flavorful, moderately acidy, and medium-bodied.

Brown Roast   See *American Roast*.

Bucaramanga   An excellent but uncharacteristically low-acid coffee from Colombia.

Bugishu, Bugisu   Arabica coffee from the slopes of Mt. Elgon in Uganda. Considered the best Ugandan coffee, although quality is not consistent.

Caffeine   An odorless, bitter alkaloid responsible for the stimulating effect of coffee and tea.

Caracas   A class of coffees from Venezuela, ranging from fair to excellent in quality.

Caracol   See *Peaberry*.

Caturra   A relatively recently developed botanical variety of the *Coffea arabica* species that generally matures more quickly, produces more coffee, and is more disease resistant than traditional arabica varieties. Many experts contend that the caturra and other modern varieties of Coffea arabica produce coffee that is inferior in cup quality and interest to the coffee produced by the traditional "old arabica" varieties.

Celebes   See *Sulawesi*.

Chanchamayo   One of the best coffees of Peru.

Chiapas   Coffee-growing state in southern Mexico; the best Chiapas coffees are grown in the southeast corner of the state near the border with Guatemala, and may bear the market name Tapachula after the town of that name. At their best, Chiapas or Tapachula coffees display the brisk acidity, delicate flavor, and light to medium body of the better known Mexican coffees of Oaxaca and Vera Cruz States.

Chicory   The root of the endive, roasted and ground like coffee.

Chipinga   Region in Zimbabwe that produces the most admired coffees of that country.

Cibao   A good but undistinguished coffee from the Dominican Republic.

Cinnamon Roast   See *Light Roast*.

City Roast   See *Light French Roast*.

Coatepec, Altura Coatepec   Respected washed coffee from the northern slopes of the central mountain range in Veracruz State, Mexico.

Cobán   One of the best coffees of Guatemala.

Coffee Oil, Coffeol   The volatile coffee essence developed in the bean during roasting.

Cold-Water Method   Brewing method in which ground coffee is soaked in a proportionally small amount of cold water for 10 to 20 hours, then separated by the drip method.

    The resulting concentrated coffee is stored and mixed with hot water as needed. The cold water method produces a low-acid, light-bodied cup that some find pleasingly delicate, and others find bland.

Colombian   Straight coffee from Colombia. The best (Medellín, supremo grade) is a classic coffee probably as good as Jamaican Blue Mountain, but with a somewhat stronger, higher-pitched acidity. The Colombian coffee typically found in specialty stores (mixed Medellín, Armenia, and Manizales, or MAM, excelso grade) is usually excellent but not remarkable, with full body, complex acidity, and rich flavor.

Commercial Coffees   Packaged preground (prebrewed in the case of instant or soluble) coffees sold by brand name.

Complexity   A tasting term describing coffees whose taste sensations shift and layer pleasurably, and give the impression of depth and resonance.

Continental Roast   See *Espresso Roast.*

Continuous Roaster   Large commercial coffee roaster that roasts coffee continuously rather than in batches.

Costa Rican   Straight coffee from Costa Rica. The best Costa Rican coffees (San Marcos de Tarrazu, Tres Rios, Herediá, Alajuela) display a full body and robust richness that make them the most admired of Central American coffees.

Crema   The pale brown foam covering the surface of a well-brewed cup of espresso.

Cúcuta   A coffee grown in Colombia, but usually shipped through Maracaibo, Venezuela.

Dark French Roast   A roast of coffee almost black in color, thin-bodied, and bittersweet in flavor, with an overlay of burned or charcoal-like tones.

Dark Roast   Vague term; may describe any roast of coffee darker than the American norm, from full-city or light French roast through espresso or Italian roast to dark French roast.

Decaffeination Processes   Specialty coffees are decaffeinated in the green state, currently by one of three methods. The solvent-water method (often called *European Process* or *Traditional Process*) involves soaking the green beans in hot water, removing the caffeine from the hot water by means of a solvent, and recombining the water with the beans, which are then dried. The water-only method, which carries the proprietary name *Swiss Water Process,* involves the same steps, but removes the caffeine from the water by allowing it to percolate through a bed of activated charcoal. In the carbon dioxide method, which is only beginning to be established in the specialty-coffee trade, the caffeine is stripped directly from the beans by a highly compressed semiliquid form of carbon dioxide.

Demitasse   "Half cup" in French; a half-size cup used primarily for espresso coffee.

Djimah, Djimma, Jimma   A coffee from Ethiopia. Washed Djimah is an excellent low-acid coffee. Dry-processed Djimah is a lesser coffee often exhibiting wild or medicinal taste characteristics and is not often traded as a speciality coffee.

Dominican Republic, Santo Domingo   Straight coffee from the Dominican Republic. High-grown Dominican coffee (usually marked *Barahona*) is a fairly rich, acidy coffee with classic characteristics, making it a lesser version of the better Jamaican coffees. Other Dominican coffees (Baní, Ocoa) are softer and mellower, and resemble the better Haitian coffees.

Doser A spring-loaded device on specialized espresso grinders that dispenses single servings of ground coffee.

Drip Method Brewing method that allows hot water to settle through a bed of ground coffee.

Dry-Processed Coffee, Dry Method Coffee, Natural Coffee Coffee processed by removing the husk or fruit after the coffee berries have been dried. Frequently but not always inferior to washed coffee, or coffee processed by the wet method.

Earthiness, Wildness, Gaminess Closely related terms applied to coffees that embody just enough of the off-taste of a carelessly processed natural coffee to be interesting, but not enough to be dirty, sour, or harsh, equivalent terms applied to coffees in which these off-tastes dominate.

Ecuador Straight coffee from Ecuador. At best, Ecuador coffees are medium-bodied and fairly acidy, with a straightforward flavor typical of Central and South American coffees.

El Salvador Straight coffee from El Salvador. Usually a dependable but undistinguished coffee, with good body but rather spiritless acidity and flavor.

En Pergamino, In Parchment See *Parchment Coffee.*

Espresso Roast, After-Dinner Roast, Continental Roast, European Roast A roast of coffee darker than the American norm, with a dark brown, oily surface and a rich, bittersweet flavor.

Espresso Used to describe both a roast of coffee (see *Espresso Roast*) and a method of brewing in which hot water is forced under pressure through a bed of finely ground coffee. In the largest sense, an entire approach to coffee cuisine, involving a traditional menu of drinks, many combining brewed espresso coffee with steam-heated, steam-frothed milk.

Estate-Grown Coffee Coffee grown on medium-sized farms, as opposed to small peasant plots or large plantations. Some specialty coffees are now identified by estate name, rather than the less specific regional or market name.

Ethiopian Straight coffee from Ethiopia. The best Ethiopian dry-processed coffee (Harrar or Harar) tends to be medium-bodied and brilliantly acidy with rough, winy tones. The best washed Ethiopian coffee (Yirgacheffe, Sidamo, some Limu, and Washed Djimah) can be fragrant, gentle, and rich.

European Preparation Used to describe coffee from which imperfect beans, pebbles, and other foreign matter have been removed by hand.

European Process See *Decaffeination Processes.*

European Roast See *Espresso Roast.*

Excelso A comprehensive grade of Colombian coffee, combining the best, or supremo, and the second-best, or extra, grades.

Extra Second-best grade of Colombian coffee.

Filter Method, Filter-Drip Method Technically, any brewing method in which water filters through a bed of ground coffee. In popular usage, describes drip method brewers utilizing a paper filter to separate grounds from brewed coffee.

Finish The aftertaste of a coffee. Finish is largely a function of body, and may be "long" or rich and lingering, flat and acidic, brief and effervescent, etc.

Flavored Coffees   Coffees that in their roasted, whole-bean form have been mixed with flavoring agents.

Flavor   What distinguishes the taste of coffee once its acidity, body, and aroma have been described.

Flip-Drip, Neapolitan Macchinetta, Macchinetta   A style of drip method brewer in which the ground coffee is secured in a two-sided strainer at the waist of the pot between two closed compartments. The brewing water is heated in one compartment, then the pot is flipped over, and the hot water drips through the coffee into the opposite compartment.

Fluid Bed Roaster, Sivitz Roaster   A roasting apparatus that works much like a giant popcorn popper, utilizing a column of forced hot air to simultaneously agitate and roast green coffee beans. These devices are also called *Sivitz roasters*, after their popularizer and American manufacturer, inventor Michael Sivitz.

French Press, Plunger Pot   Brewing method that separates spent grounds from brewed coffee by pressing them to the bottom of the brewing receptacle with a mesh plunger.

French Roast, Heavy Roast, Spanish Roast   A roast of coffee darker than the American norm; may range in color from dark brown (see *Espresso Roast*) to nearly black (see *Dark French Roast*) and in flavor from rich and bittersweet to thin-bodied and burned.

Full-City Roast   See *Light French Roast*.

Gaminess   See *Earthiness*.

Ghimbi, Gimbi   A good washed coffee from western Ethiopia, at best displaying a sharp but rich acidity and complex flavor.

Good Hard Bean   A grade of Costa Rican coffee grown at altitudes of 3,300 to 3,900 feet.

Green Coffee   Unroasted coffee.

Group, Delivery Group   The fixture protruding from the front of most espresso machines into which the filter holder and filter clamp.

Guatamalan   Straight coffee from Guatamala. The best Guatamalan coffees (Antigua, Cobán) exhibit rich, spicy acidity and excellent body.

Haitian   Straight coffee from Haiti. The best Haitian coffees are low-acid, medium-bodied, and pleasantly soft and rich.

Hard Bean   Term often used to describe coffees grown at relatively high altitudes; in the same context, coffees grown at lower altitudes are often designated *soft bean*. The higher altitudes and lower temperatures produce a slower maturing fruit and a harder, less porous bean. Hard bean coffees usually make a more acidy and more flavorful cup than do soft bean coffees, although there are many exceptions to this generalization. The hard bean/soft bean distinction is used most frequently in evaluating coffees of Central America, where it figures in grade descriptions.

Hard   Trade term for low-quality coffee, in contrast to mild coffee.

Harrar, Harar, Harer, Mocha Harrar, Moka Harar   The best of the dry-processed, or natural, coffees of Ethiopia.

Hawaiian, Hawaiian Kona See *Kona*.

Heavy Roast   See *French Roast*.

Herediá   One of the better coffees of Costa Rica.

High-Grown   Arabica coffees grown at altitudes over 2,000 feet, usually higher. Such coffees are generally superior to coffees grown at lower altitudes. The term *high-grown* is also used in many Latin American grade descriptions.

High Roast   See *Light French Roast.*

Huehuetenango   One of the better coffees of Guatemala.

Indian, Indian Mysore, Mysore Straight   Coffee from India, usually from Karnataka State, formerly Mysore. The best Indian coffee is low-key, with moderate body and acidity. At best it is rich; at worst bland. Also see *Monsooned Coffee.*

Indonesian   Straight coffee from Indonesia. Indonesian coffees are usually marketed under the name of the island of origin; see *Sumatra, Sulawesi, Java.* All are distinguished by full body, rich flavor, and a low-toned, vibrant acidity.

Italian Roast   A roast of coffee considerably darker than the American norm. Usually dark brown in color and rich and bittersweet in flavor, but may range in color to almost black and in flavor to nearly burned.

Jamaican Blue Mountain Style Various blends of coffee intended by their originators to approximate the qualities of true estate-grown Jamaican Blue Mountain. They may contain no actual Jamaican coffee.

Jamaican Blue Mountain Celebrated, estate-grown straight coffee from above 3,000 feet in the Blue Mountain District of Jamaica. The best known is Wallensford Estate Blue Mountain. Also see *Jamaican.*

Jamaican High Mountain Straight coffee grown in the mountains of Jamaica and exported under the market names *High Mountain Supreme* or *Blue Mountain* Valley. Both are considered excellent coffees, but less distinguished than the true, high-grown Jamaican Blue Mountain.

Jamaican   Straight coffee from Jamaica. The best (Jamaican Blue Mountain) is, or was, a balanced, classic coffee with rich flavor, full body, and a smooth yet vibrant acidity. These characteristics and its relatively short supply have made it one of the world's most celebrated coffees. Whether it still merits this distinction is subject to debate among importers and roasters. Lower-grown Jamaican coffees (Jamaican High Mountain) tend to be less acidy and lighter in body. Other Jamaican coffees are undistinguished.

Java, Java Arabica   Straight coffee from Java. The best displays the low-toned richness characteristic of Indonesian and New Guinea coffees, but is usually lighter in body and more acidy. Old Java, Old Government, or Old Brown are mature coffees from Java, created to mimic the flavor characteristics of the original Java coffee, which was inadvertently aged in the holds of eighteenth- and nineteenth-century ships during their passage to Europe.

Jimma, Djimma.   See *Djimah.*

Jinotega   One of the better coffees of Nicaragua.

Kenyan   Straight coffee from Kenya. The best Kenyan coffees are consistently full-bodied and flavorful, with a deep, winy acidity. Of the world's great coffees, Kenyan probably is the most consistent in quality and most widely available.

Kilimanjaro   Coffee from the slopes of Mt. Kilimanjaro in Tanzania.

Kona, Hawaiian Kona, Hawaiian   Straight coffee from the

Kona coast of the Island of Hawaii. The best Kona coffee has classic balance, with medium body, good acidity, and rich, complex aroma and flavor.

La Minita, La Minita Farm Well-publicized estate in the Tarrazu district of Costa Rica that produces an excellent, meticulously prepared coffee.

Lavado Fino Best grade of Venezuelan coffee.

Light Espresso Roast See *Light French Roast.*

Light French Roast, Full-City Roast, Viennese Roast, Light Espresso Roast, City Roast, High Roast A roast of coffee slightly darker in color than the American norm, but lighter than the classic dark roast variously called *espresso, French,* or *Italian.* In the cup, light French or full-city roast is less acidy and smoother than the characteristic American roast, but may display fewer of the distinctive taste characteristics of the original coffee. In parts of the United States, such as Northern California or the Pacific Northwest, light French or full-city may be the typical roast of coffee.

Light Roast, Cinnamon Roast, New England Roast A roast of coffee lighter in color than the American norm, and grainlike in taste, with a sharp, almost sour acidity.

Limu Good low-acid, washed coffee from Ethiopia.

Lintong, Mandheling Lintong Market name for the most admired coffee of Sumatra, Indonesia.

Longberry Harrar Grade of Harrar coffee from Ethiopia; beans are larger than Shortberry Harrar, but there may be no discernable difference between the two in terms of cup quality.

Macchinetta, Neapolitan Macchinetta See *Flip-Drip.*

MAM Acronym for Medellín, Armenia, and Manizales, three of the most famous and best coffees of Colombia. To simplify large-scale coffee contracts, coffees from these three regions are sold together as MAMs.

Mandheling The most famous coffee of Sumatra.

Manizales One of the better coffees of Colombia.

Maracaibo A class of coffees from Venezuela, including many of the most characteristic and distinguished coffees of that country.

Maragogipe (MAH-rah-goh-SHZEE-peh) A variety of *Coffea arabica* distinguished by extremely large, porous beans. It first appeared in Maragogipe, Brazil, and has since been planted all over the world.

Matagalpa One of the better coffees of Nicaragua.

Mattari, Matari One of the best coffees of Yemen. Usually a winier, sharper version of the Yemen style.

Mature Coffee Coffee held in warehouses for two to three years in order to mildly reduce acidity and increase body. Mature coffee is held longer than old crop coffee, but not as long as aged or vintage coffee.

Mbeya, Pare Coffee from the south of Tanzania.

Medellín One of the best coffees of Colombia.

Medium Roast, Medium-High Roast See *American Roast.*

Mexican Straight coffee from Mexico. The best (Oaxaca Pluma, Coatepec, some Chiapas) are distinguished by a light body and a delicate, pleasant acidity.

Microwave Brewers   Brewing apparatus designed to take advantage of the unique properties of the microwave oven. Current microwave brewers use a variety of technical means, ranging from open-pot through various approaches to filter-drip.

Middle Eastern Coffee, Turkish Coffee   Coffee ground to a powder, sweetened, brought to a boil, and served grounds and all.

Mild   A trade term for high-quality arabica coffees. Often contrasted with hard, or inferior, coffees.

Mocha Harrar, Moka Harar Name for the peaberry grade of Harrar coffee from Ethiopia.

Mocha, Moka   Straight coffee from Yemen; also a drink combining chocolate and coffee. The coffee, also called *Arabian Mocha, Yemen*, or *Yemen Mocha*, takes its name from the ancient port of Mocha. It is the world's oldest cultivated coffee, distinguished by its full body and distinctively rich, winy acidity.

Mocha-Java   Traditionally, a blend of Yemen Mocha and Java Arabica coffees, usually one part Yemen Mocha and two parts Java Arabica. All commercial Mocha-Java blends and many specialty versions no longer follow this recipe. Commercial blends may combine any of a variety of heavy-bodied coffees in place of the Java, and any of a variety of highly acidy coffees in place of the Mocha, while changing proportions to maintain a uniform taste. Versions offered by specialty roasters may blend a true Java with a true Yemen Mocha, or may substitute another (often better) Indonesian coffee for the Java, or an Ethiopian Harrar for the Yemen. Most specialty blends do maintain the original two-thirds, one-third formula, however, and probably represent the classic blend accurately. In its traditional form, Mocha-Java is the world's oldest coffee blend.

Monsooned Coffee, Monsooned Malabar Indian   Mysore coffee deliberately exposed to monsoon winds in open warehouses, with the aim of increasing body and reducing acidity. Monsooned Malabar is the best grade of this coffee.

Moshi   Market name for coffee from the slopes of Mt. Kilimanjaro in Tanzania.

Mysore, Indian Mysore   See *Indian.*

Mérida   One of the best and most characteristic Venezuelan coffees, delicate and sweet in the cup.

Nairobi   Coffee from the slopes of Mt. Kenya in Kenya.

Natural Coffee, Dry Method Coffee   See *Dry-Processed Coffee.*

Neapolitan Macchinetta, Macchinetta   See *Flip-Drip.*

Neapolitan Roast   Sometimes used to describe a roast of coffee darker than the normal espresso roast, but not quite black.

New Crop   Coffee delivered for roasting soon after harvesting and processing. Coffees are at their brightest (or rawest) and most acidy in this state. Also see *Old Crop.*

New England Roast See *Light Roast.*

New Guinea   Straight coffee from Papua, New Guinea. The best New Guinea coffee is moderately rich and full-bodied, with the low-key acidity that distinguishes all of the coffees of the Malay Archipelago and Indonesia.

New Orleans Coffee   Traditionally, dark-roast coffee blended with up to 40 percent roast and ground chicory root. Most New Orleans blends sold in specialty stores today contain no chicory, however. They are essentially dark-roast blends, perhaps incorporating some wild- or earthy-tasting coffees from Brazil.

Nicaraguan   Straight coffee from Nicaragua. The best (Jinotega, Matagalpa) are excellent but not distinguished coffees in the classic Central-American style: medium-bodied, straightforwardly acidy, and flavorful.

Oaxaca, Oaxaca Pluma (Wah-HAH-kuh)   Straight coffee from the southern Mexican state of Oaxaca. Oaxaca coffees are among Mexico's best.

Ocoa   One of the better coffees of the Dominican Republic.

Old Arabicas   Botanical varieties of the *Coffea arabica* species that appeared relatively early in the history of coffee, such as *var. bourbon, var. blue mountain,* or *var. typica,* as opposed to varieties that have been developed more recently in deliberate efforts to increase production. Many experts contend that the modern varieties of *Coffea arabica* produce coffee that is inferior in cup quality and interest to the coffee produced by the arabica varieties.

Old Crop   Coffee that has been held in warehouses before shipping. Old crop differs from aged or vintage, and mature coffees in two ways: First, it has not been held for as long a period, and second, it may not have been handled with as much deliberateness. Depending on the characteristics of the original coffee and the quality of the handling, old crop may or may not be considered superior in cup characteristics to a new crop version of the same coffee. See also *New Crop.*

Old Java, Old Government, Old Brown   Arabica coffee from Java that, like mature coffee, has been held in warehouses for two to three years, reducing acidity and increasing body. The purpose is to mimic the flavor characteristics of the original Java coffee, which was inadvertently aged in the holds of eighteenth- and nineteenth-century sailing ships during their passage to Europe.

Open-Pot Method   Brewing method in which the ground coffee is steeped (not boiled) in an open pot, and separated from the brewed coffee by settling or straining.

Organic Coffee, Certified Organic Coffee   Coffee that has been certified by a third-party agency as having been grown and processed without the use of pesticides, herbicides, or similar chemicals.

Parchment Coffee, In Parchment, En Pergamino   Describes washed coffee shipped with the parchment covering still adhering to the bean. The parchment is removed and the beans polished prior to roasting in the consuming country.

Parchment   A final thin, crumbly skin covering wet-processed coffee beans after the coffee berries have been skinned, the pulp removed, and the beans dried.

Pare   See *Mbeya.*

Peaberry, Caracol   A small, round bean formed when only one seed, rather than the usual two, develops at the heart of the coffee berry. Peaberry beans are often separated from normal beans and sold as a distinct grade of a given coffee.

Percolation   Technically, any method of coffee brewing in which hot water percolates, or filters down through, a bed of ground coffee. The pumping percolator utilizes the power of boiling water to force water up a tube and over a bed of ground coffee.

Pergamino   See *Parchment.*

Peruvian   Straight coffee from Peru. The best (from the Chanchamayo valley) is flavorful, aromatic, and mildly acidy. At its best it displays the quality and characteristics of the better Central American coffees.

Plunger Pot   See *French Press.*

Primo Lavado, Prime Washed A grade of Mexican coffee that includes most of the fine coffees of that country.

Pyrolysis   The chemical breakdown, during roasting, of fats and carbohydrates into the delicate oils that provide the aroma and most of the flavor of coffee.

Quakers   Discolored or deformed coffee beans.

Regular Roast   See *American Roast.*

Richness   A satisfying fullness in flavor, body, or acidity.

Rio   A class of carelessly picked and prepared coffees from southern Brazil with a characteristic medicinal, iodine-like flavor deriving from the poor handling of the berries. The term *Rioy* or *Rio-y* has come to be applied to any coffee with similar taste characteristics.

Rioy, Rio-y   See *Rio.*

Robusta, Coffea Robusta   Currently the only significant competitor among cultivated coffee species to Coffea arabica. Robusta is a lower-growing, higher-bearing tree that produces coffee of inferior cup quality and higher caffeine content than Coffea arabica. It is used as a basis for blends of instant coffee, and for less expensive blends of preground commercial coffee. It is not a factor in the specialty coffee trade. See also *Coffea Arabica.*

Sanani   One of the best coffees of Yemen. Usually a lower-toned, somewhat less acidy version of the Yemen style.

Santo Domingo   See *Dominican Republic*

Santos, Bourbon Santos   A high-quality, washed coffee from Brazil, often but not always shipped through the port of Santos, and usually grown in the state of São Paulo or the northern part of Minas Gerais State. The term *Bourbon Santos* is sometimes used to refer to any high-quality Santos coffee, but it properly describes Santos coffee from the first three or four years of growth of the Bourbon variety of the arabica tree.

Sharki   One of the better coffees of Yemen.

Shortberry Harrar   Coffee grade from Ethiopia; beans are smaller than longberry Harrar, but there may be no discernable difference between the two in terms of cup quality.

Sidamo, Washed Sidamo   A distinguished low-acid, washed coffee from Ethiopia.

Sivitz Roaster   See *Fluid Bed Roaster.*

Soft Bean   Often used to describe coffees grown at relatively low altitudes; in the same context, coffees grown at higher altitudes are often designated *hard bean.* The lower altitudes and consequently warmer temperatures produce a faster maturing fruit and a lighter, more porous bean. Soft bean coffees usually make a less acidy and less flavorful cup than do hard-bean coffees, although there are many exceptions to this generalization. The hard bean/soft bean distinction is used most frequently in evaluating coffees of Central America, where it figures in grade descriptions.

Spanish Roast   See *French Roast.*

Specialty Coffee Association of America   An association of specialty coffee roasters, wholesalers, retailers and importers headquartered in Long Beach, California.

Specialty Coffee   Whole-bean coffee retailed in bulk by small-scale roasters and merchandisers. Such coffees are usually sold by country of origin, roast, flavoring, or special blend, rather than by brand or trademark. The term *specialty coffee* also suggests the trade and culture that has grown up around this merchandising practice.

Steam Wand, Nozzle, Pipe, Stylus The small protruding pipe on most espresso machines that provides live steam for the milk-frothing operation.

Straight Coffee, Varietal Coffee An unblended coffee from a single country, region, and crop.

Strictly High-Grown Washed Highest grade of Haitian coffee.

Strictly High-Grown   Highest grade of El Salvador coffee.

Sulawesi, Celebes   Straight coffee from the island of Sulawesi (formerly Celebes), Indonesia. The best Sulawesi coffee (Toraja) is rich with the same vibrant, low-key acidity as the much-admired Sumatra coffees, but may display less body and a higher-toned acidity.

Sumatra   Straight coffee from the island of Sumatra, Indonesia. The best Sumatra coffees (Mandheling, Mandheling Lintong, Ankola) are among the world's finest, displaying rich flavor, extraordinarily full body, and a distinctively vibrant, low-key acidity.

Supremo   Highest grade of Colombian coffee.

Swiss Water Process   See *Decaffeination Processes.*

Tamper   In espresso brewing, the small, pestle-like device used to distribute and compress the ground coffee inside the filter basket.

Tanzanian   Straight coffee from Tanzania. The best and most characteristic Tanzanian coffees display a rich flavor and full body, with a vibrantly winy acidity that makes them

resemble the coffees of neighboring Kenya. They are less admired than the coffees of Kenya, however, owing to a somewhat lighter body and less consistent quality.

Tapachula   See *Chiapas.*

Tarrazu, San Marcos de Tarrazu One of the better coffees of Costa Rica.

Thermal Block   A system for heating water in espresso brewers that uses coils of pipe enclosed inside a heating element, rather than the usual small tank or boiler.

Toraja   Coffee from central Sulawesi (formerly Celebes), Indonesia. With Sumatran Mandheling and Ankola one of the most admired coffees of Indonesia.

Traditional Process   See *Decaffeination Processes.*

Tres Rios   One of the better coffees of Costa Rica.

Turkish Coffee   See *Middle Eastern Coffee.*

Ugandan   Straight coffee from Uganda. The finest Ugandan arabica (Bugishu or Bugisu) displays the winy acidity and other flavor characteristics of the best East African coffees, but is less admired than the finest Tanzanian, Kenyan, and Zimbabwe, owing to generally lighter body and less complex flavor.

Vacuum-Filter Method   A brewing method that differs from other filter methods in that the brewing water is drawn through the ground coffee by means of a partial vacuum.

Varietal Coffee   See *Straight Coffee.*

Varietal Distinction, Varietal Character   A tasting term describing positive characteristics that distinguish a given coffee from coffee from other regions. Examples are the winy acidity of Kenyan coffees and the heavy, complex body of Sumatran and Celebes coffees.

Venezuelan   Straight coffee from Venezuela. Some Venezuelan coffees (Tachira, Cúcuta) resemble Colombian coffees; however, the most characteristic (Mérida) is sweet and delicately flavored.

Viennese Coffee   Ambiguous term; sometimes refers to coffee brewed by the drip or filter method from Viennese roast or light French roast beans; also refers to brewed coffee of any

roast topped with whipped cream.

Viennese Roast   A roast of coffee slightly darker in color than the American norm, but lighter than the classic dark roast variously called *espresso, French,* or *Italian.* In the cup, Viennese roast (also called *light French, full-city,* or *light espresso* roast) is less acidy and smoother than the characteristic American roast, but may display fewer of the distinctive taste characteristics of the original coffee. Viennese roast may also refer to a mixture of one-third beans roasted to a dark brown and two-thirds roasted to the typical American medium brown.

Vintage Coffee   See *Aged Coffee.*

Wallensford Estate Blue Mountain   See *Jamaican.*

Washed Coffee   See *Wet-Processed Coffee.*

Wet-Processed Coffee, Wet Method Coffee, Washed Coffee   Coffee prepared by removing the skin and pulp from the bean while the coffee berry is still moist. Most of the world's great coffees are processed by the wet method. Yemen Mocha and Ethiopian Harrar, two exceptions, are processed by the more

primitive dry method; the great Sumatra and Celebes or Sulawesi coffees are processed by a combination of dry and wet methods.

Whole-Bean Coffee   Coffee that has been roasted but not yet ground.

Wildness   See *Earthiness.*

Yemen, Yemen Mocha, Mocha, Arabian Mocha   Straight coffee from the southwestern tip of the Arabian peninsula, bordering the Red Sea, in the mountainous regions of present-day Yemen. The world's oldest cultivated coffee, distinguished by its full body and distinctively rich, winy acidity.

Yirgacheffe, Yrgacheffe   One of the most admired washed coffees of Ethiopia, distinguished by its fruit-like acidity and complex flavor.

Zimbabwe   Straight coffee from Zimbabwe. The best (from the Chipinga region) exhibits excellent body and the vibrant, winy acidity characteristic of East African coffees. Some rank it second in quality only to Kenyan among African coffees.

Coffee Index

Strictly high grown, 55, 244
Strictly high grown washed, 57, 244
Sugar in coffee, 186–187
Sulawesi coffee, 69, 71 72, 74, 244
Sumatran coffee, 69, 71, 244
Supremo, 30, 58, 244
"Swiss Water Process" decaffeination method, 196–198, 236

Táchira coffee, 60
Tamper, espresso, 143, 154, 175
Tanzanian coffee, 67–68, 244
Tapachula coffee *See* Chiapas coffee
Tarrazu coffee, 31, 55, 244
Tasting procedure, 45, 46
Tasting terms, 43
Taylor & Ng Amore espresso machine, 164–165
Thermal block, 167, 171, 179, 244
Thermal coffee mugs, 185
Thermos brewers, 124, 126, 129
Thermos carafe, 117, 122, 126, 128, 134, 135, 184
Thomas Cara, 230, 231
Toddy cold-water brewer, 134–135, 184
Toraja coffee, 71, 244
Toshiba filter brewer, 126, 129
"Traditional" decaffeination process, 30, 195, 236, 244
Tres Rios coffee, 55, 244
Trichlorethylene, 196
Trier, 93
Trujillo coffee, 60
turbo cappuccino frothing device, 159, 162
Turbo Frother frothing device, 170
Turkish-style coffee *See* Middle Eastern-style coffee
Turkish-style grinder, 102, 107

Ugandan coffee, 68, 244–245
Ukers, William, 73

U.S. Food and Drug Administration, 192, 198, 204
Urubamba coffee, 62

Vacuum pot, 110–111, 120, 131, 133
Vacuum-filter coffee, 118, 119, 245
Varietal Coffee, 46, 244
Varietal distinction, 50
Venetian Coffee, 225
Venezuelan coffee, 60, 245
Veracruz coffee, 52
Vermont Country Store, The, 123
Via Veneto espresso maker, 163
Victorian House concentrate coffee, 133
Viennese coffee, 37, 223
Viennese roast, 38, 39, 41, 245
Vintage coffees *See* Aged coffees

Wagners flavorings, 85
Wallensford Estate Blue Mountain coffee, 31, 56–57, 245
Washed coffee *See* Wet-processed coffee
Water quality for brewing, 113, 123
Water softening devices, 113
Water temperature for brewing, 109–110, 113, 124, 125, 127
Welker microwave brewer, 130, 131
Wellman, Fredrick, 181
Wet-processed coffee, 58, 210–211, 245
Whole-bean coffee, 245
Wildness, 51, 237, 245
Winy taste, 46, 48, 60, 65–69, 73
Woodard & Charles grinder, 102, 106, 107

Yemen coffee *See* Yemen Mocha coffee
Yemen Mocha coffee, 10, 64–65, 75, 245
Yirgacheffe, Yrgacheffe coffee, 65–66, 245

Zassenhaus grinder, 103, 106, 107, 135
Zimbabwe coffee, 68, 245

Biographical Notes

Kenneth Davids' vocation of writing and his avocation of coffee drinking inevitably culminated in this book. His fascination with coffee began in Europe in 1958; he admits to having spent much of his life since in coffee houses and cafés, drinking coffee, talking, and writing. Born in Chicago, Davids graduated from Northwestern University and later received his master's degree in English from the University of California at Berkeley. He has lived in Europe, Mexico, and Hawaii, his travels including several weeks spent among coffee roasters and fanciers in Great Britain preparing the British edition of this book. He eventually carried his love for cafés to the point of co-owning and managing one in Berkeley. At present he teaches at California College of Arts and Crafts in Oakland.

M. L. Duniec was born in Germany and raised in Longview, Washington. She received a bachelor of Fine Arts degree at California College of Arts and Crafts. She worked in Washington State, teaching art at Lower Columbia College and as Art Director for *The Edmonds Paper*. Currently living near Pittsburgh, Pennsylvania, with her husband and daughter, she works as a free-lance artist, etcher, and quilt designer.